PSYCHOLOGY AND PROFESSIONAL PRACTICE

New Titles from
QUORUM BOOKS

PSYCHOLOGY AND PROFESSIONAL PRACTICE

The Interface of Psychology and the Law

Edited by
FRANCIS R. J. FIELDS
and
RUDY J. HORWITZ

Q

QUORUM BOOKS
WESTPORT, CONNECTICUT • LONDON, ENGLAND

Library of Congress Cataloging in Publication Data

Main entry under title:

Psychology and professional practice.

Bibliography: p.
Includes index.
1. Psychology — Practice.   2. Psychologists — Legal
status, laws, etc.   I. Fields, Francis R. J.   II. Horwitz,
Rudy J.
BF75.P75   150'.23'73   81-19899
ISBN 0-89930-015-4 (lib. bdg.)   AACR2

Library of Congress Catalog Card Number: 81-19899
ISBN: 0-89930-015-4

First published in 1982 by Quorum Books

Greenwood Press
A division of Congressional Information Service, Inc.
88 Post Road West, Westport, Connecticut 06881

Printed in the United States of America

10 9 8 7 6 5 4 3 2 1

Contents

Acknowledgments

The authors wish to acknowledge their sincere appreciation for the excellent cooperation and valuable time rendered by our psychology and legal colleagues in this endeavor. Sincere appreciation is acknowledged to Jean Trostle for her proofreading and typing of this manuscript. The authors also wish to acknowledge the editorial assistance in chapter 7 of Francene Z. Taylor.

FRANCIS R. J. FIELDS

Introduction

Throughout the country there has emerged a strong emphasis upon a phenomenon that has profound implications for practitioners in fields encompassed by mental health and behavioral sciences. This emphasis, of course, is upon accountability by service providers in general. Patient and public rights continue to represent major focal points of interest among consumers at all levels of American society. The issue of accountability is directly related to a major objective of this book, namely, an explication of the varied roles and qualifications of psychologists as emerging independent service providers. As the reader proceeds, it will become apparent that health services are but one of the varied services provided by psychologist specialists.

In all considerations of the provision of services to the public, one must confront an ineluctable interface with the law. Nowhere is this more apparent than in the provision of professional services, in which there is a high standard of expected performance. The failure to meet such standards by the professional practitioner will raise the specter of negligence with attendant damages as a possible legal remedy. As is the case in the provision of services to the public at all levels, there are ethical and moral considerations that must be addressed. This book will also speak to such issues. Another major emphasis will be the impact of legal considerations upon the provision of psychological services.

Our psychologist colleagues have been joined by two distinguished legal colleagues in this endeavor. The jurist member of our contributors will address his expertise to a variety of critical issues encountered by psychologists pursuing their varied roles. He will also devote a chapter to his general assessment of psychology as it assumes its place among the more traditional service-providing professions such as medicine, dentistry, law, and education.

An appropriate way to introduce the reader to the variegated specialty interest areas in psychology is to list the various divisions included in the American Psychological Association. These are as follows:

1. General Psychology
2. Teaching of Psychology
3. Experimental Psychology

[no division numbered 4]

5. Evaluation and Measurement
6. Physiological and Comparative Psychology
7. Developmental Psychology
9. Personality and Social Psychology
9. The Society for the Psychological Study of Social Issues
10. Psychology and the Arts

[no division numbered 11]

12. Clinical Psychology
13. Consulting Psychology
14. Industrial and Organizational Psychology
15. Educational Psychology
16. School Psychology
17. Counseling Psychology
18. Psychologists in Public Service
19. Military Psychology
20. Adult Development and Aging
21. The Society of Engineering Psychologists
22. Rehabilitation Psychology
23. Consumer Psychology
24. Theoretical and Philosophical Psychology
25. Experimental Analysis of Behavior
26. History of Psychology
27. Community Psychology
28. Psychopharmacology
29. Psychotherapy
30. Hypnosis
31. State Psychological Association Affairs
32. Humanistic Psychology

Historically, most accounts date the inception of psychology as a separate discipline back to the laboratory of Wilhelm Wundt in Leipzig, Germany, in 1879. Prior to that time, the field was considered as being under the umbrella of biology. Indeed, the biological roots of psychology are rather firmly established and reflected in general psychology textbooks. Such textbooks invariably contain chapters on physiology and anatomy, as well as on sensation and perception. At times, such chapters consider these subjects in significant detail. From the mid-nineteenth century until well into the twentieth century, the major thrust of psychology had been reflected in academe. Thus, the bulk of psychologists were employed in institutions of higher learning where they engaged in teaching and conducting research in animal learning behavior and brain behavior relations. It was in the mid-1940s that the psychologist practitioner role within the health field began to emerge in a significant manner. The large-scale employment of clinical and counseling psychologists by the Veterans Administration during the World War II era is widely accepted as providing a significant impetus to the emergence of psychologists as practitioners in the health area (Wolman, 1965). In the mental health area, the initial functioning of the psychologist was within the framework of the mental health team. This was particularly the case within health service delivery systems such as hospitals and mental health clinics. Such teams usually were comprised of a psychiatrist (who was frequently the team leader), a social worker, a nurse (whose special interest and training were in psychiatric nursing), and usually a clinical psychologist. Subsequently, members of a variety of other health service disciplines joined the basic team. It is now not uncommon to observe the mental hygiene team being comprised of specialists in occupational therapy, speech pathology, physical therapy, and corrective therapy, in addition to psychiatry, social work, psychology, and psychiatric nursing. Such augmented multidisciplinary treatment teams are most frequently observed in psychiatrically oriented health service delivery systems.

Notwithstanding the psychologist's historical roots in the mental hygiene team, there are abundant signs presaging the development of a more independent role for the psychologist. This development is not limited to the mental health arena, as it is observed in various other areas of psychology.

Currently, forty-seven states and the District of Columbia have existing statutes providing for the certification or licensure of psychologists. At one point all fifty states possessed such legislation. However, three states — South Dakota, Alaska, and Florida — rescinded their statutes by means of sunset legislation. The issue of sunset legislation is a separate topic and it will undoubtedly have a profound impact upon the issue of quality of care and accountability to the consumer. The present authors will not address this issue in any detail in this book.

By April 1977, twenty-three states and the District of Columbia had enacted legislation that provided for the direct payment by insurance carriers to licensed psychologist practitioners for services rendered policyholders of the specific insurance carrier. This trend has been buttressed by the recent decision by the U.S. Court of Appeals (Fourth Circuit) on June 16, 1980 (*Virginia Academy of Clinical Psychologists and Robert J. Resnick, Ph.D., v. Blue Shield of Southwestern Virginia and Neuropsychiatric Society of Virginia, Inc.*). This decision affirmed the independent status of the psychologist practitioner by decreeing that Blue Shield must cease requiring psychologists to bill through physicians and render psychological services under the supervision of a physician. These were agency (Blue Shield of Virginia and Blue Shield of Southwestern Virginia) requirements that had to exist before a psychologist would be eligible to receive compensation from the agency for services rendered its policyholders. On February 23, 1981, the subsequent appeal to the U.S. Supreme Court by the defendants was in effect rejected as the court refused to hear the case. The Supreme Court thereby allowed the lower tribunal's decision to stand and thus afforded substantial support to the "emerged" independence of the licensed psychologist practitioner. The independent practitioner trend for psychologists is further presaged by implementation in 1976 of the National Register for Health Service Providers in Psychology. This register defines who is a health service provider in psychology. In addition, it delineates academic and experiential requirements the psychologists must meet in order to be listed. The significance of the National Register lies in its formulation of national standards that must be met by individual psychologist practitioners who desire to be listed on it. Such an approach carries with it profound implications for the quality and level of service rendered by the psychologist practitioner. As early as 1947, the American Psychological Association established professional standards for guaranteeing the level of services provided by the psychologist practitioner. In that year, the American Board of Examiners in Professional Psychology was formed. This approach, modeled after the medical profession, established the requirements of the

Ph.D. degree and five years' experience in one of three specialty areas, clinical psychology, counseling psychology, and industrial psychology.

In 1953, the American Psychological Association, again recognizing the increasing service role of the psychologist practitioner, established its code of ethics. In this, an attempt was made to establish standards of ethics for psychologists who were functioning in various specialty areas. In 1963, the association published a booklet entitled *Ethical Standards of Psychology*. There have emerged subsequent editions. The 1981 edition is that which is currently accepted. The issues of ethical standards will be discussed in detail in a subsequent chapter.

Succinctly, the purposes of this book are threefold: (1) role explications of a variety of psychologist services being rendered to the public with increasing frequency; (2) articulation of critical legal issues in the various psychology specialty areas that have implications for the psychologist practitioner; and (3) assessment of some of these legal issues by an experienced jurist.

The format this book follows addresses these issues. In some instances, the legal issues will be discussed within the specific chapter, whereas in others, legal issues will be treated in a separate chapter.

A chapter on entering private practice is included. Although this relates to the psychologist practitioner, the authors feel that there is sufficient general information to allow for applicability to practitioners in other disciplines. The segments on partnerships, incorporation, and potential legal problems certainly have universal applicability.

BIBLIOGRAPHY

Wolman, Benjamin B. *Handbook of clinical psychology.* New York: McGraw-Hill, 1965.

PSYCHOLOGY AND PROFESSIONAL PRACTICE

1 ALLAN M. HORWITZ and RUDY J. HORWITZ

Independent Practice of Psychology

The independent or "private" practice is often considered representative of an individual's professional maturity. By "hanging the shingle" an individual proclaims his or her preparedness and willingness to assume responsibility for providing quality services to the public. However, the ability to provide high quality services is not fully dependent upon the degree of academic education successfully completed by an individual. Very simply, some professionals succeed while others fail at operating an independent practice. This paper will focus on the mechanics of developing an independent practice of psychology and may serve as a comprehensive guide. Also, it may help stimulate ideas for attorneys, accountants, and other concerned professionals in performing their role as advisor for independent psychological practitioners.

GENERAL CONSIDERATIONS

The independent practice of psychology, or of any discipline, is fraught with promises and problems. It is important to examine not only the benefits of operating independently, but the negatives as well. It is only after an individual weighs the pros and cons of an independent practice that the best decision can be determined. At best, an independent practice can be financially rewarding and personally gratifying. At worst, it can spell disaster for a professional career.

In order to operate an independent practice of psychology, an individual should possess certain characteristics and skills. Licensing laws, which will be discussed later in this chapter, can only go so far in defining the educational and practical requirements of an independent practitioner. In fact, licensing laws merely establish the minimum standards that are assumed to reflect competence for operating independently.

In terms of academic education, the master's degree is currently considered to be the minimum standard for licensing eligibility. In the past, individuals even without bachelor's degrees could practice psychological techniques—prior to licensing laws. The purpose for imposing educational requirements was to eliminate charlatans from the professional community. Charlatans were considered to be those individuals who did not employ scientific principles and techniques in providing services to the public. Therefore, the educational system was charged with the task of "weeding out" individuals deemed incapable of scientifically applying the techniques of psychology. It is recognized that this task can be adequately accomplished by the rigors of a master's level program. However, viewing the nature of the independent practitioner's work, having to deal with a multitude of psychological problems, licensing requirements shift to establishing the doctorate as the minimum educational requirement.

A psychologist who desires to develop an independent practice has to be eclectic and well-rounded as to abilities and skills. It is insufficient to possess the knowledge and skills for applying psychological techniques. The psychologist may also have to perform clerical, managerial, sales, and even janitorial work while operating an independent practice. Flexibility in performing various roles and tasks is essential.

Independent practitioners have to develop an ongoing regimen of education. They subscribe to and read professional journals that contain articles related to their work. They attend professional workshops and conferences for the purpose of improving their psychological techniques. Such activities must be scheduled regularly and should avoid disrupting the normal routine of providing professional services. Continuing education has become a requirement for maintaining licensure in the medical profession. It is currently being considered by the psychological profession for inclusion into the licensing laws. Such laws require a professional to complete an established number of hours in educational activity aimed at improving or enhancing professional skills. In many states, continuing education is not law but is informally imposed by the state psychological association.

Independent practitioners usually do not have the benefit of colleagues being close at hand to consult with for professional advice. Psychologists in institutional settings have regularly scheduled formal meetings and informal meetings in an office or cafeteria, at which time they can solicit the advice of co-workers. Therefore, independent practitioners have to develop and maintain channels of communication with colleagues in order to obtain the information and/or support needed to develop professional opinions. It is out of this need that the concept of peer review arose. On a periodic basis, a panel composed of colleagues reviews the independent practitioners' work in order to judge the quality of service provided to the public and to make suggestions for improvement, if necessary. Peer review is regulated by the state psychological association and is not a requirement of the licensing law.

When a psychologist works in an institutional setting, the workload, for the most part, has already been structured. He or she is assigned certain duties and referred people to whom the practitioner provides services. The work is usually scheduled with clearly defined time demands. The independent practitioner has to develop and maintain workload structuring on his or her own which challenges organizational skills. Scheduling work activities usually has to be dealt with daily, especially when starting an independent practice. Not wanting to lose a prospective client, an independent practitioner may be tempted to "drop everything" in order to be of service. Such behavior, while serving benefit in the short run, may eventually lead to schedule chaos and independent practice disaster.

Perhaps the greatest challenge to the independent practitioner's organizational skills is the problem of self-regulation. The independent practitioner has to resist the temptations of taking time off whenever the urge arises or of buying a luxury item rather than a good typewriter. There is a need to control "splurge" spending and to instill budget measures. Time off may be personally required but may be harmful to the practice.

The independent practitioner must learn entrepreneurial skills and how to treat the practice as a business; how to establish goals and limits for the practice; and to organize and unite the efforts of friends, relatives, and staff. He or she must learn how to manage people as well as the practice.

Psychologists in practice must become masters of their knowledge. They have to be authoritative about the techniques they apply in order to gain the respect of their clientele and the professional community. Clients seek the services of an independent practitioner because they expect the best treatment their money can buy. Psychologists who utilize outdated techniques can not expect to maintain an independent practice for very long since referrals will likely dwindle. Psychologists who appear unknowledgeable as to their techniques can not command the attention or respect of their clientele. Self-confidence is necessary for the successful results of an independent practice — namely, the belief that the psychologist's abilities and methods of treatment of the practice are conducive to success.

Of the numerous necessary sacrifices made in order to establish an independent practice, perhaps the most difficult is severing the "umbilical cord." Psychologists who desire independence must be willing to fend for themselves. By announcing the independent practice they are proclaiming their professional maturity and understanding that they alone assume responsibility for their actions. However, this does not imply they have to rely on their own resources completely. Rather, this indicates their desire to organize their professional life as they believe best. As often is the case, there exists a fine line between dependence and independence as between immaturity and maturity. Some psychologists attempt to start an independent practice as a sideline. It is an attempt to get "feet wet" — to either determine their suitability for independent practice or to maintain the security of an income from full-time employment. This situation may be considered analogous to the college student who moves away from home and has his own apartment but has all expenses paid by his parents. In such cases, the pains and pleasures of independence cannot be fully experienced. By maintaining ties with an institution, a psychologist can not fully declare he or she is practicing independently. However, such ties serve a protective function for the psychologist and the public, as well. Ties developed or maintained with institutions should be symbiotic rather than parasitic.

Increasing the circle of professional friends is essential for operating independently. This is important to do in order to develop informal channels of communication for obtaining advice on problems you may encounter. Scheduling regular informal get-togethers over breakfast, lunch, dinner, or the after-work "happy hour" with a colleague, can serve to allow a mutual exchange of ideas and information which may lead to satisfactory solutions of a problem. This would serve a similar function as informal meetings in an institutional setting described above.

Finally, regarding assembling the professional services that may be required, the professional should obtain recommendations from colleagues, family, and friends as to lawyers and accountants who may be of service. An informal meeting should be arranged with several lawyers and accountants to select one of each with whom working relationships may be developed. The attorney may offer suggestions on professional contracts, malpractice insurance, and office lease questions. An accountant can offer advice on record keeping of finances, investments, employees' records, and tax records. Also, both can serve as referral sources and recommend their friends and clients to the psychologist.

LICENSURE

The major purpose of professional licensing is to assure the public that an individual meets the minimum standards required by law to practice a profession. Although every one of the fifty states enacted a certification-licensing law regulating the practice of psychology, several states' laws contain "sunset" clauses which disband the board of psychological examiners if their efficacy cannot be demonstrated. In effect, the licensing law would become null and void. This, in fact, occurred in Florida, South Dakota, and Alaska.

The standard of minimum competence is part of the licensing law. This defines, fairly clearly, the educational and experiential requirements necessary for obtaining a license. In order to allow for a period of transition, "grandfather" clauses permit individuals who may not meet the educational standard, but who have been practicing and possess experiential knowledge, to apply for licensure. Grandfather clauses are in effect for a specific period of time following the effective date of the law. After the expiration date of the grandfather clause, the specified minimum standards are in effect.

The state board of psychological examiners meets to hear violation incidents of the licensing law. Also, it determines needs for revisions to the law. Amendments to licensing laws are to fill the needs created by inadequacies in the original law. The board of psychological examiners usually works closely with the ethics committee of the state psychological association. The ethics committee hears complaint cases of ethical misconduct. If there is any question of licensing law violations, the state board of psychological examiners has the power to revoke a license. It is important to differentiate between ethical misconduct and licensing law violation. For example, an industrial psychologist who may be licensed as a psychologist may utilize psychotherapy techniques within the definition of the licensing law. However, if the industrial psychologist has not had any training in psychotherapeutic techniques, this would constitute a case of ethical misconduct.

Licensing laws vary, from state to state, as to the included scope of activities and clarity of definitions. The use of the title "psychologist" may be restricted in a broad or narrow range. The activities or services may also be either specifically or generally spelled out. Not only is it important for a law to define clearly the characteristics included, but it should also clearly describe the sanctioning or penalty system. The penalties for violating licensing laws vary from state to state.

Most state licensing laws allow for reciprocity. In other words, if an individual is licensed in one state, he or she can usually become licensed in another state with minimum effort. However, it is usually required that the individual meets the minimum standards described in the law. Due to variations in the minimum requirements, it is easier to obtain licensure in a state with lesser standards than attempting to do so in a state with more stringent standards than those of the state in which the license has already been obtained.

Professional licenses usually have to be renewed. The renewal fees help pay for the services of the board of psychological examiners and the general administration costs. Fee payment is usually required annually or biannually. License renewal is usually automatic, as long as the fee is paid.

In summary, due to variations in the states' licensing laws, it is necessary to obtain a copy of the law in order to avoid violations. Although a licensed psychologist may not necessarily violate the tenets of the law, violations of ethical conduct must also be considered. It is necessary to become familiar with the licensing law of the state in which you intend to practice. The code of ethical standards can be obtained from the American Psychological Association (APA, 1967).

SETTING UP AN OFFICE

After obtaining a license for independent practice, attention can be given to establishing the practice. Essentially, this is a twofold task. One phase deals with choosing a location, decorating, and determining needed services and equipment. The other phase deals with developing clientele. Usually out of financial necessity, these phases occur simultaneously. However, with careful forethought and planning, establishing the practice does not have to be a monumental task.

Financial considerations are likely the major stumbling block for plunging into an independent practice. Although the eventual financial rewards would be gratifying, the initial financial drain could prove devastating. The cash flow problem during the early stages of practice development can be quite difficult to control. At this point, it is beneficial to obtain the services of an accountant. The accountant can offer assistance in budgeting and suggestions for obtaining loans. Asking professional friends for recommendations is the best way to find a suitable accountant.

The practitioner should consider several factors when determining the amount of a loan. Quite often, it is expected a new business will lose money the first year of operation. It should break even, or be slightly ahead, by the end of the second year. Therefore, it would be advantageous to secure a loan equal to the amount necessary to sustain the individual for at least a two-year period, arranging to repay the loan within a five-year period. Besides banks and finance companies, relatives and friends may provide loans at a more favorable interest rate. The effect of having to repay a loan may also serve as a motivating force to make an all-out effort in developing the practice.

Choosing an Office Location

By no means is choosing an office location an easy task. Certain rules for dealing with this problem can help the decision-making process. There is a tendency to believe that the office should be located where clientele are bountiful. Such locations include offices in close proximity to businesses, schools, and churches. Success is not necessarily guaranteed by being near the mainstream of clientele. It is first essential for practitioners to evaluate their own needs and preferences. First considerations should be given to their own lifestyle. This is not only important for determining the type of office setting, but the geographic location as well. If an individual enjoys water sports, he or she should consider settling in a water resort area. Nor should a practitioner settle in a small town if he or she enjoys the cultural activities of the big city. In regard to specific office locations, psychologists would be ill-advised to establish their practice in a high pedestrian-traffic area, such as a center city office building, if they do not like crowds and noise. In general, personal preferences should guide in determining the general and specific office locations.

Zoning restrictions may exist in certain neighborhoods and business areas that may exclude operation of an independent practice. Specific local laws or ordinances may be checked with the building manager or property owner. For example, some communities are zoned strictly residential and it is a violation to operate a practice even though the practitioner lives in the building. It is best to describe accurately the nature of the practice in order to obtain the best advice possible.

It is possible to share space in an existing professional building. This does offer certain advantages including bypassing initial office setup, shared expenses, shared services and the possibility of intraoffice referrals. As mentioned earlier, the initial setup of an office can be costly and time-consuming. By renting space in an existing professional office, the setup problem is virtually eliminated. The independent practitioner can personalize his or her own office area but would have to compromise as to the other areas. The benefits apply also to sharing the costs of clerical services and general equipment. As there are advantages to sharing operating costs, there may exist disadvantages as well. For example, should all utilities' costs be divided equally among the occupants, or should it be based upon the actual amount of use? How about wear and tear on the reception area furnishings? One practitioner may see fifteen clients during the course of a day, whereas another practitioner may only see five. In effect, the office furnishings may be worn out more by the clients of one practitioner than by the clients of another. The general rule in a shared office environment is to agree fully to a formula for dividing operational costs on an equitable basis.

Another problem regarding shared office space is the sharing of liability. For example, one practitioner's client might trip on a lamp cord in the reception area. This may result in all occupants being held liable for any personal injury to the client of one of the practitioners. Therefore, a practitioner upon entering a shared office arrangement should clarify in writing the extent of shared responsibility.

In any office environment, the practitioner has to assume responsibility for clientele safety. Therefore, the practitioner has to become familiar with workers' compensation regulations, OSHA standards, local fire safety regulations, and general building safety codes. It is not sufficient to merely have a "good-looking" office — it must also be safe. Electrical wiring, heating and air conditioning, plumbing, and lighting must all meet standards of safety.

Working out of the practitioner's private residence may be appealing in certain aspects but does pose certain problems. In terms of appeal, setting up an office in the home can be less expensive, more convenient (in terms of transportation), and may offer certain tax advantages. The spouse, if at home, could also serve as a telephone and office receptionist. However, one of the major problems in combining office with residence is the possible compromise of privacy, not only for the practitioner's family and personal life, but for the client as well. Clients can justifiably feel "short-changed" if their sessions are interrupted by the practitioner's family members who may accidentally or unintentionally intrude. On the other hand, a client could intrude on the practitioner's personal life by knowing the office is located within or adjoining the residence. In general, it is most likely best to segregate personal from business matters and environments.

Specific Needs for Office Services and Equipment

To assist in the provision of services, the practitioner must give careful consideration to the selection of clerical equipment (including typewriters and dictation equipment), telephone equipment and services, and general office supplies. Careful planning of supportive office needs promotes the smooth operation of the office.

Typewriters and dictation equipment can significantly add to the business-like quality of the professional office. Today's rapid technological changes are leading to major improvements in office equipment. Word processing equipment, being sophisticated computerized typewriters, can offer various time-saving and accuracy advantages over equipment that was available five or ten years ago. However, it is important to assess the anticipated needs for typewriting equipment and weigh this against the cost for the equipment. A nonelectric standard office typewriter may satisfactorily fulfill the practitioner's needs for the first five years. This is especially true if the practice is limited to the provision of services rather than the communication of information regarding the services.

Dictation equipment, like typewriters, has undergone significant improvements. A variety of recording types exist. It is best to experiment and try out various models that are appealing and personally rate them on ability to satisfy needs of convenience, ease of operation, recording capacity, and sound quality. The basic popular types of dictation equipment include magnetic belts, discs, standard cassettes, and micro- or mini-cassettes. The types of power sources have to be considered since some are A.C. operated only (desk-top type) whereas others are standard battery, rechargeable battery, and even car battery operable.

In general, office equipment should be evaluated in terms of ability to satisfy needs. Practitioners who have minimum demands can make do with low-cost and basic equipment. However, as volume increases based upon clerical output, it would be advisable to consider more sophisticated equipment. Practitioners need to explain their needs to the office equipment representatives in order to match the needs with the characteristics of the equipment. Also, individuals should get the opinion of equipment users as to dependability and servicing. Maintenance contracts should be considered when purchasing equipment and are usually included under leasing arrangements. Purchasing less expensive equipment may be appealing in terms of initial cost but this may be overriden by the high cost of frequent repairs and lost time. Legal recourse may be taken if the equipment does not meet promised expectations.

Telephone answering equipment is a significant asset to the practitioner who spends time out of the office or who does not have a full-time secretary. Live answering services are available and offer certain advantages over answering equipment. The live answering service can contact the psychologist if the caller has an emergency problem. Also, it can arrange appointments. On the other hand, live answering services can create problems by not answering quickly and by incorrectly relaying the information given by the caller. Modern answering equipment offers features which permit remote retrieval of messages, remote change of outgoing messages, and even a call forwarding or paging system. When considering answering services, it is best to consult with professional friends who have either the live or equipment answering services. Demonstrations of answering equipment can usually be arranged for a short period of time, perhaps for several days to several weeks. The local phone company has equipment available for rental and should be consulted in any event for answering equipment hookup.

ANNOUNCING SERVICES

Once an office has been established in which the practitioner can conduct business and provide services, attention should then be directed to techniques for obtaining referrals. Essentially, psychologists must make their name known in the community in which they are practicing. The major concerns include giving the impression of soliciting business, inappropriate or unprofessional advertising methods, and "puffing" the extent of personal abilities.

The techniques for announcing the availability of services generally follow those guidelines as established by the legal and medical professions. The announcement should clearly state the practitioner's name, highest degree of education, office address and telephone number, specific area(s) of expertise, and office hours. It is generally unacceptable to include a fee schedule in an announcement. Also, it is not proper to include laudatory statements from satisfied clients. The printed media are generally acceptable for service announcements; however, radio and television are not. Although recent changes have occurred in the "ethics of advertising" professional services, the taboo of solicitation remains in effect. The content and method of announcement should not be such that it would negatively influence the reputation of the profession. There should be no claims as to "better" quality of service. In general, sensationalism has to be avoided. However, with certain media, namely, radio and television, this may prove difficult to avoid. Advertisement in the telephone directory is seemingly increasing in popularity. The listing in the Yellow Pages section under the heading "Psychologists" has to be limited to the basic information of name, degree, address, phone number, and specialty area.

"Puffing" the extent of services refers to a practitioner's attempt to "bite off more than can be chewed." There may be a tendency to undertake a service for which the required expertise is not possessed. The practitioner must resist the temptation to overstep the boundaries of his or her skills. Although an individual may possess a license that describes him or her as a "clinical psychologist," the practitioner's education and experience may have been in another area of psychology. It is the ethical responsibility of the practitioner to provide only those services for which skills are possessed.

Receiving referrals can be a sensitive area in regard to the technique employed in requesting such referrals from another individual or organization. There appears to exist a fine line between the ethical referral procedure and solicitation. The basic definitions of ethical referral include that the referral is necessary and service will be provided that meets the standards of quality. The only reward is to be the knowledge that the client is receiving the required treatment provided by a skillful practitioner. The relationship between the practitioner and the referring individual is developed over a period of time and is based on the areas of trust and confidence. The notion of solicitation implies an active attempt on the practitioner's part to "ask" directly for referrals — usually, prior to the establishment of trust conditions. Also, financial remuneration is often involved.

Announcement cards, which state the basic information of the services, tend to be the most popular method of advising the public of the intention to practice independently. Statements on the card should inform the recipient of the scope of services, office location, telephone number(s), and office hours.

Business cards offer another means of announcing the availability of services. Information should be brief and explicit. The card may also serve as an appointment reminder. It is advisable to design the card in a conservative fashion, depicting professionalism, avoiding sensationalism that may be construed as a solicitation tactic. Business cards should be carried in sufficient quantity and given frequently to referral source contacts.

DEVELOPING REFERRAL SOURCES

Referral sources are often labeled the "gate-keepers" of professional clientele. In developing a practice, it is essential to maintain a high quality of professional service so that the referral sources can rely on the knowledge that the clients they are referring will receive quality treatment. Word has a way of "getting back" to the referral source regarding the quality of the service. If satisfaction is not received in regard to treatment, future referrals will likely not be made. It is important to develop and maintain communication with the referral source to inform them of the progress being made with each referral. This communication will help to indicate an appreciation of referrals. Satisfied referral sources can also serve as a means of advertisement for a practice. Unfortunately, dissatisfaction with a professional service has a tendency to be more easily communicated than satisfaction.

With certain organizational referral sources, such as the Department of Labor and Industries Division of Vocational Rehabilitation, certification as a provider of professional services is offered. This may serve to attest to a standard of competence.

A variety of potential referral sources exists for the private practitioner. To discover these potential referral sources, the private practitioner should take the time to get advice from professional friends. Various federal, state, and city government agencies utilize psychological services. Contacting the supervisors of such governmental organizations, and informing them of a private practice, may lead to receiving referrals and consultations.

As mentioned above, the Department of Labor and Industries Division of Vocational Rehabilitation relies on psychological services for the provision of vocational rehabilitation services to its clientele. Each state agency varies slightly in regard to its referral procedure. However, assistance in regard to obtaining information about the provision of services can be obtained from the agency's "liaison to providers of professional service."

The Disability Determination Division of the Social Security Administration also relies on psychological services. Often, this agency works closely with the Division of Vocational Rehabilitation. Referral and billing procedures for this particular agency vary from those of the Division of Vocational Rehabilitation. However, once again, assistance in regard to providing services is available from the agency's professional service liaison.

The judicial court system utilizes psychological services for determination of competency to stand trial, marital and family counseling in divorce proceedings, and to testify as to the psychological impact of personal injury in negligence matters. Therefore, it would likely prove beneficial to forward announcement cards to attorneys in general practice and the court system. In some states, medical assistance programs, such as Medicaid and Medicare, provide coverage for psychological services. It is necessary to check with the local office in order to ascertain whether psychological services are covered.

"Freedom of choice" legislation in various states has had the impact of increasing referral sources for private practitioners. Essentially, such legislation permits individuals who have insurance coverage to choose whom they want as a provider of services. In the past, such services usually had to be at least supervised by a physician. Each insurance company has its own billing procedure. The insurance company should be contacted in advance of the provision of the service in order to determine if the treatment is included under the coverage. Also, the fee amount covered by the insurance company is usually a percentage of the total fee. These matters should be clarified in advance for the client as well as the service provider.

PROVIDING SERVICES

A client is anyone or any group to whom services are provided. Although a fee is customarily exchanged for the service provided, a client can actually be anyone to whom professional advice is given — even for free. Therefore, although a fee may not be charged, this does not negate responsibility for the service. This legal responsibility should serve the private practitioner as a caution for not straying away from the realm of competency.

It is essential to communicate to the client the plan of action, treatment, or the scope of service that will be provided. If the service that is required or requested is not within the realm of competence, the potential client should be referred elsewhere for the services.

Establishing the fee for the service rendered requires the consideration of various factors: the practitioner's overhead for maintaining the office, "profit margin," and consideration of the prevailing rates of service fees in the local area. A "provider of service-client" contract may be developed in order to limit the scope of liability. Such a contract would serve to specify the commitments of the provider and the client, to each other.

A recordkeeping system has to be adequately maintained in case there is any question as to the nature of the service provided. For Internal Revenue Service purposes, records have to be maintained for the fees charged and actually received. The recordkeeping system also has to protect the confidentiality of the client. Therefore, the rules of an adequate recordkeeping system should be carefully determined in advance and adhered to stringently.

MALPRACTICE LIABILITY AND INSURANCE

Although a private practitioner has all good intentions for providing a quality service, errors and problems can occur. A psychologist who provides diagnostic testing services may misdiagnose, leading to inappropriate treatment. A therapist conceivably could create more problems for a client, resulting in unsatisfactory treatment outcome. To protect the private practitioner, in terms of financial liability, malpractice insurance is available. The insurance division of the American Psychological Association offers coverage for the practitioner and assistants. The premium rate for a malpractice policy is quite reasonable in view of the extent of coverage. In order to select insurance, copies should be obtained from the various companies offering the policies. The practitioner should select the policy that best satisfies individual needs. Colleagues should be consulted for advice on malpractice insurance coverage. Also, if a practitioner already has an insurance agent, advice regarding malpractice insurance may be obtained from the agent.

LEGAL PROTECTION FOR THE PROFESSIONAL PRACTICE

The private practitioner has many concerns to deal with that are apart from the quality of service. Such concerns involve office operational costs, zoning requirements, IRS rules and regulations, and Department of Labor and Industry Standards regarding employee salaries and safety. Because the private practitioner has to perform in a variety of roles, advice should be obtained as early and as frequently as possible. The private practitioner should obtain the professional services of and befriend an attorney, accountant, insurance agent, and perhaps even a business management consultant, in addition to referral source contacts.

Corporation law provides certain benefits to private practitioners. The most essential benefit, perhaps, is the separation of personal and professional liability. An unincorporated practitioner may place in jeopardy personal assets if he or she becomes the subject of a malpractice suit. Corporation laws vary from state to state. Therefore, it is essential to discuss such matters with a local attorney. The private practitioner should develop a list of other questions to discuss from a legal standpoint. An attorney should be quite helpful in terms of developing form contracts for various aspects of the practice.

CONCLUSION

Developing a professional relationship with an attorney, accountant, and insurance agent can prove to be beneficial by increasing the number of potential referral sources. By developing mutual trust and respect for other professionals, a psychologist increases the chances for success in independent practice. Independent practitioners should not allow themselves to become isolated.

BIBLIOGRAPHY

American Psychological Association. *The ethical standards of psychologists.* Washington, D.C.: American Psychological Association, 1967.

Lewin, M. H. *Establishing and maintaining a successful professional practice.* Rochester, N.Y.: Professional Development Institute, 1977.

Testing:
The Armamentarium of
Psychology

GENERAL CONSIDERATIONS

Almost everyone is familiar with psychological tests. Testing is performed in schools, hospitals, the armed services, business, and industry. Test results are used to assess personality and intellectual functioning, level of academic achievement, and vocational interests and aptitudes. The basic function of psychological tests is to measure differences that exist between the behavior of individuals or of the same individual at different times. In order to appreciate the value of psychological testing, some information should be known regarding the development or history of testing, administration, and statistical techniques for analysis and interpretation. Tests and results can be used inappropriately, thus infringing upon the legal rights of individuals and groups. This chapter will approach the problems of testing as viewed by psychologists and attorneys. Statistics and other esoteric concepts will not be discussed in detail. Rather, an overview of psychological testing as a science and art will be presented.

Schools are probably the largest test users. Students are classified according to their abilities to benefit from certain instructional programs, they are counseled for career purposes, and are either granted or denied admission to colleges or professional schools — at least in part by their test scores. School psychologists play an important role in the guidance of students based upon the professionals' skill in interpreting test results. They are often called upon to defend their interpretations and knowledge of the testing instruments that are commonly used in making school-related decisions.

The personnel departments of business and industry control the hiring, promoting, and firing of individuals, often based upon test scores as well as rated job performances. The assumption is that a definite relationship exists between test score and expected job performance. This is the basic assumption in defense of state professional licensing examinations. Individuals can understandably develop a negative attitude toward testing if they "just missed" the passing mark by "a couple of points." Industrial and consulting psychologists usually have to shoulder the decision of job placement which often excludes qualified individuals due to a "margin of error."

Clinical psychologists deal with the personality functioning of individuals. Tests are used to support or refute diagnostic impressions usually obtained by interview techniques. In addition, tests deal with questions of legality such as sanity and competence. Test results are used to show whether a prison or a mental institution would provide a better therapeutic milieu, whether or not there has been any significant change in personality functioning, and whether an individual has gone as far as possible with therapy and is ready for discharge. Clinical decisions, whether based on the results or not, are highly responsible for and control the treatment provided to patients. Once again, knowledge of test results and statistical analysis is essential in order to minimize the "margin of error" in making decisions.

As may be gathered from the above comments, testing and its power should not be taken lightly. Psychologists, counselors, therapists, school administrators, test publishers—anyone who uses test results for decisions —all have the responsibility of safeguarding the appropriate use of tests. Anyone who assumes responsibility for administering, scoring, and interpreting test results should be aware of the legal implications if any part of the testing process is violated. In order to defend the rights of individuals who have been scrutinized by tests, attorneys and other interpreters of the law should be familiar with the characteristics of tests in terms of value and shortcoming. Tests are merely a tool for measuring human behavior. Although tests may accurately measure and reflect various aspects of behavior, they may only be as good as the examiner's ability to administer and interpret them. As the saying goes, "If the carpenter knows his tools and materials, he can build anything."

THE DEVELOPMENT OF PSYCHOLOGICAL TESTING

Mental Abilities and Intelligence

Testing grew out of the need to differentiate and classify people who were considered insane or feebleminded. Nineteenth-century Europe and America attempted to develop a means for caring for abnormal individuals. Special institutions were built to provide care. However, it was essential to establish admission standards and a means for efficiently classifying individuals in need of care. In 1838, Jean Etienne Esquirol, a French physician, had published a work that dealt with the differentiation between feeblemindedness and attempted to differentiate categories according to linguistic standards or verbal ability, which he felt were the most reliable measures. Edouard Seguin, another French physician, worked with the idea of muscle control and sensory discrimination as being essential in the classification of feeblemindedness. He developed sense and muscle training techniques, which are still in use in institutions today. Esquirol's efforts developed into the verbal approaches to understanding intellectual functioning, whereas Seguin's work led to the performance or nonverbal aspects.

For the most part, the nineteenth-century scientific study of psychology focused upon generalities of human behavior rather than differences. Wundt's laboratory, established in 1879, developed the experimental approach to studying behavior. Besides increasing knowledge about responses to sensory stimuli, such experimental laboratories aided in establishing the importance of standardized procedures for the measuring and comparing of human behavior.

Sir Francis Galton, the English biologist, perhaps gave the first major impetus to testing. He developed a laboratory in 1884 in London to accumulate "anthropometric" data on simple sensorimotor behavior. Galton believed a strong relationship exists between sensorimotor function and intellect. He also was responsible for the development of various statistical techniques for analyzing data of individual differences.

During the late 1800s, emphasis was placed on the development of "mental tests," and this term was first published in an article by James Cattell, an American psychologist. His approach was similar to Galton's, utilizing data obtained from sensory discrimination and reaction time tests. However, results were discouraging in the analysis of linking such measures to other indicators of intellectual functioning, such as academic grades and teacher's ratings. Other names associated with pioneering efforts in mental testing include Emil Kraepelin, Herman Ebbinghaus, and G. C. Ferrari.

The individual most often associated with the early development of intelligence tests was Alfred Binet. In 1904, a commission was assigned the task of studying the education of subnormal students in Paris schools. The first intelligence scale was developed in 1905 by Binet and Theodore Simon. Refinements of this first scale were presented in the 1908 scale. The concept of "mental age" debuted in this scale. The popularity of the Binet-Simon scale led to revisions and translations such as the Stanford-Binet (developed by L. M. Terman) which introduced the concept of I.Q. or intelligence quotient. The Kuhlmann-Binet was one of the early attempts to develop infant and young children's measures of intelligence.

The emphasis from individual to group testing most likely shifted as a result of World War I. A practical problem existed for the U.S. Army to classify and assign to duty one and one-half million men quickly. The result was the Army Alpha and Army Beta tests. The Army Alpha was a general purpose group test used with men who were literate. The Beta examination was developed for use with illiterate and foreign language-speaking men and was essentially nonverbal. Following the war, revisions of these tests were made for various and special purposes and the "testing boom" was underway. Unfortunately, the techniques for interpreting the results of these tests were not sufficiently advanced to meet the demand. Unrealistic expectations led to frustrations which eventually caused strong criticism of testing and hindered its development.

Aptitudes

It was soon to be realized that intelligence tests were limited in scope and were measuring verbal, numerical, and abstract reasoning abilities. Perhaps a more appropriate title may have been Scholastic Aptitude Tests. The need for a variety of measures to reflect aptitudes led to the development of screening tests. Measures were developed for general clerical, mechanical, artistic, and musical aptitudes. The Army General Classification Test (AGCT), developed during World War II, served a similar purpose as the World War I Army Alpha. This test roughly and quickly screened large numbers of men who were then classified for further special testing.

World War I test development efforts emphasized group screening techniques. World War II efforts focused upon individual and specialized measures for almost every job in the military. The military psychologists are credited with developing test construction and standardization techniques through extensive research.

The value of multiple aptitude test batteries was seen in their power to differentiate an individual's strengths and weaknesses. Intelligence tests usually offered a single score, which could not be readily translated into a performance "profile." With multiple aptitude test batteries, not only could interindividual comparisons be made, but intraindividual comparisons as well. The importance of statistics for the analysis of test scores increased by the investigation of differential aptitudes. The work of psychologists such as L. L. Thurstone paved the way for the concept of "factor analysis." In a sense, multiple aptitude test batteries are the ultimate in psychological assessment. Although the military was responsible for the initial thrust, the development of multiple aptitude test batteries continued for civilian use as well.

Personality

Measures of personality usually focus upon the nonintellectual components of psychological functioning such as interests, attitudes, motivation, interpersonal relationships, and emotion. Kraepelin developed the technique of free association for use with abnormal people. Selected words are presented as stimuli and the subject has to respond with the first word that comes to mind. By using this technique, Kraepelin studied the effect various factors had on this psychological functioning. The free association technique was developed further for use with the differential diagnosis of mental disorders.

Other forerunners of personality measurement tools include standardized questionnaire and rating scales. Cattell, Karl Pearson, and Galton developed these techniques. During World War I, R. S. Woodworth developed the personal data sheet, a self-report inventory, for screening out severely neurotic men from the military. Following the war, splinter versions of this inventory developed in the civilian sector. These versions focused upon home, school, and vocational adjustment.

Hugh Hartshorne and Mark A. May developed a personality measurement technique known as "situational testing." Simulation of an everyday task is presented and a subject's performance is observed. They employed this technique with school children to study cheating, cooperativeness, persistence, lying, and stealing. The administration of such a technique requires extensive training for the examiner. Usually, the purpose of the task is disguised. Scoring is essentially objective.

Another approach to personality measurement is projective technique questionnaires. The test stimuli are basically unstructured, requiring the structuring to be performed by the subject. It is the structuring of the task which is the behavior being observed. Incomplete sentences, drawings, arranging objects to create a scene, dramatic enactments, and responding to pictures and inkblots are examples of projective techniques.

Although personality assessment research has been quite extensive in recent years, the value derived in terms of the improvement of such measures has been generally questionable. In this area progress in research appears to be hindered more by the characteristic problems of personality assessment than by the quality of applicable statistical techniques.

STATISTICAL CONSIDERATIONS

Comparison of responses, whether inter- or intra-subject responses, is the crux of the skill for analyzing psychological test data. Test scores can be expressed as age scores, standard scores, and percentiles. Raw scores alone are virtually meaningless. Meaning is supplied by comparing scores to a reference or norm group.

The procedure for developing a norm group and generally organizing data can be explained in relatively simple terms. First, scores are tabulated into a frequency distribution. This information may also be graphically displayed by a distributive curve. Histograms are bar representations on the graph that cover an area equal to the number of subjects in a particular category. A frequency polygon is a straight line drawing that also represents the number of subjects in a category.

The bell-shaped normal curve is the ideal frequency polygon. It is this curve that serves as the basis for the development of various statistical procedures and techniques. Almost all psychological traits and characteristics can be represented by the normal curve. It is symmetrical and has a single central peak. The normal curve theoretically reaches its perfect shape as more normally distributed data are added to the sample.

Another description of data is central tendency. Included in this group of statistics are the mean, median, and mode. The central tendency figure is the single most representative score of the group of data. The mean (M), or average score, is obtained by summing all of the scores and dividing by the number of scores (N). The mode, or most frequent score, is obtained by finding the midpoint value of scores in the class interval that contains the highest frequency of a score. The median is obtained by arranging all the scores of a group in order, bisecting the list of scores, and finding the value that falls in the middle of the list.

Measures of variability compose another set of descriptors for scores. These values reflect the degree of individual score differences relative to the central tendency. Measures of variability include the range, average deviation, and standard deviation. The range reflects the lowest and highest scores of a group. However, as a representative value, the range may be poor due to the possibility of unusually high or low scores. The average deviation is derived from the sum of all the deviations, or differences between each score and the mean, without regard to whether it is a positive or negative sign difference. The sum of all the deviations should equal zero. Because sign value is disregarded, the average deviation has limited value in terms of involvement in mathematical computations. Therefore, its value as a statistic is also limited. Perhaps the most usable variability statistic is the standard deviation. It is symbolized by SD or σ. The variance is equal to the sum of the deviations, which have been squared to eliminate negative sign values and divided by the number of scores. To obtain the SD, the square root of the variance is computed as follows:

$$SD = \sqrt{\frac{\Sigma x^2}{N}}$$

The shape of the distribution or frequency curve is dependent upon the size of the SD. If the deviations from the means are large, the value of the SD will be large and the distribution will be flat. The concept of SD is essential to the statistical comparison of two or more groups.

Percentiles

The percentile score represents the location of an individual's score in the group. The higher the percentile rating, the higher the score. Rank values are in a sense opposite, in that the lower the numerical value, the higher the score. The 50th percentile corresponds to the median score value. The graphic representation of a percentile norm group is called an ogive curve. The percentile rating is useful for comparing an individual's performance to the group as well as comparing the same individual's performances on several tests to the norm group. Raw scores are meaningless until they are converted into percentile ratings. Percentile ratings are easily computed, understandable, and have wide application for different types of tests and different types of people. Unfortunately, percentile ratings can only represent the location of an individual's score in a group; they cannot show the differences or distance between the scores.

Standard Scores

Perhaps the most useful method of presenting test scores is by utilizing information about the standard deviation. Standard scores are computed in a manner that represents the distance of the individual's raw score from the group mean. Types of standard scores include linear, normalized, deviation I.Q., and normal percentile graphs. Due to the statistical derivation of standard scores, and the stringent requirement imposed, they offer flexibility for reconversion to other types of score reporting, test construction, and statistical analysis.

Linear standard scores are usually referred to as standard scores or Z scores. Linear scores are computed by dividing the difference between the score and the mean of the group by the standard deviation. Tests employing this method of score reporting include the Wechsler Intelligence Scale and the College Entrance Examination Board.

Normalized standard scores deal with data that have been translated to fit the normal curve. Certain data may be represented by a frequency distribution that is skewed, or nonbell-shaped. Therefore, the scores of such a distribution must first be converted to a value that will lead to a normal or bell-shaped distribution. Robert McCall devised the *T* score, which is computed by multiplying the normalized standard score by ten and adding to or subtracting from fifty. The Stanine Scale, developed by the U.S. Air Force, has scores from one to nine.

The normal percentile graph method is a combination of percentile ratings and normalized standard scores. Arthur S. Otis developed The Normal Percentile Chart, which permits recording of scores of a group and facilitates norm group development and other means of test score analysis. The normal percentile graph technique can also be used for developing individual score profiles. Therefore, an individual's strengths and weaknesses can be individually presented. The Psychological Corporation's Differential Aptitude Tests employ the normal percentile graph for reporting test scores.

The deviation I.Q. method is different from the ratio I.Q. method. Ratio I.Q.'s express the relationship between the "mental age" score and the chronological age value. Deviation I.Q.'s are computed by using the standard score deviation, as described above, with a mean of 100 and a SD of sixteen. The Wechsler Intelligence Scales and the 1960 Stanford-Binet revision use the deviation I.Q. method.

Age Scores

The ratio I.Q. is perhaps the most significant example of an age score. It was first employed by the 1916 Stanford-Binet form. The mental age, determined by the score, is divided by the chronological age of the individual and multiplied by 100 to eliminate decimal values. One of the major problems with ratio I.Q. is the ability to maintain meaning and I.Q. value at different age levels. In general, age scores have a limited value in describing psychological traits, since not all characteristics are dependent upon age.

GENERAL CHARACTERISTICS OF PSYCHOLOGICAL TESTS

As mentioned above, a psychological test is a scientific observation of behavior. Since not all behavior of a particular type can be monitored for observation purposes, a sample of the behavior is selected. The sample selected should be reflective of the observed behavior. The diagnostic value or predictive ability of a test is the degree to which the test reflects the general behavior. It is not essential that the sample test be similar to the general behavior. What is important, however, is that some definite and repeatable relationship exists between the sample and general behavior.

Standardization refers to the establishment of uniform procedures for test administration and scoring. All factors have to be considered regarding the uniformity of environmental conditions, test instructions, and test presentations. The test should be constructed in such a manner that it can be objectively administered. An individual's score should be the same on a test regardless of the examiner. The test's level of difficulty should be matched to the level of the group to which it is administered. For example, if a test of simple arithmetic is given to college students, the score distribution will be skewed, not normal. This would violate requirements of the normal-shaped curve necessary for performing statistical analysis. The goal, therefore, in test construction is to provide only those items that will result in a normal distribution for the group.

Reliability

Reliability in a test refers to the consistency or stability of the measured behavior, or score; if the behavior being measured is stable over time; and whether an individual will obtain a similar score over a period of time. For example, intelligence is assumed to be a stable psychological behavior, especially for adults. If there would occur a large discrepancy between an individual's I.Q. scores, at different times, the test would not be considered reliable. Methods for determining reliability include test-retest, split half, inter-item, and equivalent form. The method for reporting the reliability of a test is the coefficient of correlation.

The coefficient of correlation represents the extent of the relationship between sets of scores. The distribution of scores is referred to as the scatter diagram or bivariate distribution. The range of correlation is from -1 to $+1$.

A negative correlation ranges between -1 and zero. Positive correlations range between zero and $+1$. The value of zero suggests that no relationship exists between two sets of scores. For purposes of reliability, higher negative values are as important in terms of meaning as higher positive values. The Pearson Product-Moment correlation coefficient is perhaps the most common method of computing a correlation coefficient. This can be performed in various ways, using different formulas. Essentially, it represents the mean of the product of the standard scores on two tests.

Test-retest reliability is based on using the same test after a period of time. This type of reliability is often referred to as the coefficient of stability. Various problems enter into computing such a coefficient, including practice effects and memory.

Split-half reliability coefficients are derived from a single test administration. It is essential to "split" the test questions into equally representative halves. Both content and difficulty should be equivalent. The Spearman-Brown method is perhaps the most frequently used formula for determining a split-half reliability coefficient.

Inter-item consistency combines the aspects of test item equivalence and homogeneity. In a sense, it is similar to split-half reliability in terms of requiring equivalence, but also requires the uniformity or homogeneity of items throughout the test. The Kuder-Richardson method is perhaps the most popular for determining inter-item correlation coefficients. It represents the mean of all possible split-half coefficients that can be obtained by various test splittings. Coefficient of internal consistency is the general term applied to any correlation coefficient derived by any split-half method. Equivalent form reliability refers to the relationship between two tests that appear to have similar items of equivalent difficulty. Essentially, "parallel" tests are constructed and administered close in time to each other. This type of correlation is referred to as the coefficient of equivalence. In general, alternate test forms are desirable for several reasons. They can be administered to measure the effects of intervening variables, to minimize practice effects, and to avoid unauthorized exchange of test information if more than one group is being treated.

In general, it is important to employ a measure of reliability appropriately. Certain tests cannot be assessed according to specific correlation techniques. In order to appreciate the appropriateness of a test for a particular purpose, the reliability should be established.

Validity

Validity is the test characteristic that describes how well a test measures that behavior which it is stated to measure. Essentially, there are four types of validity: content, concurrent, construct, and predictive. Validity information is important for determining the appropriateness of a test for a special purpose. Also, it is important to compare the results obtained by the user of a test for a local group of subjects to the results obtained by the test constructor.

Content validity deals with the test items' representativeness of the general behavior being measured. For example, if the test's purpose is to measure achievement level in arithmetic, the obvious assumption is for the test to contain arithmetic problems. The test samples, or compilation of items, should represent the items available in the general group in the same proportion. Therefore, content has to be divided in a manner that covers all aspects of a particular behavior, both in terms of theoretical and practical knowledge. Content validity has particular value for achievement tests. However, it is not practical for personality and aptitude tests. The term *face validity* is not the same as content validity but is often confused with it. It simply refers to whether or not a test appears valid to the taker. It is not a substitute for content validity, which has actually been derived or computed.

Concurrent validity refers to the relationship between the test scores and some criterion index obtained almost simultaneously. Examples of criterion indices include academic grades, job performance ratings, and other validated test scores. Contrasting groups may also be administered the same test and their scores compared. This method thus leads to the discrimination of test scores between the two groups. This particular approach is often used for the validation of personality and interest tests. Ratings are another method for developing criteria for validation. This approach is often utilized for personality measures but can be used for all psychological tests. Ratings are only as good a criterion as the skill of the rater and the rating method. Other test scores may be used for validation purposes, especially if that test has already been validated. This method is particularly useful for similar tests, parallel forms, and abbreviated test forms.

Construct validity deals with the ability of a test to measure a theoretical construct. Spelling and arithmetic tests are definite in content, for example, whereas the concept of intelligence and personality tend to be more abstract. Age differentiation assumes that the construct measured depends upon age of the subjects tested. However, this may pose difficulties in analysis, for different cultural groups have varying expectations for different aged individuals. Factor analysis, as mentioned earlier in this chapter, is a statistical technique for grouping traits and analyzing data. Essentially, this method narrows down what may be considered a large number of characteristics into a few categories. Internal consistency deals with the similarities of each test item to the purpose of the test. This approach often is employed in comparing the value of each subtest for the purpose purported by the whole test. Essentially, these are measures of homogeneity.

Predictive validity is concerned with the ability of a test to predict some future behavior. Often, concurrent information is used for criterion purposes. Academic achievement records are frequently employed for validating intelligence tests. These would include grades, honors and awards, extracurricular activities, and teacher's ratings. Scores achieved at the end of some specialized training may also serve as criteria for predictive validity. Job performance ratings compared to scores obtained on a related test may also lead to developing a test's predictive ability.

Utilizing Statistical Information

The main goal of psychological testing is to develop efficient measurement instruments that work quickly, accurately, and inexpensively. Statistical techniques have played a major role in accomplishing this goal. The main methods include expectancy tables, validity coefficients, decision theory item analysis, cross validation, and multiple test scores.

Expectancy tables are a simple method of graphically displaying the likely outcomes for each score on a test. Expectancy tables can be developed for dichotomous or continuous data. Dichotomous criteria offer twofold possibilities. Continuous data criteria represent a single relationship outcome.

Validity coefficients show the strength of the relationship between the test and the criterion. Such coefficients are computed in a similar fashion as mentioned before, by using the Pearson Product-Moment Correlation formula. A biserial correlation may be computed for a dichotomized criterion.

Decision theory deals with establishing the amount of percentage of errors that will be permitted. It requires developing a strategy for the passing and failing of borderline test scores. Statistical decision theory was developed during the 1940s by A. Wald. The goal is to formalize the decision process in order to develop an efficient decision within specific conditions. Taylor-Russell tables offer one method of maximizing efficiency in the decision-making process. These tables require information about the proportion of "passes" prior to using a specific test, the proportion of "passes" that can be permitted, and the validity coefficient of the test selected for use. Problems with decision theory application include insensitivity to outcomes that are difficult to assign to such values as moral values and good will, the finality of the decision, and the availability and assigning to specific training based on a specific score. In 1955, Paul E. Meehl and E. Rosen discussed the possibility that use of decision theory in certain cases may actually increase the number of errors. This occurs in situations in which tests alone may be utilized for decisions, avoiding other sources of information.

Item analysis and cross-validation offer the possibility of shortening a test, making it more reliable and valid. Usually, lengthening a test makes it more reliable and valid, if done so in a random way. However, by using the Spearman-Brown statistical technique, items that add little to the overall validity and reliability coefficients may be discarded and actually increase the coefficients. Tetrachoric and phi coefficients are used for a dichotomous criterion and dichotomous item response. Biserial correlations are used if the criterion is not dichotomous. Performing an item analysis leads to homogenizing the test. However, this may sometimes lead to lowering the validity coefficient as well, for certain situations.

Perhaps the best approach for psychological assessment through testing is to combine the information obtained from several tests. This can be accomplished through use of a multiple regression equation and multiple cutoff scores. The multiple regression equation is used to predict a single criterion score based on a subject's scores on the individual tests. Multiple cutoff scores is a technique by which a minimum cutoff score is determined for each test. The General Aptitude Test Battery (GATB), mentioned above, utilizes this approach. Meehl (1954) discusses the value, in terms of accuracy, speed, and cost of employing statistical techniques over that of "clinical judgment" in the decision-prediction process. He concluded that statistical information of known validity should be the basis for decisions rather than clinical judgment. Sawyer (1966) reanalyzed Meehl's work and concluded that the clinician's subjective judgments are valuable sources of information which should be included in a "statistical" formula for decision purposes.

Concluding Remarks Regarding Statistics

In order to appreciate an individual's test scores, knowledge of the statistical methods employed for interpreting the scores is essential. The assumption is made that statistics are a forte area for a psychologist who uses tests. The psychologist, as a statistical expert, has the responsibility of communicating this knowledge in a manner that is clearly understood by laymen. The psychologist, as a statistician, assumes responsibility for utilizing the appropriate statistical methods in order to develop the most realistic representation of the data. Attorneys should recognize the need for retaining the services of a statistical expert to serve as interpreter and clarifier, if the case deals with psychological testing.

THE CURRENT STATUS OF PSYCHOLOGICAL TESTING

With what may appear to be growing disillusionment with psychological testing in almost all corners, what is the status of psychological testing from the standpoints of university training programs and service delivery systems? This question was approached by a group of members of the American Society of Psychologists in Private Practice (ASPPP). At the American Psychological Association's annual convention in 1977, a series of papers was presented addressing the testing status question. Emphasis was placed upon studying the attitude changes in teaching psychological assessment techniques at the graduate level and the utilization of assessment techniques by psychologists in private practice.

The general trend of psychology developing as the scientific discipline appeared to change during the 1960s and 1970s. An almost simplistic approach to understanding human behavior began to appear in the form of radical therapeutic fads which promised quick and thorough cures for those problems that seem to be constantly increasing and immune to traditional forms of therapy. Thus, assessment was deemphasized and exotic therapy glorified. Apparently, the instructional staff and student sentiments and curiosities favored learning more about the avant garde therapies which denied any need for assessment. A survey of graduate psychology training programs suggested that the problem was due to the "elective" status of assessment courses. Students declined taking assessment courses if such were not required for graduation. The survey also suggested that the instructional staff at many of the universities surveyed displayed negative attitudes regarding the value of psychodiagnostic assessment, in terms of training and service.

The ASPPP Survey was also conducted of a group of private psychological practitioners. The conclusions drawn from the information supplied by this sampling suggested that there was a tendency to utilize testing for specific purpose classification rather than general screening. The therapeutic orientations of the practitioners in the survey appeared to play an insignificant role in determining the need for testing. The trend appears to be a desire to select and administer tests in a theoretical fashion — namely, the test results should answer specific questions regarding an individual's functioning rather than offering vague or global reflection of behavior. In other words, the informational needs fulfilled by test results should apply to specific questions regarding the likely outcomes of therapeutic intervention.

The question seems to fall back to the methods of training professional psychologists. The general trend is to prepare students of psychology to think rather than to function as a psychologist. Rigorous scientific methods are taught in graduate programs, but it appears to be up to the students to integrate this training with their mode of service provision. Perhaps, this integration of scientific training should occur during a practicum or intern training period. The goal of training students of psychology is to integrate scientific knowledge, treatment, and research.

The level of training is an important issue regarding the purchase and utilization of tests. Private psychological practitioners generally restrict the more complex usages of tests to the Ph.D.-level practitioners. Objective tests and noncomplex roles are under the domain of the M.A.-level practitioners. This division of training requirements was suggested by the ASPPP survey information. However, test publishers require test users to register their qualifications prior to purchasing tests. A code system defining levels of responsibility is employed for each published test. The training requirements needed to purchase restricted tests are clearly defined. In practice, however, such control may have little effect, for the control ends with the sale and not with the actual usage.

Testing is flourishing and increasing in some areas and declining in others. In some states, governmental agencies are requiring psychological evaluations for certain types of cases in which such evaluations were not required in the past. The trend appears to be toward public health rather than mental health services only. In Pennsylvania, the Lethal Weapons Training Act requires a psychiatric or psychological examination to be performed for every individual who would utilize a lethal weapon during the course of employment. The target population for this law is security guards who heretofore were given guns and other lethal weapons without any structured screening procedure. However, the use of tests is restricted in other areas. For example, in California, school children could not be classified as retarded based on standard psychological test results. Therefore, other assessment methods have to be developed for classification purposes. In the landmark case, *Griggs v. Duke Power Company*, the Supreme Court ruled that tests used for personnel selection should contain questions that directly apply to the elements of the job to be filled. In the past, tests were often used in a biased manner to deny hiring individuals. The same was true, perhaps, in many other areas where psychological tests were used inappropriately.

SUMMARY AND CONCLUDING REMARKS

Psychological assessment glorified the development and utilization of testing instruments as being the epitome for understanding human behavior. The testing concept requires statistical methods for interpretation and analysis. The statistical procedures, required for a truly scientific approach to testing, were perhaps a little late coming, for the early years of testing led to traumatic incidents. Also, safeguards for the restrictions of test users and usages may be considered inadequate. The problems likely led to frustrations and fears related to testing. Since testing is the forte of psychologists, they should be charged with the responsibility of safeguarding its use. The American Psychological Association developed the book, *Standards for Educational and Psychological Tests and Manuals* (APA, 1966). The contents of the standards book should be fully comprehended by anyone who uses tests for decision-making purposes. The value of statistically derived testing procedures can be realized in terms of accuracy, speed, and economy. The general trend appears to be toward administering tests on a selective basis for the purpose of determining therapeutic treatment and predicting likely outcomes. However, quite often, the test is only as good as the skills of the person who administers it. Therefore, psychologists should be fully familiar with a test if the results of it are going to be the basis of a decision. Their ability to defend a decision based on test results is strongly related to their knowledge of and familiarity with the test and procedures.

Even with safeguards, testing biases can exist. Lawyers and the legal system have the responsibility of defending the rights of individuals who may have been wronged by testing. It may be difficult to demonstrate that methods other than testing would not have resulted in an equal or even greater wronging. Emphasis should be placed upon encouraging the continuing scientific development of testing and testing procedures, rather than impeding it. Caution should be exercised in order to avoid over-restriction of test procedures.

Lawyers and psychologists should promote teamwork for improving the status of testing for decision purposes. Psychologists can communicate understanding of statistical and other technical testing information to lawyers. In return, lawyers can interpret the laws that control the usage of testing in order to avoid potential problems for the psychologists at some future time.

BIBLIOGRAPHY

American Psychological Association. *Standards for educational and psychological tests and manuals.* Washington, D.C.: American Psychological Association, 1966.

Fein, L. G., ed. Current status of psychological diagnostic testing in university training programs and in delivery of service systems. *Psychological Reports*, 1979, *44*, 863-879.

Ivnik, R. J. Uncertain status of psychological tests in clinical psychology. *Professional Psychology*, 1977, *8*, 206-213.

Meehl, P. E. *Clinical versus statistical prediction: A theoretical review of the evidence.* Minneapolis: University of Minnesota Press, 1954.

Sawyer, J. Measurement and prediction, clinical and statistical. *Psychological Bulletin*, 1966, *66*, 178-200.

Sundberg, N. D. *Assessment of persons.* Englewood Cliffs, N.J.: Prentice-Hall, 1977.

3 THOMAS N. TUMILTY

The Clinical Psychologist

THE PROFESSION OF CLINICAL PSYCHOLOGY

Psychology and Psychiatry — Training and Competency

The clinical psychologist, via the traditional team approach, has been involved most intimately with two other professions — psychiatry and social work. Although the functions of these team members were once quite specific and delineated, such is no longer the case and the team approach is no longer reflected in the specialization of the past. More and more the functions of these three professions, as well as the training to carry out those functions, have come to overlap.

The public, as well as many professionals, is understandably confused about the training, qualifications, and limitations of these health providers. Few clinical psychologists in private practice can claim never to have had to explain to a perplexed client how they were different from a psychiatrist.

Several service professional disputes (primarily between clinical psychologists and psychiatrists) have arisen regarding professional boundary rights as clinical psychology has struggled for autonomy and freedom from the expectations engendered by the traditional "team approach." Fuel for the maintenance of such disputes has come partly from a lack of knowledge and recognition of the training and competencies of the respective professions, particularly psychology and psychiatry.

In the February 1977 issue of *American Psychologist* (Kiesler), an editorial pointed out several of the distinguishing features of clinical psychology versus psychiatry, including differences in training and competency of its practitioners. In essence, a psychiatrist is a physician who, after undergraduate training in medical science, has gone through three to four years of medical school training leading to the M.D. degree plus a one-year internship. Actual training relevant to later professional practice comes through a three-year residency consisting primarily of actual treatment of patients under the supervision of an experienced psychiatrist certified by the American Psychiatric Association. Full membership in the American Psychiatric Association depends on this residency, but any physician legally and ethically can limit his or her practice to psychiatry without the benefit of the full program of residency training in that area. In the three-year residency, however, there is little or no training in research and statistics. An additional consideration is the relatively high percentage of foreign-born psychiatrists with the attendant difficulties in communication and divergent value systems.

According to Kiesler's citation of the 1972 American Psychological Association Manpower Survey of 21,000 doctorate-level members, these psychologists, after earning undergraduate degrees, spent 5.4 years registered time (and 6.7 years total elapsed time) in their doctoral training. This time typically includes the master's thesis and the doctoral dissertation, which comprise two comprehensive research projects.

Also, as recommended by the recent Education and Credentialing in Psychology meeting (Wellner, 1977), doctoral training in psychology typically includes instruction in scientific and professional ethics and standards, research design and methodology, statistics, and psychometrics, as well as some work in each of four substantive content areas: biological bases of behavior (physiological psychology, comparative psychology, neuropsychology, sensation and perception, psychopharmacology); cognitive-affective bases of behavior (learning, thinking, motivation, emotion); social bases of behavior (social psychology, group processes, organizational and systems theory); and individual differences (personality theory, human development, abnormal psychology).

In addition to practicum work done concurrently with this broad study of human behavior, the clinical psychologist must have one year of intensive internship training involving assessment and treatment of psychological problems under the guidance of experienced clinical psychologists. This is typically followed by at least two years of supervised experience before the practitioner is eligible to take the examinations required for certification or licensure in his or her particular state. After five years of experience, the psychologist is eligible for the examinations of the American Board in Professional Psychology (ABPP) which, if passed, earn him or her a diploma of specialization in clinical psychology.

Psychiatrists are usually in a better position, due to their medical training, to detect and give attention to any physical problem that may be contributing to or resulting from the psychological difficulties. In addition, the psychiatrist usually can be expected to have a greater knowledge of and access to biological forms of treatment, such as medications, electroconvulsive therapy, and psychosurgery. While sometimes indicated, particularly for more severe forms of psychopathology, such forms of treatment have at times been abused and unnecessarily prescribed with attendant side effects, some permanently debilitating or life threatening.

More conservative forms of treatment, some of which (such as behavior therapy) a psychologist is more likely to be expert in administering, are often ignored by the psychiatrist in favor of time-consuming and expensive psychotherapy or drugs, the latter temporarily relieving symptomatology while doing little to enhance the patient's feelings of self-worth and sense of competency.

The psychologist, with broad training in the study of human behavior and a scientific background, may be in a better position to assess the usefulness of various behavioral forms of therapy for a particular problem. Also, through expertise in the use of psychological assessment devices, the psychologist may be better able to determine a client's needs in treatment.

How Clinical Psychologists Spend Their Professional Time

The American Psychological Association is the organization representing the interests of nearly 47,000 psychologists as of 1978. It sponsors annual conventions, publishes *Psychological Abstracts* and 17 other psychological journals, and, through its boards and committees, seeks to meet the professional, scientific, and educational concerns and needs of its members.

Division 12, The Division of Clinical Psychology, is the largest in membership of the forty-one divisions in the association. The interests of the members of this division are many and varied, as suggested by a 1977 American Psychological Association Directory survey, which requested that respondents supply information on major fields of interest as well as more specialized areas of competence. Major fields of interest under Clinical Psychology included psychotherapy, clinical child psychology, behavior and mental disorders, neurological disorder, mental retardation, speech disorder, psychosomatic disorder, medical psychology, and gerontology, (see Introduction). Some of the specialized areas of competence listed under one of these major areas (Psychotherapy) included behavior and conditioning therapy, group therapy, hypnotherapy, adolescent therapy, Gestalt therapy, biofeedback, existential therapy, psychodrama, rational-emotive therapy, sex/marital therapy, and transactional therapy.

A recent survey of approximately 23 percent of the membership of the Division of Clinical Psychology (Garfield and Kurtz, 1976) sheds some light on the way clinical psychologists tend to apportion their professional time. These authors found that about 35 percent of their sample were employed in institutional settings; 30 percent were employed in university settings; just over 23 percent listed private practice as their main occupational setting; and 11.5 percent indicated a variety of other settings. Just over 47 percent indicated that they engaged in some part-time private practice. In terms of specific professional activities, therapy (individual and group psychotherapy; behavior modification) accounted for 31.4 percent of the professional time of clinical psychologists. The three areas accounting for the next largest portions of such time were teaching (13.8 percent), administration

(13.2 percent), and diagnosis and assessment (9.8 percent). It is apparent that today's clinical psychologist is primarily a therapist, and not the tester that fit the stereotype of yesterday.

A more recent survey of all identified licensed/certified psychologists in the United States by the National Register (Wellner and Mills, 1977) yielded similar results, in terms of private practice and psychotherapy, from a much larger sample (approximately 19,000). About 73.8 percent of the respondents reported they are currently providing health services and, of these, almost 25 percent reported being in full-time private practice (80 percent of these are self-employed) and over 55 percent in some form of private practice. Over 90 percent of the private practitioners provide psychotherapy services.

Apparently, most licensed/certified psychologists are in some form of private practice and are providing psychotherapy, independent of inter-profession supervision, as an integral part of the health services they deliver. Furthermore, it is obvious that professional psychology is a national resource of considerable importance. According to a survey of American Psychological Association members for the year 1976 (Gottfredson and Dyer, 1978), an estimated two to four million people annually received approximately nineteen million hours of health services from doctoral-level association members.

Specialized Expertise of the Clinical Psychologist

In order to qualify as a profession, a field such as psychology must include specialized expertise. Its practitioners must have at their disposal techniques of demonstrable utility. There is good evidence that such techniques now exist in the profession of psychology (Peterson, 1976). These include test batteries useful in the diagnosis of brain dysfunction; valid and reliable tests of intelligence; achievement, aptitude, and interest tests useful in vocational counseling; and certain measures of psychopathology that bear some relationship to clinically important behaviors such as suicide.

Behavioral assessment measures of direct relevance to treatment planning and assessment are now available (Cautela, 1977). General Forms provide background information and aid in the general identification of possible maladaptive behaviors. Process Forms are concerned with agreed upon target behaviors, motivation for change, and the treatment plan and its outcome. Techniques Forms provide information for the implementation of the therapeutic strategies, and Specific Forms provide specific information on the target behaviors to aid in the behavioral analysis of those behaviors.

Such techniques as biofeedback training, especially electromyographic (EMG); progressive muscle relaxation techniques; hypnosis; and some forms of meditation have in many instances proven useful in relieving tension and its accompanying pain. Behavior therapy procedures such as systematic desensitization have demonstrated their utility in helping people face up to anxiety-arousing stimuli and overcome their fears. Assertion training is useful in getting people to develop more ego-enhancing ways of interacting with others. Modeling can teach individuals skills in areas of deficiency, such as appropriate behavior in relation to certain classes of people (members of opposite sex, prospective employers, etc.).

Covert procedures are available to reinforce positive thoughts or punish negative thoughts so that self-esteem is increased and negative affect is reduced. Aversive conditioning has shown its utility in dealing with self-destructive behavior and sexual disorders. Operant conditioning has allowed for dramatic reductions in the bizarre behavior and the development of more adaptive behavior in schizophrenic children and adults. Many other techniques are used to therapeutic advantage by professional psychologists when dealing with a patient's problems in a clinical setting.

Quality Control of Members of the Profession

Through statutory regulations of the states, through state psychological associations and their committees, and through guidelines and individual specialty designation by the American Psychological Association, the public is provided a high degree of assurance that the providers of psychological services are competent and responsible.

With the passage of a licensure bill by the Missouri General Assembly in 1977, the practice of psychology came to be regulated by law in all fifty states. It had taken thirty-two years for statutory regulations to be enacted in every state since Connecticut first "certified" psychologists in 1945. Sunset legislation has become the basis for the recision of statutes in three states. This has been alluded to earlier and will not be treated here. Psychologists are now recognized by statute as independent practitioners for the diagnosis and treatment of emotional or mental disorders in forty-seven states in the United States, the District of Columbia, and six Canadian provinces. The national standard for licensing of the American Psychological Association consists of a doctoral degree, a comprehensive written and oral examination, and supervised experience. Only a few states deviate from this standard in recognizing the master's degree as the minimally acceptable educational requirement with additional experience to compensate for this lower educational level.

The distinction between *certification* and *licensure* laws is an important one for the profession and the public. Certification laws may merely provide for the restriction of the title "psychologist" to persons who have met certain standards. A licensure law additionally defines the practice of the profession of psychology and limits the use of psychological techniques to persons determined to be properly qualified. Most states have enacted the more inclusive licensure type of regulation which better represents psychology as an independent, autonomous health profession.

Dörken (1976) discusses some of the desirable features in the wording of these statutory regulations that would be consistent with psychology's claim that it is a health profession. He also discusses the growing momentum to have continuing education as a requirement for relicensure, as has already been enacted in several states.

The knowledge and skill of the members of a profession is often attested to by certification from a major organization representing that profession. The American Board of Professional Psychology (ABPP), established by the American Psychological Association as the American Board of Examiners in Professional Psychology in 1947, certifies the professional competence of psychologists in the areas of clinical, counseling, industrial and organizational, and school psychology. This is done through an oral examination by five "diplomates" (individuals already so certified) who evaluate the candidates' knowledge and skill in the particular area as well as by observing the individual's skill interacting with a patient in a therapeutic encounter. Clinical protocols also are offered by the candidate as evidence of clinical expertise.

Another type of what might be called "specialty certification" was initiated through the establishment in 1975 of the *National Register of Health Service Providers in Psychology* by the American Psychological Association (see Introduction). On the basis of a credentials review of applicants, a directory of those found meeting fairly strict criteria was issued in 1975 and is being continually updated. Those criteria as of January 1, 1978 are: (1) currently licensed or certified by the state board of examiners of psychology at the independent practice level of psychology; (2) a doctorate in psychology from a regionally accredited educational institution; and (3) two years of supervised experience in health service, of which at least one year is postdoctoral and one year (may be postdoctoral year) is in an organized health service training program.

Identification of those psychologists who have voluntarily applied for inclusion and who meet these criteria provides a register that is useful to consumers, third party payers, and health planners. It identifies qualified health providers and, thereby, facilitates insurance claim processing and reimbursement for those listed, as well as delineating currently available manpower resources of psychology as a health profession. It has already been accepted as a criterion guideline by several insurance carriers and agencies at both federal and state levels.

Organized psychology, as a means of self-regulation to protect the public interest, established standards and published them in the book *Standards for Providers of Psychological Services* (APA, 1974). In January 1975, the Committee on Standards for Providers of Psychological Services was created and charged with updating and revising the standards adopted in September 1974. One year later, this committee was further charged with reviewing the standards and recommending revisions applying to a more limited range of services, namely, those ordinarily involved in the practice of clinical, counseling, industrial-organizational, and school psychology. In addition, these revised standards were to specify uniformly the *minimally acceptable levels* of quality assurance and performance providers must reach or exceed.

These revised standards (APA, 1977c) provide guidelines for providers, programs, and service environments as well as areas of accountability for practitioners. As with the original standards, the revised version has been used as an authoritative reference in organizing and staffing psychology services, in supporting legislation, in increasing confidence in the competence and responsibility of psychologist service providers in federal and state health programs, and in guiding changes in governmental and private accreditation manuals that affect the functioning of psychologists in varied human service settings (Jacobs, 1976).

The American Psychological Association has supported the establishment of state Professional Standards Review Committees (PSRC). These "peer review" committees handle questions concerning whether the psychological services provided were necessary, whether such services were the most appropriate that could have been provided, whether they met or exceeded professionally recognized standards, and whether the charges were usual, customary, or reasonable. Although such committees are not disciplinary bodies and their decisions do not carry the force of law, they may provide disinterested opinions that may resolve disagreements involving psychologist service providers, clients, or third party payers.

The American Psychological Association developed a set of ethical standards to guide the conduct of psychologists in their professional activities in 1953, which was updated in 1959 and 1962. In 1975 (APA, 1975), the Committee on Scientific and Professional Ethics and Conduct approved the seventh draft, *Ethical Standards of Psychologists*.

This draft, and subsequent revisions in 1977, 1979, and 1981, included nine principles covering responsibility, competence, moral and legal standards, public statements, confidentiality, welfare of the consumer, professional relationships, utilization of assessment techniques, and the pursuit of research activities. These principles are designed to maintain confidence in the integrity of psychology and to protect and maximize the benefit to consumers of psychological services.

Psychology then, as a profession, is regulated by state law; provides for certification of members in specialty areas; identifies qualified health providers; promulgates standards to improve the quality, effectiveness, and accessibility of psychological services; provides for review of the quality and cost of services; and enjoins members to adhere to a code of ethics in their professional activities.

Professional Independence and Autonomy

According to the publication *Standards for Providers of Psychological Services* (APA, 1977c), "Psychologists shall pursue their activities as members of an independent, autonomous profession." Further, "They shall seek to eliminate discriminatory practices instituted for self-serving purposes that are not in the interest of the user (e.g., arbitrary requirements for referral and supervision by another profession.)" Psychology has been struggling for over thirty years to free itself of domination by the medical profession and, although the struggle is being won, many problem areas still exist that are inimical to the interests of psychology as a profession and to the welfare of the American public.

With the establishment of the Council for the Advancement of Psychological Professions and Sciences (CAPPS) in 1971 and the Association for the Advancement of Psychology (AAP) in 1973, psychology finally had advocacy organizations at the federal level. State psychological associations had been fighting for legislation in the interests of psychology and the public before this, but often their financial resources and personnel were insufficient to have great input into the legislative process.

Most of the legislative issues involve giving psychologists parity with psychiatrists, or at least nonpsychiatrist physicians, and eliminating the requirement of medical supervision or referral. A recent survey of American Psychological Association members by the AAP (AAP, 1977a) found clear support for AAP's advocacy efforts to include therapeutic services by psychologists without medical referral and supervision in the existing Medicaid and Medicare programs (84 percent) and to oppose the "medical psychotherapy" concept in federal laws and regulations (85 percent). In addition, support of such advocacy was apparent in efforts to include psychological services and adequate mental health benefits in any national health insurance legislation enacted by Congress (84 percent) and to petition the Federal Trade Commission to change hospital staffing policies that allow medical domination of essential health services (82 percent).

Psychological services under Medicaid were not provided for by most states as of 1977. Only a few accepted qualified psychologists as independent providers of therapy and testing services. A few others limited autonomy to testing, while some required medical referral for either therapy or testing. Psychologists are not now included as therapists under Medicare, and psychological testing is only covered on medical referral. Federal legislation was pending in 1977 (S. 123, H.R.2270) that would make psychologists independent providers under Medicare and remove any arbitrary provisions of physician referral.

As of 1977, several federal-level programs had endorsed psychologists as autonomous providers of health services, establishing parity between psychologists and other qualified providers of such covered services. These programs included the Federal Employees Health Benefits contracts; the Rehabilitation Act of 1973 (Public Law 93-112); the Civilian Health and Medical Program of the Uniformed Services (CHAMPUS); CHAMPVA, a program for the dependents of totally disabled veterans; Work Incentive Program (WIN); Federal Employees Compensation Act; Health Maintenance Organization (HMO) legislation; and Head Start Manual (July 1975) health performance standards (Dörken and Morrison, 1976). Regulations provide that a psychologist may serve as a program director of a community mental health center as well as of specialized programs (mental hygiene clinics, day treatment centers) within the Veterans Administration.

At the state level, freedom-of-choice legislation had been enacted by twenty-nine states, covering over 70 percent of the U.S. population, by 1978. This legislation provides for direct recognition of psychologists as providers under private health insurance plans and removes any necessity of medical referral for covered services. Freedom-of-choice or direct recognition legislation allows the individual seeking treatment direct access to a psychologist, as well as a psychiatrist.

Evidence from cost/utilization studies show that general medical hospital costs drop when psychological treatment is freely available (Kaiser-Permanente Medical Group, San Francisco), further arguing for the desirability of the consumer's free access to a psychologist's services (Cummings and Follette, 1976).

The requirement of medical referral or supervision at times adds unnecessary professional visits and increases the cost of services. Restriction of the availability of psychological services also serves to reduce the supply of mental health resources, thereby inflating the rates of medical services. The struggle continues to end this discriminatory practice and make health resources more readily available and at lower cost to the consumer.

Another struggle for independence is being waged with the Joint Commission for the Accreditation of Hospitals (JCAH). The commission has recently established for psychiatric facilities accreditation requirements that discriminate against psychology as an independent, autonomous profession and against the public's right to quality health services. Although there has been some recent tempering of this policy in certain states, JCAH accreditation requirements have prohibited psychologists from exercising independent staff privileges in hospitals, long-term care and psychiatric facilities and maintain that patient care is the ultimate responsibility of the physician. These requirements go so far as to require that the medical staff assess the competence of nonmedical staff and delineate their privileges, a subordination that psychology as an established health profession finds unacceptable.

These arbitrary restrictions favoring the medical profession are not difficult to understand given the evidence that the JCAH, to some extent, has been playing the role of a self-serving extension of the American Medical Association, the American Hospital Association, and the College of Physicians and College of Surgeons. The power wielded by JCAH derives from the fact that many federal and state statutes require that health care facilities have accreditation from JCAH in order for them to qualify for benefits under a variety of programs. Interestingly, even though JCAH standards are incorporated in such statutes, these standards are in violation of all those state and federal laws that provide for psychology as an independent, autonomous profession as well as giving specific authorization for qualified psychologists to direct clinical services and programs (Dörken and Morrison, 1976).

In order to remedy this untenable situation, AAP has petitioned the Federal Trade Commission (FTC) to investigate certain JCAH practices. The petition is based on the allegation that JCAH and the American Medical Association are guilty of monopoly, conspiracy, and boycott, and of violations of the Clayton Act, the Sherman Act, and Section IV of the FTC Act. The AAP has alleged that JCAH imposes restrictions that are inimical to the public interest by stifling competition and that artificial and predatory barriers have been erected that exclude qualified and recognized professional services without medical, social, or economic justification, for the exclusive benefit of physicians and hospitals. The FTC has undertaken an investigation based on these complaints and the outcome is still pending (AAP, 1977b).

Psychology's fight for independence and autonomy as a profession continues but progress often seems painfully slow. We have a fruitful history of development, thorough training of those who enter the profession, techniques "that work," and quality control of our members. Yet, what we, as practitioners, spend most of our time doing (psychotherapy) is often restricted unnecessarily and unfairly by other professions and, through their influence, by federal and state regulations. The advent of consumerism helps to highlight these inequities, however, since the public as well as the profession suffers from the restriction of psychological services. The public has the right to better access to quality health care and the need to realize this right is the main force in helping psychology become a truly independent and autonomous profession.

THE CLINICAL PSYCHOLOGIST IN THE LEGAL SYSTEM

Laws Affecting the Psychologist's Participation in Judicial Matters

In the judicial system psychology is slowly being accorded respect as a profession with an important contribution to make in arriving at informed legal decisions. Dörken (1970) reported that twelve states required and fifteen other states permitted the involvement of a qualified psychologist in the commitment process of the mentally retarded. A psychologist's participation was not required in any state, though possible in four, in the case of commitment proceedings for the mentally disordered.

In late 1975 and early 1976, another survey was conducted of state officials that requested information as to whether psychologists could sign papers committing an individual to a state owned and operated psychiatric inpatient treatment facility/mental retardation facility (Dörken, 1977). The results of this updated survey showed little change in terms of commitment of the mentally retarded but a dramatic shift toward greater participation of psychologists in the commitment of the "mentally ill." Twenty-three states now allowed such participation, twelve only on a second opinion/signature basis, five on a first opinion/signature basis, and six in which no distinction was made as to order.

More elaborate and slightly updated findings are reported by Sobel (1978b) based on a review of the statutes of the fifty states and the District of Columbia through the spring 1977 legislative sessions. She found that twenty-four states *permit* a psychological evaluation to be part of the process for involuntary commitment for mental illness. Only Arizona has a specific *requirement* for a psychological evaluation as part of this legal process. In the case of only one of the twenty-four states (Maine) will a psychologist's testimony by itself be sufficient for judicial commitment. Twenty-six states and the District of Columbia have statutory provisions that do not permit psychological testimony to be primary evidence in commitment proceedings, and in these jurisdictions psychological test reports are usually attached to the physician's report.

Sobel (1978a), as part of the same review, also reported on state statutes regulating the procedures for determining whether a person is judged to be competent to stand trial (pretrial competency) and whether the law specifies the inclusion of psychological testimony. Assessments of pretrial competency address the question of whether the defendant has the capacity to understand the nature and object of the proceedings going on against him or her and whether the defendant is capable of assisting in the defense. As of spring 1977, seventeen states either specified psychological certification in their provisions or included psychologists as a mental health expert. As Sobel points out, this is a somewhat poorer record than that of inclusion of psychological testimony in commitment procedures for the mentally ill.

Psychologists still are not being accorded parity with psychiatrists (despite the fact that both are trained to diagnose and treat mental disorders), or even nonpsychiatrist physicians for that matter, in the area of civil commitment and competency to stand trial. Some gains have been evident, however, that point to a greater appreciation of the psychologist's expertise and the role a psychologist can play in the commitment process and as an expert witness in pretrial competency hearings.

The Clinical Psychologist as an Expert Witness

The right of psychologists to serve as expert witnesses, in the same capacity as a psychiatrist, is firmly established in both statutory law and case law in at least half of the states. In those jurisdictions in which he or she does act as an expert witness, the psychologist can expect to be required, at least initially, to establish his or her personal qualifications. Such qualifications are determined by questions at the beginning of courtroom testimony from the attorney relating to such areas as identity; place of residence and/or business; highest degree earned, in what field, and from what institution; licensure/certification status; amount and type of experience in the field of psychology; and, perhaps, any special skills, recognition, or awards relevant to professional competence.

Most often the psychologist will be providing testimony based primarily on psychological test results. Testimony based on an extensive interview with a client without any use of psychological assessment devices, however, seems to be becoming more common. Such testimony may be quite useful if the raw data (interview responses of the client) are placed within a theoretical framework more easily understood and supported by more empirical evidence than that observed in some psychiatric and psychological testimony. Moreover, the psychologist may often perform a service by providing detailed interview data and avoiding much of the speculative inferences and uninformative labeling that are often associated with psychiatric and psychological testimony. Testimony by psychologists, without test results, is not inappropriate in civil commitment proceedings.

The psychologist can find use for tests to make an "educated guess" as to whether a defendant met the court's criterion of insanity at the time a crime was committed. Such a question generally requires that inferences be made concerning the client's mental state at the time of the illegal act. Insofar as projective assessment devices of questionable validity will be requested by the psychiatrist and used by the psychologist in an attempt to answer this question, however, it becomes debatable as to whether the psychologist will be providing any useful service. The attorney on the opposing side will almost surely question the psychologist's testimony, beyond that derived from the projective tests, based on quotations from authoritative sources that such tests lack reliability and/or validity. If "projectives" are used, one should be prepared to account for important conclusions based on more "psychometrically respectable" tests so that the credibility of the entire testimony is not jeopardized.

Other questions frequently asked of the psychologist involve parental fitness, disability resulting from an accident, and competence of a person to manage his or her own affairs. Such questions often require psychological assessment not only at the present time but also inferences about mental states probable in the past or likely in the future. Pope and Scott (1967) address themselves to the use of psychological tests in the pursuit of answers to such questions.

Whatever the nature of the courtroom testimony, certain points are well to keep in mind:

1. It is important that the lawyer specify before the trial the questions the

psychologist will be expected to answer on the stand. If such questions are not clearly formulated, the most appropriate information may not be gathered via certain tests and interviews and the psychologist's conclusions may "miss the mark."

2. If not already aware of the law as it pertains to the issue about which he or she is going to testify, the psychologist should ensure that the lawyer provide information on this matter at a pretrial conference. The expert witness needs to be familiar with the legal definition of the terms relevant to the case so that the testimony is in accord with the legal formulations.

3. The psychologist similarly needs to inform the lawyer briefly of the nature of the tests being administered, particularly information relating to their purpose and validity. The opposing attorney may isolate for criticism one small part of the administration, scoring, or interpretation of the tests or of the client's response to one of the tests. Strict adherence to the standardized administration procedure for each test will give protection against an otherwise potential source of criticism. Such attempts to discredit psychological testimony should be countered by the lawyer who has contracted for the psychologist's services, possibly by reference to the widespread and established utilization of such tests in the manner of usage followed by the psychologist.

4. The opposing attorney may also suggest that the testimony is biased because the psychologist is being paid to testify on the client's behalf. It should be made clear that the psychologist is being paid for the time involved and services provided and not for the testimony itself. Being paid in advance, and so reporting if questioned, is one practice that allows the practitioner to counter the criticism of being paid to support a particular position.

5. The psychologist should be prepared to distinguish himself or herself from a psychiatrist. Since such a question could be asked so as to demean the psychologist's testimony relative to that of a psychiatrist on the opposing side, certain of the differences and relative strengths of the psychologist mentioned earlier in this chapter should be kept in mind.

6. The cross-examination should not be taken personally. Anger or sarcasm on the part of the expert witness may compromise the effectiveness of the testimony. In the adversary process, opposing counsel can be expected to do everything possible to prove the case. This includes ordinarily unwarranted attacks on the psychologist's qualifications, findings, and perhaps even the psychologist personally.

7. Findings do not speak for themselves. The ability to express oneself so as to be readily understood with a presentation in a calm, confident manner has a great deal to do with the effectiveness of the psychologist's testimony. Psychologists are not in court to defend a client, but they do have an ethical obligation to defend their testimony so that it has the effect on the audience that it should.

8. In the scientific pursuit of psychology we learned that most variables

are continuous and that "black and white" thinking was a less sophisticated form of cognition. In court one will have to revert to the more primitive form of thinking necessitated by the decision processes of the judicial system. It may be necessary to say yes or no, perhaps without any opportunity to clarify or qualify the response, unless the attorney for whom the psychologist is testifying sees fit to ask the questions necessary to provide that luxury.

9. It is probably a good rule to place more emphasis on observations and less on inferences, providing multiple observations to substantiate each inference that is made.

The Clinical Psychologist as a Consultant to the Attorney

The role of the psychologist in jury selection has as its goal a fair group of men and women who will not be hostile and prejudicial, prior to the presentation of evidence, toward the attorney, the client, or the cause of action. Such characteristics of prospective jurors as socioeconomic status, physical features and constitutional factors, ethnicity, age, sex, religion, and marital status may be relevant in jury selection depending on the nature of the case. A good knowledge of psychological studies relating such demographic characteristics to predispositions to respond certain ways, given certain stimuli, is essential if the psychologist is to be of maximum effectiveness in ensuring for the attorney a jury that will be sympathetic to the client and his or her cause.

Gordon (1975) presents an eight-step approach to jury selection which includes: (1) counsel's solicitation of the client's approval for the forensic psychologist to be consulted on the matter of jury selection; (2) the attorney's provision to the psychologist of a fact situation summary which includes critical witnesses and their anticipated testimony; (3) a briefing of the attorney by the psychologist on matters relevant to courtroom style, including observation of dress, speech patterns, and personality dynamics; (4) psychological evaluation of the client, including speech patterns, physical appearance, personality characteristics, etc.; (5) the psychologist's construction of an ideal juror profile based on several weighted factors, such as: age, education, marital status, children, occupation, geographical background, race, religion, sex, and clinical observation and inference; (6) observation by the psychologist of interactions between the attorney, clients, and the panel during which the psychologist makes the ratings and watches for cues to rapport, body language, etc.; (7) the preparation by the psychologist of the eleven questions for the attorney to ask that will elicit the factor information required; and (8) tabulation by the psychologist of the scoring sheets and presentation to counsel of recommendations for strikes.

In addition to jury selection, the psychologist may also advise the attorney as to which witnesses could be called upon to corroborate the psychological testimony or other aspects of the case and the questions counsel could ask them to ensure effective presentation of their views. Taking advantage of the observations of the opponent's witnesses to support one's own position is yet another area in which the psychologist may usefully advise the attorney.

ETHICAL RESPONSIBILITY AND PROFESSIONAL LIABILITY

Legal and Ethical Implications of Therapy

In order to safeguard the rights of clients and ensure professional responsibility, it has been suggested that several factors must be taken into account before, during, and following treatment. One of these factors is *informed consent*. In reference to behavior modification in particular, Stolz, Wienckowski, and Brown (1975) suggest that evaluation of the extent to which individual clients or members of a target population can give truly informed consent involves preparation of a description of the treatment or program and its goals so that clients or participants know what is involved; assessment of the extent to which clients or participants are competent to understand the proposed therapy and make an appropriate judgment about it; and evaluation of the degree to which their consent can be truly voluntary.

If competence to understand the proposed therapy is in question (for example, an actively psychotic patient), the concept of *best interest* becomes a central focus. Best interest requires that the benefits of the contemplated therapy clearly outweigh both the known harms and possible risks or side effects, that the proposed procedure is in fact efficacious, and that this procedure is the least intrusive or restrictive one still available (Friedman, 1976). Optimally, the treatment of choice would be one high in potential benefit, low in risk or side effects, strongly supported as efficacious by experimental investigations, and minimal in its infringement on the individual's freedom of expression and choice.

Voluntary consent to treatment is strongly influenced by the setting in which such treatment takes place. Institutional settings (prisons and mental hospitals) are often viewed as providing maximum infringement on voluntary consent because of their pervasive influence over the lives of those they attempt to rehabilitate or treat. In reference to such settings, it is often recommended that certain committees be established to ensure that the client's rights are protected (Friedman, 1976).

One of these, a statewide peer review committee, would consider the appropriateness of proposed treatments based on their proven efficacy, whether the design of the procedure is professionally sound, the risks or side-effects involved, and the availability of less hazardous or intrusive procedures. A human rights committee (for various regions in the state) would have such duties as investigating complaints regarding treatment programs; categorizing and monitoring procedures with a diligence increasing with the hazardousness and intrusiveness of the procedures and divergence of the treatment goals from those of the client; determination that the client has the capacity to consent to the particular procedure and that the client and/or his or her guardian has given a valid informed consent or waiver in writing to the proposed procedure; ensuring that the client has been apprised of the procedure and its implications and informed that no benefits or penalties will be contingent upon participation in the proposed program or agreement to undergo the proposed procedure.

Such review committees as have been described can be initiated at the institutional level as well to protect patient rights through evaluation of the appropriateness of proposed treatment programs and through monitoring of such programs once they are put into effect.

Often, the person who will undergo treatment is able to negotiate the proposed goals and procedures of therapy directly with the professional personnel who will carry out such treatment. A mutual agreement or contract that specifies the responsibilities and rights of both the client and therapist would then be worked out between them. A simple therapeutic contract suggested by Schwitzgebel (1975) might state that "The therapist will treat the patient with the degree of care which similar therapists would exercise under the circumstances, and the patient agrees to follow instructions and pay the therapist the reasonable value of his professional services."

Beyond this, a contract could specify such factors as the mutually agreed upon goals of treatment, the procedures that will be used to reach those goals, the anticipated duration of treatment, and how the outcome of treatment will be measured. Prior to initiation of such a contract, the client should be apprised of such factors as probable benefits of therapy, possible risks or side effects of the procedures to be employed, and available alternative types of treatment.

Most of the guidelines suggested for psychological treatment and the protection of patient rights have grown out of the concern about one particular form of therapy, behavior modification. An important reason for such concern would seem to be the relative effectiveness of this form of treatment as compared with other forms. People fear control when they believe the means for effective control exists and when they have developed a distrust in those in whom the means for such control is invested. While the extent of this concern by the public is probably unwarranted, occasional abuses under the guise of the term *behavior modification* have occurred and have fueled the move to increase the extent to which clients are involved in determining the goals and procedures of their own treatment.

The draft of the American Psychological Association Commission on Behavior Modification (APA, 1976) recommended that persons engaged in any type of psychological intervention subscribe to and follow the ethics code and standards of their professions. The commission also recommended that the association consider adopting a checklist of issues that could be used in the evaluation of ethics of any psychological intervention, including but not restricted to behavior modification. The intention of the commission was to focus attention on those aspects of the therapeutic process in which clients are potentially at risk and, thereby, increase attention to the client's rights.

The checklist recommended by the commission for issues relevant to all settings includes: (1) selection of goals that are realistic, explicit, positive, and serve the client's best interests, and that are chosen through consideration of what the client sees as the problem; (2) selection of methods that are consistent with current legal rulings and with the American Psychological Association ethical standards, after the client and psychologist have discussed the intrusiveness and efficacy of alternative approaches; (3) informing the client that the intervention can be refused or terminated without prejudice of any kind; (4) opportunity for outside review of interventions used and goals chosen; (5) selection of the least coercive, punitive, and intrusive intervention methods currently available; (6) mutually agreed upon explicit and realistic plans for the transition to the postintervention period; (7) accountability achieved through monitoring the effects of the intervention, evaluating progress systematically, and sharing results with the client; (8) confidentiality maintained through access to records controlled by the client; and (9) insurance that the person conducting the intervention is qualified to offer the service or has appropriate supervision and that the client has been made aware of such qualifications. The committee suggests consideration of further issues when the psychologist has dual allegiances, when the client's competency is in question, and when the voluntary nature of the client's consent is questioned.

While the preceding recommendations have been suggested as applicable to any therapeutic intervention, their use in actual fact is probably most oriented to such forms of therapy as behavior modification in which humans are assumed to be controlled by relatively conscious and rational motives. Therapists of other persuasions might very well consider quite naive and outdated the assumption that a client can be expected to be aware of and act in his or her own best interests in a cooperative approach to the problems.

In actual fact, there is doubt that any client ever comes to therapy 100 percent motivated to cure the problems. External pressures or a sudden increase in symptoms may bring the client into therapy and cause him or her to express a desire to eliminate a problem. Motivations counteracting achievement of such an expressed goal, however, frequently include the reinforcing attention that the maladaptive behavior provokes, the utility of the behavior in allowing for avoidance of feared or disliked responses that would represent more responsible behavior, and the need to maintain the behavior as confirmation of a negative and yet valued and supported self-image.

We as therapists may accept the client's expressed intention to eliminate problem behavior, but we cannot realistically expect complete cooperation in pursuit of these stated therapeutic goals. Appointments, instructions, self-control techniques, etc., will be conveniently "forgotton." Blame for lack of progress will be externalized.

Understanding, feelings, and behavior that threaten the status quo will be filtered out by the client, if possible. Clients are often the greatest threat to their own best interests, not some institution or some presumed Machiavellian therapist.

In light of the antitherapeutic motivations that clients bring to therapy, guidelines and checklists to ensure accountability of the therapist and protect the "rights" of the client sometimes fall short of being in the best interest of positive therapeutic outcome. There are techniques that utilize the client's resistance rather than enlist "cooperation" and these cannot easily be incorporated into a contract. Suggesting that a client maintain or even encourage certain maladaptive behavior often results in elimination of such behavior and would be one example of such a technique.

Guidelines and checklists are convenient but they do encourage us to content ourselves with certain rather naive assumptions — client commitment to therapeutic change. There needs to be room for techniques that are less straightforward and upfront but that in many cases are the only recourse when we are put in the double bind of dealing with a client who expresses positive expectations but subconsciously plots sabotage of therapy. The intrusion of excessive and unnecessary legal and ethical impositions on providers of therapeutic services can load the dice in favor of realization of the client's self-destructive motivations and, as such, do not themselves meet the criteria they encourage us to meet — being in the client's "best interests."

Confidentiality

In 1977, the American Psychological Association Committee on Scientific and Professional Ethics and Conduct proposed, as part of the psychologist's revised code of ethics, that "Confidential information may be disclosed without authorization from the client only when and to the extent that the psychologist reasonably determines that such disclosure is necessary to protect against a clear and substantial risk of imminent serious injury or disease or death being inflicted by the client on him/herself or another." Some prominent clinicians have argued that confidentiality should never be broken because it is essential to the development of trust and openness in psychotherapy and, in fact, to successful psychotherapy itself. These clinicians further feel that any danger to the client or someone else can be handled in ways other than the violation of confidentiality.

Despite such assertions, however, the courts have seen fit to establish conditions under which the psychotherapist must violate confidentiality or expose himself or herself to civil liability. In the summer of 1976, the California Supreme Court issued a new opinion in regard to the case of *Tarasoff v. Regents of the University of California* which had direct bearing on such conditions. In this opinion, the court holds that the psychotherapist who has, in fact, determined that a patient poses a serious danger to an ascertainable third party has a legal duty to take steps to warn and protect the potential victim. The warning can apparently be to the potential victim, to others likely to inform the potential victim of the danger, or to the police. (In this particular case, however, warning the police was not seen as sufficient.)

Such a court decision brings to focus such problems as the accurate prediction of violence, whether the responsibility for protection resides with the mental health worker or the police, the deleterious effects of potential violation of confidentiality on the process of psychotherapy and on the likelihood of violence-prone persons seeking therapeutic interventions, the therapist's responsibility in determining a potential victim's existence and identity, and the potential liability that could be incurred by the therapist if adverse consequences to the patient follow upon such violations of confidentiality (Whiteley and Whiteley, 1977).

Apparently, proposed ethical guidelines for psychologists and court opinion are in agreement that the doctor-patient relationship is of special significance as regards responsibility not only for the client, but also to some degree for any person in danger of harm from such client. Such considerations of human life supersede the therapist's commitment to confidentiality and legal liability can be incurred if one's priorities are otherwise.

Outside of special circumstances, such as where danger exists to a client or potential victim or a legal duty exists to report a battered child, the information gained by a therapist in evaluation and psychotherapy is owned by the client and may be revealed only when the client has given written consent that it may be released to a specified third party. Such a position is supported by national ethical guidelines and, in many cases, by state legislation embodied in licensure laws. Violation of confidentiality exposes the therapist to professional censure and the possibility of a claim for damages in a tort action for breach of privacy.

Unless there exists a statutory bar to testifying about confidential information, however, the court may compel the psychologist to provide such information in the course of a trial even in the absence of consent for release by the client. States not providing explicit guarantees for patient — practitioner communications through state psychology laws as of 1978 included California, District of Columbia, Maryland, Nevada, New York, North Dakota, Rhode Island, South Carolina, Texas, Vermont, Virginia, West Virginia, Iowa, and Wyoming.

If privileged communication covering psychologists has been legislated in a state, then usually only the client has the right to decide if such information will be allowed to be brought into evidence at the trial. Of course, such right by the client is automatically waived when the client has raised the issue of his or her psychological condition in certain legal proceedings, as in the filing of a suit claiming emotional damages.

Malpractice Liability

Malpractice in psychology is generally based on the legal concept of "negligence." Negligence is proved when the psychologist, being an individual from whom a high level of knowledge and skill could be expected, had a responsibility to the client to provide services; the psychologist failed to fulfill that responsibility through a "reasonable standard of care" (that level of skill expected of practitioners offering the same treatment modality on a national level); and, as a direct result of such failure, physical or psychological injury (which was reasonably foreseeable) was incurred by the client or by someone else who was affected by the client's actions.

Taking care not to deviate too far from established standards of practice and adhering to professional ethical guidelines are important in protecting the psychologist from the threat of malpractice. Physical contact with a client, especially if it involves an aggressive response by the therapist, and sexual relations with the client are areas that would put the psychologist at a high degree of risk as regards malpractice. In addition, malpractice insurance frequently does not cover the psychologist when he steps outside established standards of practice and engages in such actions. The Psychologist Professional Liability Policy presently being endorsed by the American Psychological Association, for instance, excludes coverage when liability is incurred by "licentious, immoral or sexual behavior intended to lead to or culminating in any sexual act" and "assault and battery by or at the direction of the insured except in the act of self-defense."

In the case of suicide, the liability risk to the therapist increases with the severity of the intent for self-destruction demonstrated by the client in the absence of proper precautions being exercised by the therapist. As severity of intent increases, one would expect that the foreseeability of the event should also increase and it would be incumbent on the therapist to ensure the development of a relevant treatment plan and that such a plan was faithfully carried out. Foreseeing suicide as having a high potential of actual occurrence but not providing a reasonable treatment plan or not ensuring its execution would expose the therapist to maximum liability risk.

A therapist exposes himself or herself to liability to the extent that the therapist is judged to have intentionally manipulated a client for personal gain and especially when a third party has vested interest in a decision made by the client. Such could be the case when the therapist, named a beneficiary in a will, may have to prove to the court's satisfaction that there was no manipulatory intent on his or her part if the third party contests the will. Even in the absence of personal gain, a liability risk is incurred by therapists in those cases in which they encourage client actions in opposition to the wishes of a third party. The client in this case could be a minor and the third party his or her parents.

In the defense of one's professional behavior, keeping accurate and detailed client records can be quite important. Such records could offer self-protection, by way of documenting what did or did not occur in therapy, in the event that the psychologist has to defend himself or herself against a liability claim. Included in these records might be informed consent forms signed by the client attesting to understanding of and willingness to be involved in psychotherapy and any particular techniques a part thereof. The greater the degree to which techniques deviate from standard practice, the greater the need for such formal consent as protection against malpractice suits.

The following case is illustrative of the psychologist in expert witness testimony. In this case names have been changed to maintain anonymity.

Illustration of Expert Witness Testimony

This case involved a trio of young males who were charged with the slayings of a woman and her two young children following a burglary-robbery. A change of venue was granted because of alleged undue publicity in the county in which the crime occurred.

The trial of one of the defendants was separated from that of his codefendants because he had made a confession to police that implicated them. It was the defendant who had made the confession (Jordan) who was the object of the psychological evaluation and testimony.

Prior to the trial, the author was called on by the defense attorney to evaluate Jordan with regard to his susceptibility to influence and coercion as possible corroboration of anticipated psychiatric testimony. Psychological evaluation included an interview as well as administration, scoring, and interpretation of the Wechsler Adult Intelligence Scale, the Bender-Gestalt, the 16 Personality Factor Scale, the Rotter Incomplete Sentences Blank, The Slosson Oral Reading Test, the House-Tree-Person technique, and the Rorschach technique.

Following this evaluation, a report was written for the defense attorney based on the interview and the test results. The report concluded that the defendant was indeed highly susceptible to psychological coercion based on the following points:

1. "Low intelligence in general and deficits in social judgment, word meaning, and memory in particular could increase his dependence on and susceptibility to other peoples' communications."

2. "Lower ego-strength, including feelings of inferiority and guilt proneness, create an individual who doubts himself and who readily assigns self-blame."

3. "Giving way to others, being docile and dependent is as evident on the tests as in the reported relationship with his wife" (the wife reportedly had "pressured him" into confessing).

4. "Withdrawal from others, in spite of a superficial friendliness, further describes someone who tells others what they want to hear in spite of true inner feelings and beliefs that might be quite to the contrary."

5. "And, he appears to be a threat-sensitive individual who, as he stated, 'felt they [police] would hurt me and I would have told them anything to let me go'." (He reported that the police had told him that "he flunked the lie detector," "how he had committed the crime," and how he "would get the electric chair if he didn't talk.")

The defense attorney for Jordan had offered testimony by a psychiatrist that Jordan was "easily led and influenced and that he lacked sufficient strength to resist breaking under pressure." Corroborating testimony by the psychologist was first offered in defense of commission of the crime and, following a guilty verdict, as evidence suggestive of mitigating circumstances.

During direct examination, the following points were brought out:

1. Establishment of the identity, profession, and qualifications of the psychologist.

2. Confirmation of the evaluation of the defendant, including time, date, place, and tests administered.

3. Test results, including an evaluation of intelligence, personality, perceptual-motor functioning, and reading achievement level.

4. An affirmation of the defendant's susceptibility to the influence of others with particular test results related to such judged susceptibility.

5. An affirmation of the defendant's susceptibility to threat from the police and to influence from his wife in regard to his confession.

During cross-examination, the following attempts were made to discredit the psychological testimony:

1. Challenge by the prosecution suggesting that influence by the wife could have just as easily led the defendant to tell the truth as tell a lie. The psychologist acknowledged that such influence could be in either direction.

2. An attempt by the prosecution to suggest that test results indicating the perception of a threatening, hostile environment were peculiar to his present circumstances. The psychologist replied that the defendant's history, prior to incarceration, probably could account for most of his perceptual bias.

3. The prosecution next undertook to disparage test results based on the Rorschach. While acknowledging some problems with validity and reliability, the psychologist stressed the substantiation, by more psychometrically respected assessment devices, of the results attributed to the Rorschach.

4. The next attempt to belittle the psychological testimony focused on the interpretation of the I.Q. score. This score was at the point of the Borderline Retarded Range. Based on the fact that one point would have put the defendant into a higher category of intellectual functioning (Low Normal Range), the prosecution suggested a lack of reliability to the categorization. The psychologist acknowledged that one point would have changed the category but still represented the findings as validly and reliably revealing subnormal intellectual functioning.

5. The prosecution next suggested that being charged with murder had compromised the test results, with particular reference to the one-point I.Q. change that could have placed the defendant in a higher intellectual category. The psychologist conceded that the circumstances of the testing situation can affect the test results but asserted that this generally need not be a substantial consideration in interpretation of such results.

The outcomes of the trials were that all three defendants were convicted. Jordan's brother was sentenced to three consecutive life terms for first-degree murder and consecutive ten- to twenty-year terms for robbery, burglary, and criminal conspiracy. Jordan was sentenced to three consecutive life terms for second-degree murder and consecutive ten- to twenty-year terms for robbery and burglary. The third party received consecutive ten- to twenty-year terms for three counts of third-degree murder and concurrent ten- to twenty-year terms for robbery, burglary, and criminal conspiracy.

While testimony on Jordan's behalf may have helped attenuate the severity of the murder charge, there was no practical advantage in terms of sentencing. With good behavior, it would be a minimum of eighty years before he could be paroled. This seemed to be a case in which a vigorous and quite adequate defense simply was not enough to overcome a wealth of information and testimony that convinced the jury of the defendant's guilt.

BIBLIOGRAPHY

American Psychological Association. APA-approved doctoral programs in clinical, counseling, and school psychology: 1977. *American Psychologist*, 1977a, 32, 1092-1093.

American Psychological Association, APA-approved predoctoral internships for doctoral training in clinical and counseling psychology: 1977. *American Psychologist*, 1977b, 32, 495-505.

American Psychological Association. Ethical standards of psychologists, draft #7. *APA Monitor*, November 1975, 18-19.

American Psychological Association. *Recommendations of commission on behavior modification*. Washington, D.C.; American Psychological Association, 1976.

American Psychological Association. *Standards for providers of psychological services*. Washington, D.C.; American Psychological Association, 1974.

American Psychological Association. Standards for providers of psychological services. *American Psychologist*, 1977c, *32*, 495-505.

Association for the Advancement of Psychology. Psychologists on the issues. *Advance*, 1977a, *4* (1), 10.

Association for the Advancement of Psychology. Questions and answers about the FTC proceedings. Newsletter, March, 1977b.

Cautela, J. R. *Behavior analysis forms for clinical intervention.* Champaign, Ill.: Research Press, 1977.

Cummings, N. A., and Follette, W. T. Brief psychotherapy and medical utilization: An eight year follow-up. In H. Dörken and Associates. *The professional psychologist today: New developments in law, health insurance, and health practice.* San Francisco: Jossey-Bass, 1976.

Dörken, H. Utilization of psychologist in positions of responsibility in public mental health programs: A national survey. *American Psychologist*, 1970, *25*, 953-958.

Dörken, H. Laws, regulations, and psychological practice. In H. Dörken and Associates. *The professional psychologist today: New developments in law, health insurance, and health practice.* San Francisco: Jossey-Bass, 1976.

Dörken, H. The formal involvement of psychology in the commitment process for mental and developmental disorders. *The Clinical Psychologist*, 1977, *30* (4), 5-6.

Dörken, H., and Morrison, D. JCAH standards for accreditation of psychiatric facilities: Implications for the practice of clinical psychology. *American Psychologist*, 1976, *31*, 774-784.

Friedman, P. R. Legal regulation of applied behavior analysis in mental institutions and prisons. In C. Franks and G. Wilson, eds. *Annual review of behavioral therapy: Theory and practice.* New York: Brunner/Mazel, 1976.

Garfield, S. L., and Kurtz, R. Clinical psychologists in the 1970's. *American Psychologist*, 1976, *31*, 1-9.

Gordon, R. *Forensic psychology.* Tucson, Ariz.: Lawyers and Judges Publishing *sional psychologist today: New developments in law, health insurance and*

Gottfredson, G. D., and Dyer, S. E. Health service providers in psychology. *American Psychologist*, 1978, *33*, 314-338.

Jacobs, D. F. Standards for psychologists. In H. Dörken and Associates, *The professional psychologist today: New developments in law, health insurance, and health practice.* San Francisco: Jossey-Bass, 1976.

Kiesler, C. A. The training of psychiatrists and psychologists. *American Psychologist*, 1977, *32*, 107-108.

Peterson, D. R. Is psychology a profession. *American Psychologist*, 1976, *31*, 572-581.

Pope B., and Scott, W. *Psychological diagnosis in clinical practice.* New York: Oxford University Press, 1976, 312-334.

Schwitzgebel, R. K. A contractual model for the protection of the rights of institutionalized mental patient. *American Psychologist*, 1975, *30*, 815-820.

Sobel, S. B. Professional psychologists and state statutes on pretrial competency: A review. *The Clinical Psychologist*, 1978a, *31* (3 and 4), 26-29.

Sobel, S. B. State statutes and the role of professional psychologists in commitment proceedings for the mentally ill. *The Clinical Psychologist*, 1978b, *31* (2), 21-23.

Stolz, S. B., Wienckowski, L. A., and Brown, B. S. Behavior modification: A perspective on critical issues. *American Psychologist*, 1975, *30*, 1027-1048.

Wellner, A. M. Education and credentialing in psychology, II: Report of a meeting. *The Clinical Psychologist*, 1977, *31* (1), 9.

Wellner, A. M., and Mills, D. H. *Register report #9*. Council for the National Register of Health Service Providers in Psychology. Unpublished report, 1977.

Whiteley, J., and Whiteley, R. California court expands privilege debate. *APA Monitor*, February 1977, 5-6, 18.

4 WILLIAM F. ADAMS

The Counseling Psychologist

To date, there are few cases or legal precedents that directly relate to counseling psychology. The legal profession and counseling psychology have coexisted in mutually exclusive fashion for the past several decades without any real association or confrontation. Current trends, however, suggest that the two professions cannot and will not continue to function separately. The paths of both will cross more frequently and tumultuously in the near future. The interaction is foreseeable and inevitable. What is not predictable now, however, is the extent or the outcome of the interaction between the two professions.

If, as anticipated, counseling psychology and the law will eventually encounter one another in the not-too-distant future, numerous questions on many aspects may be raised. In general, these questions deal with the areas of how, when, where, why, and over what. More specifically, some of the major issues of immediate concern might be stated as: How well prepared is counseling psychology as a profession to handle itself in legal actions? When will legislation be enacted that will protect and be beneficial to the profession and individuals utilizing our services? Where will the leadership necessary to identify problems and recommend solutions on both a national and state level be found? Why has counseling psychology remained naive, uninformed, and uninterested in legal matters for so long? What are the areas and issues of concern in counseling psychology that are likely to be susceptible to legal actions? The list of questions could obviously continue, but unfortunately, there are few answers now.

It is the thesis of this article that counseling psychology is currently very vulnerable to legal actions. This observation may invite contemplation, commentary, and reaction, but any of these responses will be welcome, since the involvement and implication of those individuals practicing in the profession are essential. Prevention of problems by taking action ourselves is far better than waiting for legal intervention and monitoring to establish direction and precedent for the profession. For the time being, there is choice, but this option may not be available much longer.

At the outset it must be pointed out that a distinction is being made between *counseling psychologist* and *counselor*. The former term is more specific and classificational, while the latter concept is more broad and general in scope. This differentiation itself may be criticized as questionable, but the discussion that follows focuses on counseling psychology with full recognition that there is overlap and similarity in some instances between the two fields.

This article has chosen two important legal issues for discussion in the practice of counseling psychology—confidentiality and accountability. These issues are of contemporary significance, and an understanding of them can provide a foundation for possible resolution of others. Before these issues are reviewed, however, some background in counseling psychology as a profession will be examined, as will what constitutes being a counseling psychologist; after discussing the issues cited above, some mutual benefits that could be derived between counseling psychology and the law through closer liaison will be discussed.

COUNSELING PSYCHOLOGY AS A PROFESSION

It would appear to be a relatively easy matter to discuss counseling psychology as a profession. In fact, the task is a formidable one beset with problems. A recent edition of *The Counseling Psychologist* (Whiteley, 1977) devoted the whole issue to "professional identity," and invited contributions from many of the leading individuals practicing in the field. The contributors presented stimulating, challenging, and interesting ideas, but agreement and unanimity on what constitutes counseling psychology as a profession is seriously lacking.

The adage that "psychology has a long past, but a short history" is probably even more appropriate to the specific area of counseling psychology. Helping relationships between people have probably existed since the advent of language and societal living. In more contemporary times, however, an individual undoubtedly gained a reputation as being an empathic, sensitive, caring listener who could provide support and counsel with elemental evaluation. Clergymen, physicians, and personal friends could probably be described as the foremost "counselors" of the times.

Historically, counseling psychology emerged as a specialty from the three distinct movements of vocational guidance, psychological measurement, and personality development. In 1951 the American Psychological Association adopted the title "counseling psychology" by Division 17, and in 1952 the name of Division 17 was officially changed to "The Division of Counseling Psychology." In the same year, the Veterans Administration chose to establish the two psychological positions of "Counseling Psychologist (Vocational)" and "Counseling Psychologist (VR & E)." A significant note of interest is that an official definition of counseling psychology was unavailable at the time the American Psychological Association adopted the title by Division 17 in 1952. It was not until 1956 that the Committee on Definition, Division of Counseling Psychology, published a quasi-formal definition (APA, 1956). Other highlights in the emergence of counseling psychology as a profession included publication of *Ethical Standards of Psychologists* by the association in 1953 (later updated several times), establishment of the *Journal of Counseling Psychology* in 1954, granting of a Diploma in Counseling Psychology by the American Board of Examiners in Professional Psychology in 1955, and publication of *Ethical Principles in the Conduct of Research with Human Participants* in 1973 (Wrenn, 1977).

The brief historical sketch above underscores the recent development of counseling psychology as a formal discipline. Although in existence on an informal level for years, counseling psychology has been recognized as a distinct specialty for only a little over a quarter century. Relative to the areas of experimental, school, clinical, industrial, educational, and developmental psychology, counseling is the "new kid on the block," so to speak. Nevertheless, even though counseling psychology is a newer addition, this does not excuse or delimit the vulnerability of the discipline. In fact, counseling psychology is probably more susceptible to legal intervention and jurisdiction because of the nature of its practice, clientele, and services.

WHAT IS A COUNSELING PSYCHOLOGIST?

The question of what is a counseling psychologist is by no means clearly resolved, and there are many individual definitions. It must be emphasized at the outset, however, that a counseling psychologist is foremost a psychologist who does counseling. This is important to recognize and remember, since a counseling psychologist is really part of the broader, more inclusive profession of psychology. The Committee on Definition, Division of Counseling Psychology, held the conviction more than twenty years ago that counseling psychology was evolving and developing as a specialty area, and "although there are discernible trends toward commonality among the present psychological specialities, it is important to underline the remaining difference among them" (APA, 1956, p. 284). Changes in counseling psychology were predicted then and can continue to be expected, but "whatever the developments, they will depend on where the functions performed by counseling psychologists find their most useful outlets" (APA, 1956, p. 284).

Although counseling psychology continues to evolve and develop as a profession in finding identity, no apologies or misgivings are necessary. In fact, it is felt this evolution is both healthy and beneficial for the profession.

However, in legal matters it may be a disadvantage, as changes may periodically develop into conflictual situations and confrontations between the two fields.

As stated by Wrenn (1977, p. 10): "It is simple to state that a counseling psychologist is a psychologist at the doctoral level (Ph.D. or Ed.D. degree) who is prepared to practice counseling. The rub comes in defining counseling." There are indeed many types of counseling, and hence, "it is easy to see how wide variations in the theory-method utilized, as well as variations in kinds of client focused upon, or kind of client setting in which the counselor operates, would lead to *many* definitions of the counseling function and the role of the counselor" (Wrenn, 1977, p. 10). Herein lies the problem in developing an inclusive definition of the counseling psychologist in a court of law — the characterization of the psychologist who practices counseling is individually defined by his or her work setting, kinds of clients, and theory-methodology employed.

The American Board of Examiners in Professional Psychology (ABEPP) conducts examinations of qualified individuals to award the Counseling Psychology diploma, and many counseling psychologists are listed in the *National Register of Health Service Providers in Psychology*. The American Psychological Association adopted specific criteria for graduating counseling psychologists in 1952. It is these common features, among others, that provide counseling psychologists with basic foundations, recognized competencies, and identity as a group.

The focus on what is a counseling psychologist when we become involved in legal matters still needs to be resolved, and the "identity diffusion" is still evident. The recommendation for a real, essential definition is proposed as a solution. In the meantime, echoes from the Greyston Conference speaking to this issue nearly twenty years ago can still be heard, that "the task of adequately communicating this fact of identity to others remains, however, to be done" (Thompson and Super, 1964, p. 28).

CONFIDENTIALITY: AN AREA OF MISUNDERSTANDING, CONFLICT, AND CONTROVERSY

The area of confidentiality is a thorny, confusing, and sensitive one for counseling psychology. It is an issue that has provoked innumerable articles (in other professions as well), and yet, still cries out for satisfactory resolution (Sommer, 1962; Schrocter, 1969; Marsh and Kinnick, 1970; Goldman, 1972; Trachtman, 1972; Joling, 1974; Plant, 1974; Roston, 1975). Before confidentiality and the counseling psychologist is dealt with, some background for better understanding is appropriate.

In the original publication of *Ethical Standards of Psychologists* published by the American Psychological Association in 1953, Section 2, dealing with client relationships, emphasized their confidential nature; confidentiality was again underscored in the 1963 revision under Principle 6. More recently, in the 1977 revision of *Ethical Standards of Psychologists*, confidentiality is cited in Principle 5, which reads "safeguarding information about an individual that has been obtained by the psychologist in the course of his teaching, practice, or investigation is a primary obligation of the psychologist. Such information is not communicated to others unless certain important conditions are not met" (APA, 1977, p. 22). Six elaborative sections follow this principle, and it would appear that Sections (a), (b), and (d) are the most pertinent for counseling psychologists. In brief, these sections indicate that confidential information can be revealed to certain other parties only after cautious deliberation about imminent danger to the individual or others, that only germane information can be provided as per questions asked, and that informed consent from the client must be obtained.

The term *confidentiality* is defined in many ways, but typically refers to the intimacy or privacy of communication between people and implies aspects of trust, consent, access to personal data, and the notion of privileged communication. Hence, a discussion of confidentiality by itself is really out of context, and is best understood only in the broader context of privilege. As Trachtman (1972, p. 38) has pointed out, "privileged communication refers to the protection of the confidential relationship between client and professional and is found in some form in the civil law of most nations today, most often as an exception granted certain professional groups from testifying in courts of law about information entrusted to them by clients in the conduct of their professional relationship." Unfortunately, privileged communication statutes in a confidential relationship vary from state to state, and "it is difficult for the law to define privileged communication for professional relationships when the profession itself still lacks clearcut legal definition" (Trachtman, 1972, p. 38).

An often-quoted legal expert (Wigmore, 1961, p. 527) has recommended that four conditions be satisfied before privileged communications are extended in relationships like counseling:

1. The communications must originate in a confidence that they will not be disclosed.

2. The element of confidentiality must be essential to the full and satisfactory maintenance of the relationship between the parties.

3. The relation must be one which in the opinions of the community ought to be sedulously fostered.

4. The injury that would inure to the relation by the disclosure of the communications must be greater than the benefit thereby gained for the correct disposal of litigation.

In response to whether counseling psychologists who work with individuals need this kind of protective privilege in a relationship, Louisell (1957, pp. 745-746) wrote, "it is hard to see how the psychodiagnostic and psycho-therapeutic functions can be adequately carried on in the absence of a pre-vailing attitude of privacy and confidentiality. Such an attitude can hardly exist without sure guarantees against disclosure of the patient's secrets." Thus, the counseling psychologist finds himself or herself in a dilemma; depending on the state, confidential communications are not necessarily granted privilege in a court of law. Moreover, in his study of privileged communication statutes in the United States, Schrocter (1969, p. 334) con-cluded "that privileged communication statutes neither follow a discernable pattern in their distribution across the country, nor equally protect the confidence of the clients or the patients of the more prestigious professionals in our society." In a final note of interest, it is worth mentioning that by 1973, thirty-seven states and the District of Columbia had laws providing for psychologist-client confidentiality, but the "holder of privilege," so to speak, is the client and never the psychologist. The statutes grant privilege to the clients of psychologists, and "the right to assert or waive the privilege to prevent disclosure [on the witness stand] of communications made to psychologists during the course of treatment for mental or emotional dis-orders" (McDermott, 1972, p. 302). In essence, the client alone determines what is released.

The preceding discourse only amplifies some of the problems of confiden-tiality for the counseling psychologist, and especially privileged protection. In assessing why more problems have not been encountered in the courts, one could probably find the answer in the essence of the helping relation-ship itself. Counseling psychologists working in a variety of settings with all kinds of individuals employing many approaches are *all* in relationships that facilitate, develop, clarify, and typically improve situations for an indi-vidual. Although the kind of professional relationship shared with a coun-seling psychologist is a helping process, it is unlikely lawmakers will be enthusiastic about granting privileged confidential communications to the profession, and, even if this could be accomplished, the extent of the grant would be limited.

In seeking to establish privileged confidential communications for coun-seling psychologists, three possible directions could be taken: (a) privilege for counseling psychologists in a recognized, approved agency; (b) privilege for the general psychotherapeutic function of the counseling psychologist; (c) privilege for the professional nature of the counseling psychologist-client relationship per se (Berven, 1968). Of the three possible routes that could be taken, the third appears to provide the best prospects. Why? In the first instance, all agencies employing counseling psychologists would not have privileged confidential communications unless the agency was protected. In the second instance, it would limit the role of the counseling psychologist to only a psychotherapeutic function which has medical terminology origins. It is the third direction that offers the most promise, and also appears to satisfy all of Wigmore's criteria of privileged communications. Again, it is emphasized that the counseling psychologist is viewed primarily as a psychologist who does counseling. In the vast majority of states and the District of Columbia, psychologists are currently recognized as a profession through licensure or certification (see chapter I on the impact of sunset legislation.) *The Ethical Standards of Psychologists* (1977) clearly satisfies the first three of Wigmore's criteria, and the fourth is ensured to the extent that disclosure is critical to avert danger to others.

If the course cited above is followed in the establishment of privileged confidential communication statutes, one problem can already be anticipated, but also averted. Specifically, the generic term of *psychologist* must be refined to specify more clearly those involved in client relationships such as clinical, school, community, rehabilitation, industrial, and counseling. Any lobbying efforts for statutes are weakened by individual factions, but collective, unified, and combined efforts of all psychologists in client relationships would offer the advantage of strength in joining forces.

ACCOUNTABILITY

The issue of accountability in the practice of any profession is both an essential and necessary component. It ensures that the practitioners are responsible, attributable, and answerable for the services provided. Recently, the American Psychological Association formally recognized the significance of accountability in "Standards for Providers of Psychological Services" (APA, 1975). Heretofore, what had been assumed to exist (with adequacy implied) was made a definitive and formal prototype. For counseling psychologists, the association standards offer substantive guidelines, but also raise questions. For example, to what degree can a counseling psychologist be held accountable for the actions of a client working with him or her? Further, accountability implies review, and raises the question of who would have the responsibility of evaluating services, and moreover, how this would be done. Finally, there are questions that would have to be resolved concerning privileged confidential communication, accountability in individual versus institutional practice, and establishing criteria that would be effective in determining the satisfaction of accountability.

Despite the multitude of questions that could be posed on various aspects of accountability, it does have merit and real value for counseling psychologists. It is increasingly evident that "people are expecting (and demanding) a higher level of care and competence, not only from physicians but from other professionals as well . . . and it is quite likely that this trend shall affect more psychologists in the future" (White and Gross, 1975, p. 268). Instead of playing the ostrich with its head in the sand, it would behoove counseling psychologists to take active steps now in the analysis, planning, and implementation of accountability standards. As Mannino and Shore (1975, p.

318) point out, "the current crisis in mental health and mental health related services may be viewed as a crisis of credibility based on an inadequate system of accountability."

It would appear that the initial question that requires an answer is to whom counseling psychologists are accountable for their services. Momentary reflection suggests there are four identifiable groups: the individual client, the counseling psychologist, the place of employment, and the overall profession of counseling psychology. Although all of these groups seek the delivery of competent and qualified service, each also places a different emphasis on what needs to be held accountable.

1. The individual client is viewed as foremost and primary in the delivery of services, and it is through and with him or her that our greatest responsibility lies. The whole raison d'être hinges on how well the goals of the client are satisfied and fulfilled. In the first of the American Psychological Association standards on accountability, this is recognized in the statement that the "psychologist's professional activity shall be primarily guided by the principle of promoting human welfare" (APA, 1975, p. 691). In the interpretation, however, the emphasis on "timely, considerate, effective, and economical" services, and facilitating "the consumer's freedom of choice" appears to underplay the *kinds* and *quality* of service, which is really what is crucial to the individual and for which practitioners will be held accountable in a court of law. In essence, the client seeking services through a counseling psychologist has certain expectations and goals (realistic and unrealistic), but it is by the degree of their satisfaction (through the kinds and quality of service) that clients hold practitioners accountable. Obviously, it is incumbent on the counseling psychologist to ensure that the client is fully apprised of his or her role, responsibility, and limitations.

2. The counseling psychologist is most likely to be the "target" of grievances concerning responsibility in the provision of services. In being held accountable for the delivery of these services with a client, recognition of certain obligations and opportunities would appear worthy of consideration. Specifically, any practicing psychologist has a duty to be licensed/ certified in the state in which he or she lives, but, probably more importantly, to realize his or her limitations of expertise and refer those clients to others who can offer more beneficial service. There are numerous opportunities to broaden and enlarge one's competence and qualifications through more extensive education, workshops, and internships. Nevertheless, in the final analysis, the individual counseling psychologist must hold himself or herself accountable for the kinds and quality of services provided. As the fourth American Psychological Association standard on accountability states: "Psychologists are accountable for all aspects of the services they provide and shall be responsive to those concerned with these services" (APA, 1975, p. 691). In short, accountability for the individual counseling psychologist is best determined through honest recognition of the "self" competencies and limitations.

3. The place of employment often defines or strongly influences the standards of accountability, and these may actually be at variance with the precepts of the client and/or counseling psychologist. Management and administration keep a keen eye on the kinds and quality of services, but, in addition, are concerned with budgets and staff. In a nutshell, for the place of employment, "accountability has to do with whether a service or program helps or hinders those to whom it is geared, and whether such help makes a difference that is not possible through services and programs already available" (Mannino and Shore, 1975, p. 315). The third standard on accountability does propose that "there shall be periodic, systematic, and objective evaluation of psychological service" (APA, 1975, p. 691), and the interpretation that "regular assessment . . . should be conducted both internally and under independent auspices" lends support and justification to involvement by those outside the counseling relationship. Thus, the educational institution, agency, or hospital seeks to ensure that the services of employed counseling psychologists can be justified, are effective, and make a difference using their own criteria of accountability.

4. Finally, the overall profession of counseling psychology has a collective interest in its individual members maintaining standards of integrity and responsibility. In Standard 4.2 on accountability it is simply and succinctly stated: "psychologists are members of an independent, autonomous profession . . . and shall be aware of their activities for the profession as a whole" (APA, 1975, p. 691). McMillan (1976, p. 13) indicates that accountability of the profession from within implies peer review, and "relates to virtually all aspects of the quality of performance of the practicing psychologist ranging from appropriateness of procedures used, to fees, to contractual understandings with the patient, . . . and even to issues of outcome and effectiveness of service." Each of these aspects deserves study, and counseling psychology as a profession would be reflecting care and concern for both clients and colleagues to monitor its services and performance from within.

COUNSELING PSYCHOLOGY AND THE LAW: WORKING TOGETHER WITH MUTUAL BENEFITS

Both the professions of law and psychology provide services to individuals, and a mutual goal is to offer the most competent, knowledgeable, and beneficial assistance to persons rendered such services. A closer liaison between these two professions would benefit the individuals seeking these services. The breadth and extent of the vast knowledge of our ever-changing culture has led to professional specialization, and neither of our professions can function independently in the best interests of the individuals requiring the services. In brief, both are helping professions which need one another to provide the best service to individuals soliciting their expertise.

There are many areas where counseling psychology and the law already have considerable overlap and interaction. Some examples of mutual interest include cases of marital discord and divorce, criminal behavior, alcoholism, child abuse, juvenile delinquency, and adoption. In these cases, as well as many others, a better understanding of the psychological factors facilitates the handling of legal matters. Bernstein (1974) has indicated how the lawyer and counseling psychologist can best function as an interdisciplinary team in family matters, and Goldenson (1970) has emphasized the importance of both professions working more closely in correctional institutions. Barton and Byrne (1975) have also written on the need to design collaborative programs involving counseling and social work services with the legal aid setting.

Counseling psychologists, and psychologists in general, can make direct contributions to the development of the law. For instance, Touster (1962) suggested that psychology could be helpful to the law in the conduct of lawsuits, in the making and administering of laws, and aiding the law as an institution in understanding the why of behavior. Plotkin (1972, p. 202) discussed a case of discrimination in the use of psychological tests in employment, and as Chief Justice Burger wrote in his ruling for the Supreme Court in 1971, "psychological tests could be used for employment only when they are demonstrably related to job performance." Mention was made later that the legal profession itself has different bar examinations from state to state, and "graduates of accredited law schools who are denied the right to practice solely on the basis of an examination . . . can challenge the decision in the courts" (Plotkin, 1972, p. 204). Counseling psychologists, in particular, with their expertise in psychological testing might readily serve as a resource in questions of validity and reliability. Several authors (Louisell, 1955; Buckhout, 1974; Nash, 1974; Gorlow, 1975) have also written on the value and significance of expert witness testimony by psychologists, and how statistical data from the profession as well as clinical judgments gained through observation can be beneficial. Finally, Goldenson (1970) has reviewed the expanding role of "forensic" psychology and the contributions made in the areas of testimony, interrogation methods, guilt detection, and being a consultant in the development of laws. In the instances cited above, counseling psychology and the broader profession of psychology have a great deal to offer the legal profession.

On the other side of the coin, lawyers can also make notable contributions to counseling psychology. For example, Ball (1973) asked whether counselors knew much about the constitutional rights of clients, what constitutes procedural due process or a hearing, and if counselors knew how to act as an advocate for a client. Her general conclusion was that counselors are woefully prepared, and, if this is the case, we need to turn to the legal profession for assistance. The significance of certification and licensure was recognized many years ago (Armstrong, 1974; Saffer, 1950; Wolfe, 1950; Kremen 1951) to protect clients from dangerous, unethical, and inferior services. Later Henderson and Hildreth (1965) pointed out that different states vary in their educational, experiential, and residence requirements for licensure, and there is conflict over reciprocity or mandatory reexamination. More recently, Stigall (1977, p. 41) stated: "as practitioners of a substantive specialty within the field of psychology, counseling psychologists expect to be accorded the same rights and privileges as all other members of the profession." Often this is not the case, and "what is needed, of course, is a greater degree of consensus among training programs, credentialing authorities, and practitioners as to minimum standards for professional preparation of all psychologists" (Stigall, 1977, p. 41). Specific "in-house" recommendations were suggested (Stigall, 1977), but, again, we will require the assistance and cooperation of lawyers to resolve problems of licensure. Another sensitive area of counseling psychology where legal advice is essential centers on the need for professional liability coverage. Brownfain (1971, p. 649) discussed the growing number of psychologists who have subscribed to American Psychological Association's Professional Liability Insurance Program established in 1955, and emphasized that "the enlightened practitioner knows that he lives in a time of growing vulnerability to legal attack on grounds of malpractice." However, White and Gross (1975) indicated that the association's policy really does not protect psychologists as well as necessary, and that a better security shield must be developed. In each of the issues reviewed above, it is clear that counseling psychologists require the services of lawyers to protect and enhance the psychologists' benefits to individuals seen by them.

In summary, it is evident that there are some problem areas in both professions that could be better resolved through capitalizing on the expertise of each. Mutual benefits could obviously be derived for counseling psychologists and lawyers in terms of the competency and quality of services afforded individuals seeking those services.

SUMMARY AND CONCLUSIONS

Although this portion of an article comes at the end, it is hoped that the tone of the content is really a beginning. Counseling psychology has come a long way in a short time in establishing itself as a profession. It is anticipated that current trends in this society will bring the counseling and legal professions into closer association, and this alliance will have marked impact on the direction counseling psychology will assume. At this point it is felt counseling psychology is ill-prepared and vulnerable. Moreover, members of the profession need to play a more active role in confirming the direction to take rather than sitting back to wait to see what outside influences may direct. The task confronting counseling psychologists is not an easy one, but it is necessary. For now, at least, there is a choice.

This article has emphasized counseling as one of the specialty areas of psychology, and that counseling psychologists are particularly susceptible to legal intervention because of the nature of their practice, clientele, and services. Instead of a broad, inclusive, descriptive definition, a real, essential definition of counseling psychology has been proposed based on competency, goals, and situation. The significance of privileged confidential communications has been reviewed, and establishing statutes based on the professional nature of the counseling psychologist-client relationship per se has been advocated. The crucial aspects of accountability from different perspectives were discussed, and the significance of well-defined objectives and performance in being accountable stressed. Finally, it was indicated that both the counseling psychologist and lawyer are involved in helping relationships with individuals, and the mutual benefits that can be derived by working together of the two professions for these clients were highlighted.

BIBLIOGRAPHY

American Psychological Association, Committee on Counselor Training, Division of Counseling and Guidance. Recommended standards for training counseling psychologists at the doctoral level. *American Psychologist*, 1952, 7, 175.-181.

American Psychological Association, Division of Counseling Psychology, Committee on Definition. Counseling psychology as a specialty. *American Psychologist*, 1956, 11, 282-285.

American Psychological Association. Standards for providers of psychological services. *American Psychologist*, 1975, 30, 685-694.

American Psychological Association, Committee on Scientific and Professional Ethics. Revised ethical standards of psychologists. *American Psychological Association Monitor*, March 1977, 22-23.

Armstrong, C. P. On defining psychology as a profession. *American Psychologist*, 1947, 2, 446-448.

Ball, M. A. Do counselors need to know about due process? *School Counselor*, 1973, 2(2), 130-136.

Barton, P. N., and Byrne, B. Social work services in a legal aid setting. *Social Casework*, 1975, 56, 226-234.

Bernstein, B. E. Lawyer and counselor as an interdisciplinary team: One lawyer's suggestions. *Family Coordinator*, 1974, 23(1), 41-44.

Berven, N. L. Privileged communication and the rehabilitation counselor. *Journal of Rehabilitation*, 1968, 34(6), 10-12.

Brownfain, J. J. The APA professional liability insurance program. *American Psychologist*, 1971, 26, 648-652.

Buckhout, R. Eyewitness testimony. *Scientific American*, 1974, 231(6), 23-31.

Goldenson, R. M. *The encyclopedia of human behavior: Psychology, psychiatry, and mental health*. New York: Doubleday & Company, Inc., 1970.

Goldman, L. Psychological secrecy and openness in the public schools. *Professional Psychology*, 1972, 3, 370-374.

Gorlow, L. The school psychologist as expert witness in due process hearings. *Journal of School Psychology*, 1975, *13*, 311-316.

Henderson, N. B., and Hildreth, J. D. Certification, licensing, and the movement of psychologists from state to state. *American Psychologist*, 1965, *20*, 418-421.

Hopke, W. E., ed. *Dictionary of personnel and guidance terms*. Chicago: J. G. Ferguson Publishing Co., 1968.

Joling, R. J. Informed consent, confidentiality and privilege in psychiatry: Legal implications. *Bulletin of the American Academy of Psychiatry and the Law*, 1974, *2*(2), 107-110.

Kremen, B. G. Counselor certification in the United States. *Occupations*, 1951, *29*, 584-586.

Louisell, D. W. The psychologist in today's legal world. *Minnesota Law Review*, 1957, *41*, 731-750.

Mannino, F. V., and Shore, M. F. Accountability in a family oriented rehabilitation program. *Family Coordinator*, 1975, *24*, 315-319.

Marsh, J. J., and Kinnick, B. C. Let's close the confidentiality game. *Personnel and Guidance Journal*, 1970, *48*, 362-365.

McDermott, P. A. Law, liability, and the school psychologist: Systems of law, privileged communication and access to records. *Journal of School Psychology*, 1972, *10*, 299-305.

McMillan, J. J. Accountability among providers of psychological services. *Clinical Psychologist*, 1976, *29*(3), 7-13.

Nash, M. M. Parameters and distinctiveness of psychological testimony. *Professional Psychology*, 1974, *5*, 239-243.

Nordberg, R. B. *Guidance: A systematic introduction*. New York: Random House, 1970.

Plant, E. A. A perspective on confidentiality. *American Journal of Psychiatry*, 1974, *131*, 1021-1024.

Plotkin, L. Coal handling, steamfitting, psychology, and the law. *American Psychologist*, 1972, *27*, 202-204.

Roston, R. A. Ethical uncertainties and "technical" validities. *Professional Psychology*, 1975, *6*, 50-54.

Saffer, M. A. Certification versus licensing legislation. *American Psychologist*, 1950, *5*, 105-106.

Schrocter, G. Protection of confidentiality in the courts: The professions. *Social Problems*, 1969, *16*, 376-385.

Shertzer, B., and Stone, S. *Fundamentals of counseling*. Boston: Houghton Mifflin Co., 1966.

Sommer, N. T. The psychologist and privileged communication. *Journal of Offender Therapy*, 1962, *6* (3), 59-61.

Stigall, T. T. Counseling psychology: Training and credentialing for professional practice. *The Counseling Psychologist*, 1977, *7*(2), 41-42.

Super, D. E. The identity crises of counseling psychologists. *The Counseling Psychologist*, 1977, *7*(2), 13-15.

Thompson, A. S., and Super, D. E., eds. *The professional preparation of counseling psychologists: Report of the 1964 Greyston Conference*. New York: Teachers College Press, 1964.

Touster, S. Law and psychology: How the twain might meet. *American Behavioral Scientist*, 1962, *5*(9), 3-6.

Trachtman, G. M. Pupils, parents, privacy, and the school psychologist. *American Psychologist*, 1972, 27, 37-45.

Tyler, L. E. *The work of the counselor*. New York: Appleton-Century-Crofts, Inc., 1961.

White, A. E., and Gross, R. B. Professional liability insurance and the psychologist. *Professional Psychology*, 1975, 6, 267-271.

Whiteley, J. M., ed. Professional identity. *The Counseling Psychologist*, 1977 7(2), 110.

Wigmore, J. H. *Evidence in trials at common law*. Boston: Little Brown, 1961, 8.

Wolfe, D. Legal control of psychological practice. *American Psychologist*, 1950, 5, 651-655.

Wrenn, C. G. Landmarks and the growing edge. *The Counseling Psychologist*, 1977, 7(2), 10-13.

5 JOSEPH G. ROSENFELD

The School Psychologist

One can say that the field of school psychology dates back to the beginning of the psychological testing movement. This originated in Germany in the psychophysics laboratories of Ernst H. Weber in 1834, Gustav T. Fechner in 1860, and Wilhelm Wundt in 1879.

There have been two major areas in the field of psychology that have also had great influence on school psychology. One of the areas has been in learning theory, a major contribution of the experimental psychologist. Prominent among the experimental psychologists was W. L. Thorndike. His work in animal learning and in the development of psychological tests is frequently credited with providing definition for the emerging field of educational psychology in this country. John B. Watson, founder of "behaviorism," influenced classroom procedures and child-raising methods throughout the nation. In many ways, Watson had a profound effect on American educational theory. Watson promoted child-raising and educational practices based on a pragmatic theory concerning how learning and behavioral modifications occur. He made parents and teachers alike aware of the effect of controlled learning conditions on behavior and its use in behavior modification. Another prominent American psychologist who has contributed markedly to educational practices is B. F. Skinner. His theories are the basis of most behavioral modification approaches used in the United States. He is also one of the major advocates of the teaching machine. He felt that the instructional results in the past were too slow to satisfy learning requirements based on stimulus response theory. With machine teaching a student gets immediate feedback in terms of the correctness of his or her response. In this controlled situation, the student does not repeat mistakes and is able to identify errors more quickly. Skinner also feels that the teaching machines are uniquely adapted to the individual learner in a way not possible for a teacher in a large class.

Another major contribution to school psychology comes from the areas of clinical psychology and personality theory. School psychologists, like their counterparts in clinical psychology, must consider the whole person, his or her environment, and motivation systems, both conscious and unconscious, and be able to adapt this to the school and learning situation. Like the clinical psychologist, the school psychologist has also been greatly influenced by the mental health movement. The schools have increased their emphasis on the child-centered and problem-centered approach to teaching; awareness of mental health issues and desirable mental health practices have been seen throughout most school activities. Besides the identification and correction of mental health problems, the schools have also become sensitized to the role of prevention.

In the United States, school psychology had its early beginnings in the work of Lightner Whitmer, who directed the first psychological clinic at the University of Pennsylvania. In 1896, he recommended a program of action to the American Psychological Association in which he foresaw the need for the cooperation of education and psychology to produce a new brand of psychologists possessing the special knowledge and resourcefulness to deal successfully with problems of mental and moral retardation in school children. He believed that the training necessary for this specialist was not possessed by clinical psychologists, educators, or social workers. He saw the necessity of training a new type of professional. The other major influence in the United States after Whitmer's 1896 statement came in Chicago in 1899 when the public schools of Chicago established, through the efforts of W. S. Christopher, the Department of Child Study and Pedagogic Investigation, the forerunner of most school psychology departments.

The major organization responsible for the professional growth of school psychology has been the American Psychological Association through its Division of School Psychology. Recently, a second national organization was developed with interests specific to school psychology rather than to the field of psychology in general. This organization has called itself The National Association of School Psychologists. Both organizations have developed training programs, standards, and accreditation procedures and have attempted to define the practice of school psychology. While the national organizations are influential in the process of defining school psychology, the legal definition of school psychology has rested with state departments of education. Most states in their education codes have a category called Certified School Psychologist, attempting to define both the role and the training. As an example of one set of definitions, the one for Pennsylvania is utilized (Dept. of Educ., 1970). The state document indicates that:

The school psychologist is concerned with the learning and behavior of all children, including all types of exceptionalities. As a specialist, he is prepared to evaluate individual and group differences and prescribe courses of action. He facilitates the development of children and youth in educational settings through the application of human learning, motivation and personality theory. He is expected to be effective in his relationships with school personnel, parents and the community.

A substantial portion of the school psychologist's professional knowledge, competencies, and time are used in:

1. Collaboration, consultation and conferences with professional personnel or parents with the purpose of enhancing the learning potential of school children

2. Clinical work, including psychodiagnostics with children who have learning or associated problems

A candidate for certification as a school psychologist shall possess entry-level competency in all of the following abilities, to:

1. Establish priorities and procedures relating to the initiation of child studies

2. Conduct individual and group diagnostic studies and to develop appropriate recommendations which include the specific ability to:
   a. Evaluate the current functional level of the child
   b. Identify strengths and weaknesses in learning potential
   c. Assess personality and social factors that affect the child's learning and personal school adjustment
   d. Prepare individual prescriptions to meet the needs of children in school
   e. Identify children for special services and special educational programs where needed

3. Interpret diagnostic findings to the child, parents, teachers, and personnel of schools and agencies; to counsel with these persons about the significance of diagnostic studies and the recommendations arising from them

4. Help parents and school personnel understand the meaning and implication of "normal" and "abnormal" behavior of children

5. Provide individual and group adjustment counseling

6. Consult effectively with parents, school, professional, and community agency personnel

7. Initiate, develop, and supervise special programs and services for exceptional children and/or consult with teachers and supervisors of such programs

8. Develop in-service programs for school personnel in the application of concepts from the disciplines of psychology and education including new professional roles and operational models

9. Demonstrate a knowledge and understanding of administrative and supervisory procedures in these activities related to school psychology

10. Plan, implement, and utilize group evaluative procedures

11. Apprise the community of psychological services presently available and to help initiate the plan to develop additional program services

12. Assist in research of a psychoeducational nature which bears on the adjustment and educational performance of children and to summarize, interpret, and disseminate pertinent research findings

13. Demonstrate a knowledge and understanding of an ethical approach of psychological activities in the school aimed at protecting the rights of the individuals involved

Many state departments of education also approve university programs authorized to train school psychologists. The following are sample standards taken from Pennsylvania:

1. The program should assure the acquisition and mastery of a broad understanding of the psychology of learning and the learning disabilities of all pupils.

2. The program should provide a comprehensive understanding of personality development and in dynamics of human behavior.

3. The program should provide studies and experiences which develop competencies in psychological assessment, individual and group descriptive procedures, reporting and counseling, and consultation and guidance.

4. The program should provide studies and experience of both the performance and interpretation of research and the application of research through educational adjustment.

5. The program should provide a comprehensive understanding of the roles and functions of other pupil personnel service workers and should develop integrated concepts from related disciplines such as sociology, humanities, special education, and medicine.

6. The program should assure a comprehensive understanding of the organization, administration, and operation of public schools; various major roles of the personnel employed in public schools; and an appropriate knowledge of curriculum development in all grade levels.

7. The program should provide a broad practical experience of at least one semester of adequate supervision in an approved internship agency, usually a school or related setting.

The standards of the National Association of School Psychologists can be found in Brantley (1977) and Brantley and Brown (1978).

LEGAL ISSUES

Since the schools are charged with the legal obligation to educate children, psychologists have been used to help in this process. Lately, the law has become one of the primary vehicles used by those who feel they would like to reform education. Educational reform has come in two areas, mainly to those who have been previously excluded and discriminated against and generally in the extension in the Bill of Rights to all school children.

The Supreme Court ruled in *Brown v. The Board of Education* that education is perhaps the most important function of the state and local government and is a *right* that must be available to all on equal terms. Besides ending legal segregation in the public schools, it opened the way for a veritable flood of suits. It indicated the right of access of various kinds of children to equal educational opportunity and perhaps also extended to all children the protection of the Bill of Rights. Shortly after the Washington, D.C., schools ended their segregated system, they instituted a tracking system. However, black and poor children were vastly overrepresented in the lowest track. Federal District Court Judge J. Skelley Wright ruled in *Hobson v. Hansen* that the tracking system constituted an invidious discrimination which was unfair to private rights and the public interest. He also criticized the fact of segregation of both students and faculty and the disparity in resources available to predominantly white versus black schools. In a second *Hobson* decision, he ordered that both human and material resources be equalized across the district.

At approximately the same time (1971), the Pennsylvania Association for Retarded Children (PARC) sought to extend the right of education to all retarded children. After testimony indicating that no child is ineducable, that behavior modification techniques make even the most severely retarded child accessible to some improvement, that retarded children tend to serious regression when out of a program for even a little while, and finally, that many children in EMR classes are misclassified, the state agreed to settle the case in *Pennsylvania Association for Retarded Children v. The Commonwealth of Pennsylvania.*

The PARC decree was a landmark case which has since generated suits and reform legislation across the nation, as is noted by Theimer and Rupiper (1975). Besides requiring the state to find and include all retarded children in an appropriate program within the presumption that the closer to normal the program the better, the decree recognized the process of classification itself could result in serious harm to children; therefore, it sought to protect them through a mandatory periodic review, yearly at parental request, and for those parents dissatisfied with their child's placement, with an impartial due process hearing. In essence, it meant that the parents were entitled to adequate notice of a placement decision and that they had the right to examine their child's records, the right to counsel, the right to call and cross-examine witnesses, and the opportunity to appeal unfavorable decisions for cause. The PARC suit was followed by *Mills v. The Board of Education.* Here the plaintiff sought to establish a principle that all children from the blind to the incorrigibly disruptive, regardless of their exceptionality, were constitutionally entitled to a free public education. The judge, Joseph Wally, concurred, finding constitutional warrant for the universal right to education in both Brown (1954) and Hobson (1967). He concluded that "due process of law requires a hearing prior to exclusion, termination, or classification into a special program."

In *Larry P. v. Riles*, the plaintiff noted that the percentage of blacks in EMR classes was twice that of whites and argued that the assignment process itself was at fault. The court ordered the end to the use of pencil and paper I.Q. tests to classify children. When the percentage of blacks increased after the decision, the plaintiffs went back to court asking it to place a moratorium on all testing until either a reasonable quota system for EMR placement or a culture fair assessment instrument could be developed. Also in *Diana v. The State Board of Education*, the court ordered an end to the assignment of Chicano children to EMR classes simply because they were not fluent in English. School psychologists in California must use Spanish forms of the Wechsler Intelligence Scale for Children when testing Chicanos.

In cases involving minority groups such as in *Serna v. Portales Municipal Schools* for the Chicano-Americans and also for the Chinese-Americans in *Lau v. Nichols*, the plaintiffs have asked the courts to require schools to account in their curriculum for real differences in backgrounds, and it is no longer enough for schools to offer a general program geared to the predominant white cultural norm if some of their students cannot take advantage of it.

There is no doubt that the law is having an effect on the functioning of school psychologists. Bersoff (1975) indicated that one can identify the effect in five areas: (1) the parents' right to access the records; (2) informed consent and the right to privacy and research in assessment; (3) confidentiality of a client-clinical communication; (4) parental refusal of Proffered Educational Services; and (5) treatment of minors without parental consent.

Parental Access to Records

Parental access to records is now governed by the "Buckley Amendments," a section of the federal law extending and amending the Elementary and Secondary Education Act (ESEA) of 1965. This law is designed to protect the privacy of parents and students. It provides that all educational institutions receiving funds under any federal program administered by the U.S. Officer of Education must allow parents of students both access to official records directly related to their child and an opportunity for a hearing to challenge those records on the grounds that they are inaccurate, misleading, or otherwise inappropriate. It is the duty of a school to notify parents of these rights. In addition, the law requires that institutions obtain written consent of parents before releasing to third parties personally identifiable data about students when they become eighteen years of age and about all students regardless of age attending post-secondary education institutions. The penalty for failure to comply is termination of funds to the school systems that have a policy of practice contrary to the intent of the law. One problem was the definition of what constituted a record. Many state departments of education or local school districts tended to define what constituted a record for their district. Essentially, most jurisdictions tended to follow the Russell Sage Foundation guidelines (1970).

These recommendations have been incorporated into the recordkeeping regulations of most states. Different kinds of data require different arrangements for security and access.

Category A Data: Includes official administrative records that constitute the *minimum* personal data necessary for the operation of the educational system. This includes name and address of parent or guardian, birth date, academic work completed, level of achievement (grades, standardized achievement test scores), and attendance data. It is recommended that these records be kept in perpetuity.

Category B Data: Includes verified information of clear importance, but not absolutely necessary to the school over time, in helping the child or in protecting others. Specifically, scores on standardized intelligence and aptitude tests, interest inventory results, health data, family background information, systematically gathered teacher or counselor ratings and observations, and verified reports of serious or recurrent behavior patterns are included in this category.

School districts should give serious consideration to the elimination of unnecessary category B data at periodic intervals, for example, at points of transition from elementary to junior high school and from junior high to high school. These records should be destroyed or else retained only under conditions of anonymity (for research purposes) when the student leaves school. (Exceptions to this standard may be made in different jurisdictions.)

Category C Data: Includes potentially useful information but not yet verified or clearly needed beyond the immediate present, for example, legal or clinical findings, including certain personality test results and unevaluated reports of teachers, counselors, and others which may be needed in ongoing investigations and disciplinary and counseling actions.

Such data should be reviewed at least once a year and destroyed as soon as their usefulness is ended, or transferred to category B. Transfer to category B may be made only if two conditions are met: (1) the continuing usefulness of the information is clearly demonstrated, and (2) its validity has been verified, in which case parents must be notified and the nature of the information explained fully.

A question arises concerning the confidential, personal files of professionals in the school (school psychologists, social workers, counselors). Some professionals working in the schools may maintain personal and confidential files containing notes, raw test data, transcripts of interviews, clinical diagnosis, and other memory aids for their own use in counseling pupils. If the contract with the professional and the school board regulations permit, these may be considered the private property of the professional and need not be shared with the parents or school officials. The professional is usually bound by the code of ethics of his or her field. If the school district considers this part of the school record, then it must be classified into category B or category C data and subsequently shared with the parents and/or the student.

Schools have developed security procedures for their records. The school *may* without the consent of parents or students, release a student's permanent record file, including categories A and B, to school officials, including teachers within the district who have a legitimate educational interest. All school personnel desiring access to pupil records should be required to sign a written form, kept permanently in the file indicating specifically the legitimate educational interest in seeking this information. Others who have received the data without consent are state superintendents and their officers or subordinates, so long as the intended use of the data is consistent with their statutory powers and responsibilities; also officials of other primary or secondary school systems in which the student intends to enroll, under the condition that the student's parents be notified of the transfer, receive a copy of the record if desired, and have an opportunity to challenge the record's content through a specified judicial-like procedure. Exception to the above, school personnel may *not* divulge information in any form except with written consent from the student's parent and/or the student if he or she is over eighteen years of age. Information may be released in compliance with judicial order or orders of administrative agencies having subpoena power. Parents and/or students should be notified of all such orders and the school's compliance. When a student reaches eighteen years of age, or is married (whether eighteen or not), his or her consent alone must be obtained.

Informed Consent and Privacy in Research Assessment

In the case of *Merriken v. Cressman*, a study was proposed by a school district to identify students between the ages of twelve and eighteen who were likely to become involved with drugs. The program involved the administration of questionnaires to students and their teachers. They would be asked questions about their relationships with their mothers and fathers and about peer relationships. The researchers believed that this was related to drug abuse. Questionnaires were to be returned to a research staff for analysis and from there a list of children having a high probability of becoming drug abusers would be compiled. The final phase of the program was to provide intervention through both individual and group sessions run by guidance counselors, school psychologists, or other personnel. The idea of the program was to use it as a preventive measure by which the school district could identify potential drug abusers, prepare necessary interventions, and perhaps ward off future difficulties. A letter was to be sent to the parents notifying them that a study was being done. They were told that if they wished to examine and receive further information regarding the program to feel free to contact the principal of their school. If they did not want the child to participate in the program, they could also notify the principal of their decision. The court, however, considered the program violative of students' rights to privacy and viewed it as a usurpation of the exclusive privilege of parents since the program was intended to be administered without the knowing, intelligent, voluntary, and aware consent of the parents. Further, the program contained no provision for the students' consent and no data were to be provided whereby students could make an informed decision about participating. The court was particularly critical of the invasion of privacy represented by the questions that sought to investigate family relationships. It equated the right of privacy to that of free speech and asserted that the fact that students are juveniles does not in any way invalidate their right to assert their constitutional rights to privacy.

The lesson that most school personnel needed to learn was that the private world of students can only be invaded when there has been adequate disclosure and *informed* consent. Thus, details of the study as well as potential negative factors must be disclosed.

Bersoff (1975) also points out that there are other cases where children's rights in schools have been considered. For example, *Wood v. Strickland*, 95 S.CT. 992 (1975) indicated that school officials are not immune from liability for money damages if they know or reasonably should have known that the action they take within their sphere of official responsibility violates the constitutional rights of the student affected or if they take action with a malicious intention to cause a deprivation of constitutional rights or other injuries to students. In *Goss v. Lopez*, 95 S. CT. 729 (1975) students are entitled to informal hearings before short-term suspensions. In *Tinker v. Des Moines Indiana School District*, 393 U.S. 503 (1969), students have the right to free speech unless it produces substantial and material disruption of school discipline.

Confidentiality of Client Communication

Psychologists generally have the same rights of privileged communication as those that exist between lawyer and client. This right, however, differs from state to state and it is important for the psychologist to know the particular laws in the state in which he or she practices. Some states offer privileged communication to the licensed psychologist but not to the school psychologist. To complicate issues, a case was decided late in 1974 in California, *Tarasoff v. Regents of the University of California* (see Chapter 3), that had a profound impact on the therapist-client relationship. This involved a client who was bent on murdering a young woman, and succeeded in doing so. As the case developed, the client had confessed this to the therapist. The therapist did report this to the local authorities who investigated but took no action. The parents of the victim sued the school's governing body, the therapist, and the supervisors as well as the campus police. As far as the psychologist was concerned, the parents of the victim claimed that the psychologist had a duty to warn their daughter of the student's threat.

The clinician defended against the action on two grounds. First, he pointed out that while therapy patients often express thoughts of violence, they rarely carry them out. The very nature of psychotherapy facilitates the clients to voice this kind of ideation. Second, he argued that free and open communication is essential in psychotherapy and that unless clients are assured that the information revealed will be held in confidence, they will be reluctant to make a full disclosure of their problems, on which successful treatment depends. The court acknowledged the validity of the psychologist's arguments but found them unpersuasive. It recognized that the singling out of those few clients whose threats of violence present a serious danger and weighing that against the danger of harm to the client which might result in the revelation, involved a decision of exceptional expertise and judgment. However, the court concluded, "the public policy favoring protection of the confidential character of patient-psychotherapist communication must yield in instances in which disclosure is essential to avert danger to others. The protective privilege ends where the public peril begins." While this case is binding only in the state of California, it does indicate that there are explicit limits to the client-therapist privacy and that this relationship is not immune from scrutiny.

Parental Refusal of Proffered Educational Services

In the main, parents have been afforded more protection by the courts than have the schools. Bersoff (1975) indicated that the family union has been isolated from state intervention by a long series of Supreme Court decisions. In *Pierce v. The Society of Sisters*, the court called an Oregon statute requiring parents to send their children to public schools, to the exclusion of private alternatives, an "unreasonable interference with the liberty of parents and guardians to direct the upbringing and education of children under their control." As has already been pointed out in the *Pennsylvania Association for Retarded Children v. The Commonwealth of Pennsylvania* and in *Mills v. The Board of Education*, parents are required to receive written notice of any proposed change in status, the reason for the proposed changes, and the opportunity for a hearing at which the parents may challenge the school's recommendations and present evidence to substantiate the validity of alternate choices. Public Law 94-142 has mandated zero exclusion within educational settings, appropriate educational programming for all handicapped children, placement of all children in the least restrictive environment, assurance of extensive child identification procedures, and maintenance of an educational plan for each handicapped pupil. School psychologists are currently required by most state laws to provide the data to be used in these decision-making activities. PL 94-142 also mandates the development of individualized programs for all handicapped youngsters, stating:

The term "individualized educational program" means a written statement for each handicapped child developed in any meeting by a representative of the local educational agency or an intermediate educational unit who shall be qualified to provide, or supervise the provision of, specially designed instruction to meet the unique needs of handicapped children, the teacher, the parents or guardian of such child and whenever appropriate such child which statement shall include (a) a statement of the present level of educational performance of such child; (b) a statement of annual goals including short term instructional objectives; (c) a statement of the specific educational services to be provided to such child, and the extent to which such child will be able to participate in regular educational programs; (d) the projected date for initiation and the anticipated duration of such services and appropriate objective criteria and evaluation procedures and schedules for determining, on at least an annual basis whether instructional objectives are being achieved.

In PL 94-142 parents are becoming increasingly involved in educational planning for their children. Court mandates have enunciated the right of children and their parents of due process hearings when changes in educational programs are proposed and the parents to have the right to participate in the actual educational planning. Thus, these procedures now prevent unilateral decision making by the school, ensure greater parental involvement, and reaffirm the assumption that parents are at least equally as capable as the school staff in deciding what is best for their children.

Parents do not have absolute power, and the courts will intervene in family relationships when they consider that childrens' interests counterbalance those of their parents. For example, in 1901 the Indiana Supreme Court upheld the state's compulsory education laws despite a challenge by parents that the laws were an unauthorized invasion of their rights. The court held that the welfare of the child and the best interest of the society require that the state shall exert its sovereign authority to secure to the child an opportunity to acquire an education. It further asserted that no parent can be said to have the right to deprive his or her child of the advantages so provided (*State v. Bailey*). Also, states have allowed children to receive operations, medical treatment, blood transfusions, and vaccinations even against parental wishes when it thought such intervention served the child. Many states also require the school to report possible cases of child abuse on the part of the parents.

If a school has an appropriate program for a handicapped child and the parents consistently refuse to give permission for placement and the school firmly believes that its decision is the most advantageous for the child, it would be the right of the school administrators to initiate neglect proceedings and to obtain a court determination that their decision is indeed the one most likely to benefit the child. In some states, the right to education procedures established for the handicapped child permit the school district to ask for a due process hearing in order to establish its program for the child despite parental objection. In all of these procedures, however, the school psychologist cannot be solely responsible for working out strategies to protect everyone's rights. The courts have ruled in *Frederick L. v. Thomas* that a school district has an obligation to screen to identify all learning disabled students and cannot *just* rely on teacher referrals to the school psychologists since all learning disabled students are entitled to an "appropriate" or "proper" program. All of this further emphasizes the students' right to their education.

Treatment of Minors without Parental Consent

This has been an area that has created much consternation between parents and school authorities. Parents feel that they have a right to know about their childrens' problems in order to supervise and benefit them appropriately. The school psychologist and the guidance counselors are confronted with the fact that many children have problems that indeed can be remedied but do not wish their parents to know anything about them. The child will frequently choose not to ask for help rather than to reveal the problems to their parents. Despite this, the right of adolescents to seek help by giving valid consent is not universal and is presently confined to only certain areas, the determination of which is a matter of differing state regulations. Some states allow adolescents to seek medical treatment without parents' consent in areas of pregnancy and venereal disease. In some instances, the adolescent is permitted to seek help for a drug abuse problem in a recognized drug treatment center. Under those circumstances, parents are not required to be notified. The practitioner needs to look carefully into the regulations of his or her own state. Even though the psychologist feels he or she might be doing a great service to a teenager, the fact that this information is kept secret from the parents or even the school authorities could place the practitioner in legal jeopardy. Except in cases specifically allowed by law, the author would not treat an adolescent for any extended period of time without parental consent. While it may be appropriate to meet with someone who has asked to see you to obtain information or make a referral, long-term treatment should not be engaged in without notifying the parents.

Right to Education Hearings

Perhaps the area in which school psychologists as well as attorneys have been most involved is in the right to education hearings, especially after October 1, 1977, when Public Law 94-142 became fully effective. The federal law requires due process procedures to be followed concerning identification, evaluation, and placement in programs for handicapped students. The law indicates that all parents are entitled to legal counsel and most do obtain it. A special education hearing is a type of "administrative hearing." That is, it is like a hearing before a state agency or governmental body. At the special education hearing, a hearing officer sits as a delegate of the secretary of education. It is a responsibility of a hearing officer, on behalf of the secretary, to hear testimony and to receive documentary evidence from the parties to such a hearing. The parties are usually the parents who are considered the petitioners, and the school district or intermediate unit who are considered the respondents. The hearing officer is charged with the duty of ensuring that the hearing is conducted in an orderly, concise fashion, the parties are able to present witnesses who have relevant testimony, relevant evidence is introduced into the record, and the rulings are made on objections posed by parties during the course of a hearing. A transcript of a hearing is kept which is important to the hearing officer in order to write his or her opinion and also as the basis on which the secretary of education will consider appeals from the hearing officer's decision.

There are several different types of hearings. One is called a *preevaluation hearing*. These are available prior to the individual evaluation of a thought-to-be exceptional child for special education by either a school district or intermediate unit. If a school district feels that a child may be exceptional or in need of special education, it has to notify the parent or guardian of the district's intent to evaluate the child. The parent may refuse consent for the evaluation, and in that case, the school district may request a hearing. Under these circumstances, the questions that the hearing officer has to answer in order to resolve the issue of whether or not the proposed testing and evaluation represents a reasonable educational procedure in view of the child's school conduct and academic performance are:

1. Has the school district or intermediate unit presented evidence or testimony with regard to the student's classroom behavior or academic achievement that would show that the child may need special education and related services?

2. Does the evaluation procedure which the district proposed to use include "personalized tests," that is, tests which are not group tests?

3. Has the district or intermediate unit used these types of tests on the child before or have these types of tests been submitted to the district before? If the answer is yes, the parental consent is not required for new tests of the same type. In that case, the hearing officer will usually find for the district.

4. Are the proposed tests needed to measure or to contribute to the measurement of the child's exceptionality?

The second type of hearing is called an *evaluation hearing*. Evaluation hearings are available to parents who wish to challenge the school district or intermediate unit evaluation of an exceptional or thought-to-be exceptional child, which resulted in the conclusion that the child is not exceptional. If the parents request an evaluation hearing, the school district needs to present evidence in support of its evaluation and the reasons for finding the child to be nonexceptional. The parents may present evidence supporting their contention that the child is exceptional and/or give reasons why they should contest the district's evaluations and findings. The hearing officer must then determine whether or not the child is exceptional on the basis of the material presented at the hearing. The hearing officer also has the right to request additional testing or evaluation and then to reconvene the hearing at a later date.

The third type of hearing is called the *individualized education program hearing* (IEP). An individualized education program shall be developed for each person assigned to special education programs or services. The IEP is to be developed at a conference held jointly with the parents and the school personnel. It is not a binding contract; the IEP may be revised periodically in accordance with the special education standards without the requirement of notice and the right to a hearing. In a case of an initial IEP or where a revised IEP results in a change of educational status, special education program, or related services, the child's parents are entitled to know this and, if they disagree with the IEP, to a "due process" hearing called an IEP hearing.

At the hearing, the school district presents its proposed IEP and supporting evidence. The child's parents may present evidence concerning their disagreement with the district's IEP. Based upon a preponderance of the evidence on the record, the hearing officer must issue a report defining the assignment, program, and services in such specificity as is deemed necessary. The parties must then develop the IEP that conforms with the decision of the hearing officer. Note that the decision is based upon the preponderance of the evidence presented at the hearing. It is, therefore, extremely important for the parents who are protesting an IEP to have relevant evidence and relevant testimony. The decision is not based solely on the goodwill of the hearing officer.

The fourth kind of hearing is the *program placement hearing*. As a conclusion of the IEP conference or right before it, the school district or intermediate unit notifies the parents of the placement and program proposed for the exceptional child. If the child's parents disagree with the district's proposal, they may request a program placement hearing. The role of a hearing officer at a program placement hearing is to determine whether the school district or intermediate unit program has met its legal responsibility to provide an educational program that will appropriately and adequately address a child's special education needs. The legal responsibility of the school district or intermediate unit to provide an appropriate and adequate special education program is determined usually by state law. The hearing officer is not asked to rule on the "very best" program possible, but simply to rule on whether the program is appropriate and adequate. Key questions involved in a program placement hearing are:

1. Is the child exceptional, that is, does the child exhibit a physical or mental handicap which could influence his educational performance, or in some states is the child gifted or talented? (Gifted and talented programs are not mandated in PL 94-142 but are mandated in some states.)

2. If the child is exceptional, is he/she in need of a special education program?

3. If the child is already in a program of special education, is a change in educational assignment necessary?

4. If the above questions are answered yes, the next question becomes: Is the district's proposed program adequate and appropriate to the exceptional child?

In order to determine if the program is appropriate, the hearing officer has to see that the program addresses the degree of handicap and the particular needs of the child. If the program is not adequate, the hearing officer must then decide what modifications it requires. Also, the officer must look at the recommended IEP in order to determine whether that also reflects an adequate program. He or she may investigate whether mainstreaming is necessary, whether there is a need for vocational education, or even if there is a need for further evidence or testing. The hearing officer also looks into transportation and the mode of transportation. For example, a program may be quite appropriate but may be inadequate because the mode of transportation and the time involved getting the child to the school debilitates the child for educational purposes. In that case, the hearing officer must determine what adjustments in the district's proposals are necessary. In this situation, the hearing officer is also bound by the evidence presented at the hearing. If the hearing officer finds the proposed placement to be inadequate and/or inappropriate for the child, the hearing officer has the authority to recommend the proper type of educational assignment, but only if the recommendation can be supported by a preponderance of the evidence presented at the hearing. If the hearing officer finds that the district's program is both appropriate and adequate, then the officer must find for the district.

If the hearing officer, based on the evidence presented, cannot make a decision, he or she then may request additional information and adjourn the hearing to be reconvened after the school district has developed either a new proposal for the child or has presented additional evidence. What some parents and attorneys do not understand about a hearing is that the hearing officer's authority in rejecting a proposed assignment and making his or her own recommendations extends only to the "type" of educational program to which the child should be assigned. The hearing officer does not have the authority to assign a child to a particular school. This is the school district's duty. Thus, the hearing officer can define the program, but not say in which school the program must be carried out. The hearing officer may refer to a certain private school, explaining why that program would meet the child's needs in light of the evidence presented at the hearing. He may also refer to certain programs offered in public schools and explain why they are inadequate. Naming private schools with adequate programs could forestall the need for additional hearings and provide the school district with valuable guidance. However, the record of the hearing must contain some evidence that the programs of such schools are satisfactory. The hearing officer may use his or her own knowledge or that of those present at the hearing in discussing and considering alternative placement possibilities in both the private and public sectors. However, a particular school referred to by the hearing officer is used as only a suggestion and cannot be binding for a particular placement.

In terms of the matter of *evidence* and *testimony*, the initial burden of proof at a due process hearing rests with the school district or intermediate unit. The school district may introduce into evidence the official report recommending a change in educational assignment, and if that is not accepted, the district must also present all relevant and material evidence in support of the position which it is taking. The parent must then present evidence to contest the district's position. This can be done in either of two ways. The parent may: (1) give evidence of why the position or proposal of the school district or intermediate unit is inappropriate for the child; and/or (2) give evidence of what the parent feels is the appropriate position or proposal concerning the child. If the decision cannot be made, the hearing officer may direct the school district to develop an appropriate recommendation for the child, then reschedule the hearing at another date. The hearing officer will also try to see that recent material relating to the child is also presented.

Preponderance of the Evidence

The decision or recommendation of the hearing officer must be supported by a preponderance of the evidence on the record of the hearing taken place as a whole. A preponderance of the evidence exists when the quantity of the evidence supporting one position is greater than the evidence supporting the opposing position. All documents are also presented into evidence. At the hearing, the school district should introduce the official documents that support and substantiate positions being taken or recommendations being made by the district. Valid reasons, on the face of the document, may not be supported by additional evidence of the parents, where the hearing officer fails to challenge them.

One problem that arises at due process hearings occurs when the parents present a psychological report or test results into evidence, but the person who prepared the report is not present. It is usually too difficult and expensive for the parent to have this person present at the hearing. Nevertheless, a possible fraudulent report cannot be accepted without question. Usually, the hearing officer will ask the parties to stipulate on the record that the report was prepared by the person who signed it, stating the individual's place of appointment. However, whenever an evaluation report is submitted, it is best that the person who prepared the document is available to identify it and interpret the results or conclusions. A document that is accompanied by corroborative testimony may be given more weight than a document without such testimony.

Evidence given by the parent must be given the same consideration as the testimony of a professional witness. It is up to the hearing officer to weigh the credibility of this evidence, knowing that some children do not perform as well in a testing situation as they do at home.

Another factor that enters into hearings is medical testimony. Testimony of a medical doctor is only appropriate for the child's medical condition. What frequently happens is that the physician may recommend a specific educational placement. This placement is not binding on the hearing. Whether the child can profit from an educational program is not considered to be in the province of the physician, unless he has special expertise in that area. For example, a physician must testify as to whether a child is brain injured, but that physician is not necessarily qualified to indicate the special education needs of the child resulting from the brain injury unless his or her professional credentials so warrant.

If the parent desires the attendance of a certain school district or intermediate unit person at the hearing, the parents should request his or her attendance. If that person is unwilling to attend, a subpoena may be issued by the hearing officer. The parent, however, must give a rationale for requesting such a subpoena. The hearing officer will then determine if the presence of such person is necessary. The hearing day may be altered to allow the witness to attend, provided the parents agree to a continuance.

No less than five days prior to the hearing, the parties must list the documents and witnesses they expect to produce at the hearing and share that information with the other party. The parties should also exchange copies of documentary evidence they intend to introduce at the hearing. If one party has not complied with this, then the other party may plead surprise, requesting time at the hearing to review the documentary evidence, or if the extent of the unpreparedness is extreme, they may request a postponement of the hearing.

The hearing officer then, based on the evidence presented, weighs all the testimony, and based on procedures of state law, determines the appropriate program and the appropriate decision. If the school district's program is appropriate, then the law mandates that that particular program is the one that must be accepted rather than that of a private school placement. The law requires the child to be placed in the least restricted environment. This is interpreted by state law and by federal regulations to mean placement in a public school whenever possible (O'Connor, Alzamora, and Helling, 1978).

Once a decision is rendered, either the school district or the parents have the right to appeal the decision of the hearing officer to the secretary of education, and from there to the courts.

While some people have viewed this procedure as cumbersome and time consuming, it has worked to bring about specialized programs for those pupils who truly need them.

As can be seen, the school psychologist plays a critical role in the education of the child, especially the exceptional child. He or she is deeply involved in the appropriate educational programs and also with legal procedures, precedent, the courts, and governmental agencies. Besides working with the child, school personnel, and parents, the school psychologist needs to be able to work together with the attorney in order to help obtain appropriate programs for exceptional children.

CASES CITED

Brown v. Board of Education, 347 U.S. 483 (1954).
Hobson v. Hansen, 629 F. Supp. 401 (D.D.C. 1967).
Hobson v. Hansen, 327 F. Supp. 844 (D.D.C. 1971).
Pennsylvania Association for Retarded Children v. The Commonwealth of Pennsylvania, 343 F. Supp. 279 (E.D. Pa. 1972).
Mills v. Board of Education, 348 F. Supp. 866 (D.D.C. 1972).
Larry P. v. Riles, 343 F. Supp. 1306 (N.D. Cal. 1972).
Diana v. The State Board of Education, No. C-70-37 (N.D. Cal., E 1970).
Serna v. Portales Municipal Schools, 351 F. Supp. 1279 (D.N.M. 1972).
Lau v. Nichols, 483 F. 2d (9th Cir. 1973), Cert, granted, 412 U.S. 938 (1973).
Merriken v. Cressman, 364 F. Supp. 913 (E.B. Pa. 1973).
Wood v. Strickland, 95 S. Ct. 992 (1975).
Goss v. Lopez, 95 S.CT. 729 (1975).
Tinker v. Des Moines Indiana School District, 393 U.S. 503(1969).
Tarsoff v. Regents of University of California, 13, C.3rd 177, 529 P. 2d 553, 118 Cal. Rptr. 129 (1974).
Pierce v. Society of Sisters, 268 U.S. 510 (1925).
State v. Bailey, 157 Ind. 324, 329-330, 61 N.E. 730, 731-732 (1901).
Frederick L. v. Thomas, 557 F. 2d, 373 (1977).
Public Law 93-380, "The Elementary and Secondary Education Act of 1974," August 21, 1974.
Public Law 94-142, "The Education for All Handicapped Children Act of 1975," November 29, 1975.

BIBLIOGRAPHY

Bersoff, D. N. Professional ethics and legal responsibilities: On the horns of a dilemma. *Journal of School Psychology* 1975, *13*, 359-376.
Brantley, J. C., ed. A special issue on NASP's professional standards and continuing professional development. *School Psychology Digest*, 1977, *6*(2), 1-83.
Brantley, J. C., and Brown, D. T., eds. *Standards for training programs in school psychology*. Washington, D.C.: National Association of School Psychologists, 1978.
Kuriloff, P. Law, educational reform, and the school psychologist. *Journal of School Psychology*, 1975, *13*, 335-348.
Lupiani, D. A. The practice of defensive school psychology. *Psychology in the Schools*, 1978, *15*, 246-252.

O'Connor, L. D., Alzamora, J., and Helling E. *Hearing officers handbook*. Harrisburg, Pa.: Pennsylvania Department of Education, 1978.

Pennsylvania Department of Education. *Standards for school psychologists*. Harrisburg, Pa.: Pennsylvania Department of Education, 1970.

Russell Sage Foundation. *Guidelines for the collection, maintenance and dissemination of pupil records*. New York: Russell Sage Foundation, 1970.

Theimer, R. K., and Rupiper, O. J. Special education litigation and school psychology. *Journal of School Psychology*, 1975, *13*, 324-334.

Wallen, J. E. W., and Ferguson, D. G. The development of school psychological services. In J. F. Magary, ed. *School psychological services in theory and practice*. Englewood Cliffs, N.J.: Prentice Hall, 1967, 1-29.

Ysseldyke, J. E. Who's calling the plays in school psychology. *Psychology in the Schools*, 1978, *15*, 373-378.

Ethical and Legal Issues in Community Psychology

INTRODUCTION

Community psychology is a complex and varied branch of psychology which has been identified as a distinct field for only fifteen years. There is no agreement on the precise definition or on the exact subject matter that comprises community psychology. Therefore, this chapter will concentrate on giving the reader a broad orientation to this relatively new specialty without attempting a definitive demarkation of its boundaries. The major theme is that the two distinct origins of community psychology — clinical and social psychology — have led to a complex and confusing situation concerning its licensing, ethics, and practice.

It is suggested that more attention needs to be paid to issues such as licensing and regulation of practice if community psychology is to become a viable long-term specialty of psychology. A checklist of ethical issues that should be addressed in any community psychology intervention is also provided.

HISTORY AND DEVELOPMENT

The psychological study of people in their social environments is not new. Different psychological research approaches have dealt with this general subject since the turn of the century. Over seventy years ago, the following was written in a clinical psychology journal:

Although clinical psychology is closely related to medicine, it is quite as closely related to sociology and pedagogy. The schoolroom, the juvenile court, and the streets are a larger laboratory of psychology. An abundance of material for scientific study fails to be utilized because the interests of psychologists are elsewhere engaged (Witmer, 1907, pp. 1-9).

In the 1950s, psychologist Kurt Lewin focused his research skills upon influences of the social environment on human behavior. A major emphasis of his efforts was to understand social and community problems from a dynamic field theory. In 1951 he published his influential *Field Theory in Social Science* (Lewin, 1951).

Contemporary community psychologists agree that community psychology as a modern specialty had its origins at the Conference of the Education of Psychologists for Community Mental Health, which was held on May 4-8, 1965, in Swampscott, Massachusetts (Bennett et al., 1965). The Swampscott Conference was held in order to exchange information on the training of psychologists in community mental health. However, the more than thirty persons who attended this conference confronted the broader issue of their own identities as psychologists. Many of these participants were working in the Peace Corps, the Anti-Poverty Program, and Urban Mental Health Clinics. They were serving and studying populations that differed from those traditionally contacted by psychologists. From their struggle to identify what they had in common that differentiated them from most other psychologists, they arrived at the term *community psychology*. The term itself had been used as early as 1958 at George Peabody College in Nashville, Tennessee (Newbrough, Rhoades, and Seeman, 1970, pp. 36-51).

One of the interesting aspects of the development of community psychology in the 1960s was the major role played by government programs. Murrell, in his book *Community Psychology and Social Systems* (1973), has made this point:

More than any other specialty in the history of psychology, Community Psychology is a response to governmental activities and social reform movements. It has been particularly committed to the principle of participation by consumers in social system decisions (p.6).

It is evident from the organization of this book that psychology is divided into specialized areas. A typical psychologist has had his or her training at the graduate level in just one of these areas. The psychologists who participated in the Swampscott Conference were primarily trained in clinical psychology. Through their work in government programs and on social problems, many of them had come to see the importance of an environmental and social component to their models. Thus, there were many clinical psychologists who were adding social psychology to their clinical training. Other participants, however, had their primary training in social psychology. They had become involved in applied social/psychological research on mental health problems. Social psychologists were following the applied research approach of Kurt Lewin into new areas, particularly mental health problems in communities.

Psychologists from the two specialties, clinical and social, united their efforts to develop new social and community approaches to alleviate mental health problems. Although the psychologists united their efforts, the difference in training and practice of these two specialties caused a division and still continues to divide the field of community psychology.

DEFINITIONS

The fields of community psychiatry, social psychiatry, community mental health, and community psychology overlap considerably. A number of authors, including Zax and Specter (1974, pp. 5-8) and Heller and Monahan (1977, pp. 20-22), have attempted to clarify the subject matters of these fields. There is also considerable overlap between community psychology and social welfare, particularly the subspecialty of community organization (Frederico, 1976; Parad and Rapoport, 1972).

The definition provided by Zax and Specter emphasizes that community psychology is always concerned with a human behavior problem. This emphasis gives their definition close correspondence to the subspecialty of community mental health.

Community Psychology is regarded as an approach to human behavior problems that emphasizes contributions made to their development by environmental forces as well as the potential contributions to be made toward their alleviation by the use of these forces (Zax and Specter, 1974, p. 3).

This definition shows the expansion of the traditional clinical psychological approach from consideration of purely intrapsychic factors to consideration of individual behavior disorder. Other definitions broaden not only the factors influencing individual behavior but also the types of problems to be studied. One of these broader definitions comes from P. E. Cook. Writing in an early book, which is now out of print, Cook defines community psychology as follows:

Community Psychology represents a mixture of mental health, behavioral science, social science, psychology, sociology, and other areas. It is the application of behavioral science principles to the understanding and solution of a variety of problems and community situations, and not just those problems related to mental health and mental illness (Cook, 1970, p. 2).

Cook emphasized the different disciplines that are brought together in community psychology. It is suggested that at least three other disciplines should be added — social work, economics, and political science. Cook also highlights the problem-solving aspect of community psychology. This definition emphasizes that work in the field is almost always focused around the solution of a real or practical problem, rather than a theoretical or abstract issue.

Whereas in clinical psychology the practical application of its methodology is called *treatment*, the term generally used for applied activity in community psychology is *intervention*. The intervention is whatever the community psychologist carries out, either alone or in conjunction with other community actors, to effect a change. Thus, the word *intervention* is a broader term which can encompass traditional forms of psychological treatment (Sarason, 1974). It also includes an unlimited number of strategies to accomplish a behavioral or social change.

As was mentioned previously, there is considerable overlap among community psychiatry, social psychiatry, and community psychology. This overlap presents the natural extension of psychiatry and psychology into an approach that gives greater emphasis to social and environmental factors. At this point, the distinction between psychiatry and psychology has become one of emphasis rather than subject matter. Social psychiatry developed primarily as a field of research (by medically oriented and psychiatrically trained physicians) into the long-term solution to mental illness. Therefore, social psychiatry confines its concepts to those that fall within basic disease models of mental illness.

On the other hand, community psychiatry represents the extension of psychiatry to include social and environmental factors in its model of mental illness. Being a branch of psychiatry, community psychiatry also utilizes the basic medical disease model of mental illness.

While some practitioners in the field of psychology continue to operate with a psychiatric disease model, many do not. The majority of community psychologists are more likely to use a multidimensional behavioral and environmental model rather than a medical disease model.

TRAINING

Early Efforts

The first explicit discussion of the training of community psychologists took place at the Boston Conference on the Education of Psychologists for Community Mental Health (Bennet et al., 1965). That conference was attended primarily by clinical psychologists who were struggling to develop training for new roles of psychologists in community mental health settings.

The sole graduate training in community psychology that preceded the Boston Conference was held at the George Peabody College in Nashville, Tennessee, where the term *community psychology* had been used for several years (Newbrough, Rhoades, and Seeman, 1970). Following the Boston Conference there was a gradual growth in course work and field training in community psychology. The training typically took place as an adjunct to graduate doctoral programs in clinical psychology. In addition to the George

Peabody College, there were programs at the University of Texas at Austin, University of Colorado at Boulder, and the South Shore Medical Health Center at Swampscott, Massachusetts (Iscoe and Spielberger, 1970).

After the Boston Conference there were a number of other conferences which included the Austin Conference in 1967 (Iscoe and Spielberger, 1970), the Vail Conference in 1973 (Korman, 1974), and the National Training Conference in Community Psychology in 1975 (Iscoe, 1975).

The establishment of training was marked in 1970 by the publication of *Community Psychology Perspectives in Training and Research*, edited by Ira Iscoe of the University of Texas and Charles D. Spielberger of Florida State University. The Iscoe and Speilberger book brought together fourteen articles discussing various training programs. In addition to these programs, the training at the University of Rochester (Cowen, 1970), The City University of New York (Singer and Bard, 1970), Yale University (Sarason and Levin, 1970), and others were discussed. One major postdoctorate program at the Albert Einstein College of Medicine, Yeshiva University, was developed (Stein, 1970).

The major part of the training offered was additional course work in social and environmental aspects of mental health. This included research methods needed to study those social and environmental aspects of mental illness. The Albert Einstein program was one of the few that emphasized social and political change, rather than mental health research (Stein, 1970).

Along with different course content, there was considerable emphasis placed on getting students into internship experiences that differed from the traditional clinical psychology ones. Whereas the traditional clinical psychology internships, required of all Ph.D. candidates, trained the student to perform psychodiagnostic and psychotherapeutic services, these new community psychology internships exposed the student to program planning and development, evaluation research, and community organization. Less radical community psychology internships placed students in community mental health centers in poverty neighborhoods where they learned traditional clinical psychology skills.

In summary, early efforts in community psychology training produced a few outstanding graduates. The training was almost entirely focused on the Ph.D. candidate in clinical psychology or the postdoctoral student. Although seen as radical by the traditional academic clinicians, most early training involved experience in outpatient clinics in poverty areas where the techniques applied differed little from the traditional.

Current Status

During the 1970s, teaching and training in community psychology has steadily expanded. A survey reported by Barton et al. (1976) found that approximately 140 graduate university programs and 50 internship settings offered community psychology training. The number today probably exceeds that, although it is difficult to determine the exact number (APA, 1978b).

A few programs have developed that emphasize program planning and evaluation research. Among these is the program of the Hahnemann Medical College in Philadelphia. However, the great majority of these programs are community mental health programs. Barton et al. (1976) report that 76 percent of the community psychology programs they surveyed emphasized community mental health field work experiences. They also report that the ten most frequent course content offerings include the following list in descending order:

1. Comparison of intervention strategies

2. Crisis intervention

3. Case-consultation

4. Community mental health center, neighborhood health center organization

5. Urban community based action program

6. Mental health program planning and evaluation

7. Prevention of mental disorders

8. Group process

9. Mental health program evaluation

10. Consultee-centered consultation (Barton et al., 1976, p. 4)

Barton concluded that:

In University programs and internships substantial gains (in absolute numbers) have been made in establishing Community Psychology and Mental Health as relevant and identifiable academic and field training experiences within psychology departments. . . . Such new roles of the 1960's have become traditional community mental health roles for the 1970's largely because the choice of more traditional practicum agencies have determined the psychological techniques to be learned (Barton et al., 1976, p. 9).

As of this writing, the most recent article on training reports a survey of the members of the Community Psychology Division (27) of the American Psychological Association. The members are reported as seeing community organization, community change, interagency coordination, and human service program development as essential to community psychology. However, these are not the subjects most commonly included in community psychology curriculum (Andrulis, Barton, and Aponte, 1978).

A growing number of programs are being developed at the Master's level. At the time of this writing, the author was affiliated with the Master's Degree

Program in Psychosocial Science-Community Psychology at the Capitol Campus of the Pennsylvania State University. This program is able to escape domination by clinical psychology because it is built upon a multidisciplinary undergraduate program in social science. The undergraduate program includes sociologists, anthropologists, political scientists, statisticians, and economists in addition to psychologists. The curriculum, which is currently being expanded, has included community organization, psychopathology in a social context, social and community change processes, and techniques in action research. The majority of students take the required practicum in community and human service settings other than mental health agencies. Those who are in mental health settings learn program planning, evaluation, case management, and consultation skills, rather than diagnostic or therapeutic skills.

Clinical psychology Ph.D. programs are extremely selective and can train only a limited number of students per year. There is and will continue to be the need for training much larger numbers of human service personnel. It is predicated that the 1980s will see an expanded number of Master's-level community psychology programs which will emphasize program planning and development, evaluation research, consultation, administration, and noninstitutional treatment.

PRACTICE OF COMMUNITY PSYCHOLOGY

Introduction

The practice of community psychology takes place in many settings and takes many diverse forms. This section will describe these settings and the roles played by community psychologists. Instead of using a narrow definition of the practice, the full range of activities that are considered to comprise community psychology will be included. The influences of clinical and social psychology on the practice of community psychology will also be pointed out.

Roles

According to Wrightsman, the term *role* is usually defined as "the set of behaviors or functions appropriate for a person who holds a particular position within a particular social context" (Wrightsman, 1977, p. 16). This section will list and discuss the most important roles that community psychologists play. These roles essentially define the major functions of the psychologists.

Therapist. Some psychologists performing therapy for disturbed clients consider themselves to be community psychologists because they work in community mental health settings which serve all segments of the community. Therapy aimed at helping families and groups of people has been available for a long time. When this service is provided to a broad-based community clientele, it is viewed as community psychology. Some therapists in private practice who provide therapeutic services and charge little or no fee for poor clients consider the practice a community practice.

Behavioral therapy describes a number of methods that use the systematic application of learning principles to bring about behavior change (Brown, Wienckowski, and Stolz, 1975; Stolz, 1978). The behavioral psychologist provides skills to clients who learn through self-administered reinforcement to change their own behaviors. In some settings, institutional staff control some of these reinforcements. The behavior therapy approach is being applied by therapists in community settings. Such applications are described in greater detail in Nietzel et al. (1977). The publication of the Nietzel book has given credibility to a new and growing branch of community psychology called Behavioral Community Psychology (Turner and Goodson, 1977).

Consultant. Mental health consultation was developed and elaborated by Gerald Caplan (1970, p. 19) who has defined consultation as follows:

Consultation is used in quite a restricted sense to denote a process of interaction between two professional persons — the consultant, who is a specialist, and the consultee, who invokes the consultant's help in regard to a current work problem with which he is having some difficulty and which he has decided is within the other's area of competence. The work problem involves the management or treatment of one or more clients of the consultee, or the planning or implementation of a program to cater to such clients.

Caplan has divided consultation into four types: client-centered, consultee-centered, program-centered administrative, and consultee-centered administrative consultation.

Client-centered consultation focuses on the therapeutic needs of an individual client. An example would be giving advice to a teacher who is helping an individual child with a behavioral problem.

Consultee-centered consultation is focused on helping the professional to develop new skills or overcome his or her own deficiencies. Consultee-centered consultation often develops from client-centered case consultation into a quasi-therapeutic relationship between the consultant and the consultee (Heller and Monahan, 1977, p. 211).

Program-centered administrative consultation deals with a program of services rather than a client. In this capacity, the community psychologist offers advice concerning the structure, staffing, and administration of the program (Rappaport, 1977).

Consultee-centered administrative consultation functions to help a consultee improve his or her administrative skills.

Researcher/Evaluator. The systematic collection and analysis of information constitutes the research process. One of the major roles played by community psychologists has been research designed to answer questions about the need for and the effectiveness of treatments and other interventions. According to Heller and Monahan, "Evaluations are undertaken to provide information with which decision makers can make more rational decisions. Likewise the basic researcher formulates his/her own hypotheses while the evaluator devises questions with reference to the program and the decision maker" (1975, p. 75). Evaluation can be more formally defined as the assessment by some criteria of an activity designed to accomplish an objective.

The roles involved in evaluation are complex. In the simplest form, an independent evaluator is hired by an agency administrator to assess some aspect(s) of a program. In the course of carrying out most evaluations, the evaluator must struggle against the program's reluctance to reveal information that might be the basis for negative conclusions. The capabilities of program personnel invariably come under the evaluator's scrutiny. Therefore, relationships between evaluator and program personnel are delicate. The potential for misunderstandings and bad feelings is great on both sides. When the stakes are high, the potential for redress of misunderstandings through legal action becomes a possibility.

Teacher/Conceptualizer. Another major role is that of college or university professors who teach community psychology and conceptualize its development. Graduate training in psychology has been expanding at a steady, if not rapid, pace. Undergraduate training in community psychology also is growing. Individual courses for undergraduates in community psychology are being added to psychology and social science curricula. Goldberg reports the development of an undergraduate training program at Morehouse College in Atlanta, Georgia (1976, p. 327).

Primarily among the teachers are a growing number of writers and conceptualizers of community psychology and what it ought to be. There are presently two professional journals devoted to community psychology, the *American Journal of Community Psychology* and the *Journal of Community Psychology*. In addition, the American Psychological Association journal *Professional Psychology*, devotes a considerable amount of its space to community psychology. Furthermore, new monographs and textbooks appear constantly. For example, see the textbook *Community Psychology: Concepts and Applications* by Philip A. Mann (1978).

Change Agent/Community Organizer. During the civil rights ferment of the 1960s, some psychologists concluded that direct involvement in political action was necessary in order to bring about greater social justice. This involvement took different forms, including organizing protest demonstrations and involvement in electoral politics. Many psychologists continue to put part of their energies into the political process. Some of this political involvement continues to be a force for helping underrepresented groups. In addition, psychologists are using the political process to protect and advance the professional goals of psychology. The American Psychological Association has established a political action arm called the Association for the Advancement of Psychology (AAP, 1978). Whether acting to improve services for the mentally ill or to protect the psychologists from the domination by other professions, psychologists as citizens and professionals are lobbying, raising money for election campaigns, and organizing local and national political constituencies (Alinsky, 1972).

Practice

The practice of psychology involves the provision of a professional psychological service by a practitioner to client(s). A service is considered psychological if it is called psychological, if it is provided by a person calling himself or herself a psychologist, or if it uses the direct and systematic application of the principles of one or more psychological theories such as learning or psychoanalytic theory (APA, 1977b).

The American Psychological Association recognizes four specialty areas of psychological practice: clinical, counseling, industrial-organizational, and school. As has been mentioned, community psychology draws upon both clinical and social psychology, yet social psychology is an academic discipline, not a professional specialty.

Clinical psychologists traditionally practice in one of the several following manners:

1. They are employed by a clinic, hospital, or mental health agency and see patients in that setting for which they receive a salary.

2. They practice as private, self-employed individuals who charge fees directly to their patients or clients.

3. They join several other psychologists to form professional corporations or group practices which collect fees from patients or clients.

4. They are employed by a corporation to which they may provide a variety of services in return for a salary.

5. They are employed as university professors where they train students. However, the teaching of theory in itself is usually not considered a psychological service.

6. They carry out research and evaluation under the auspices of universities and as independent contractors to public and private agencies.

In agency or hospital settings, a branch of government or nonprofit corporation sanctioned by state or federal government takes responsibility for the service. When psychologists are self-employed or work in group practices, the professionals themselves must take that responsibility. Currently, forty-seven states and the District of Columbia require a license or certification sanctioned by the state for those psychologists who are self-employed or who are in group practice. On the other hand, the states do not require such licensing or certification for those practicing in a clinic, hospital, or mental health agency. The licensing and credentialing systems have been set up to parallel closely the states' medical licensing laws. Three states — Alaska, Florida, and South Dakota — by means of sunset legislation rescinded their licensing laws.

Social psychologists have taught and have conducted research, but historically they were not heavily involved in the provision of activities considered as psychological service. When social psychologists, such as Kurt Lewin, became involved in research on applied social and community problems, they did so as educators and researchers first and practitioners second. In fact, any applied work done by psychologists that did not directly parallel a medical or clinical practice was not considered a psychological service.

Clinical community psychologists view their activities as extensions of clinical practice and have considered themselves to be under the regulation of those laws governing the practice of clinical psychology. On the other hand, social community psychologists have considered their work to be an extension of applied social psychology and not subject to the laws and regulations governing clinical practice or the provision of psychological services.

Many of the social community psychologists are of a politically radical antigovernment orientation. Because their activities often involve organization of citizens against government, the radical social psychologists suspect that any submission to professional and state regulation would result in curtailment of their activities. In between the clinical community psychologists and the radical politically oriented social psychologists lie social psychologists who conduct applied research, evaluation, and consultation and are unsure whether or not they want to be considered psychological practitioners. In order to shed some light on this problem, let us present a rationale for the licensing and regulation of psychological activities and then apply this to community psychology.

Application of psychological principles has a potentially powerful effect upon individuals, organizations, communities, and ultimately society. The term *psychology* has become imbued with considerable power. Because of the perceived potential power, the public needs to be protected from untrained, unscrupulous persons who might portray themselves as psychologists. Licensing laws, regulations, and professional standards serve a number of functions. One is to provide the public with some minimum control of untrained or unqualified persons. This protection can be seen as simply one part of the general need to protect and inform consumers about the services and products they purchase. If the regulation of psychologists is seen only as a protection of consumers, then regulations need only apply to those instances in which a consumer is provided a service. Such has been the model typically applied in the provision of clinical psychological services. It is suggested here that responsibility should be somewhat broader. Society should be protected not only from direct consumer fraud, but also from unqualified or unethical persons carrying out a psychological intervention under their own, or educational, or governmental agency auspices.

The importance of such protection from researchers is already recognized as a federal governmental responsibility. The Department of Health, Education and Welfare (now Health and Human Services), under the direction of Congress, has established elaborate procedures to protect all subjects of psychological experiments. Federal government guidelines go beyond the guidelines drawn up by the American Psychological Association itself (APA, 1973).

The major principles in such ethical standards are informed consent, competence, and knowledge — competence of the potential subject of research to understand what will be asked of him or her and knowledge of what the research would entail. Informed consent means that the competent individual has sufficient knowledge to participate in the psychological study or experiment.

It is suggested that any psychological intervention involves human subjects who should be protected by standardized procedures codified in state laws, regulations, and professional standards.

There is no logical reason for community psychologists to be any less governed by such procedures. As a matter of fact, because of its greater potential for impacting larger numbers of persons, the activities of community psychologists have greater potential for abuse. Therefore, the activities should be closely scrutinized and regulated.

ETHICAL AND LEGAL ISSUES

Ethical Standards

Three types of problems that haunt the provision of any professional service are unethical behavior, incompetent behavior, and malpractice on the part of the professional. An unethical provider has been defined as, "one who lacks sufficient integrity, moral commitment and sound judgment to maintain standards of right and wrong actions in his professional practice" (Van Hoose, 1977).

Members of the American Psychological Association are expected to comply with a comprehensive statement of ethical standards (APA, 1977a). The preamble of the standards sets these goals:

While demanding for themselves freedom of inquiry and communication, psychologists accept the responsibility this freedom requires: competence, objectivity in the application of skills and concern for the best interests of clients, colleagues, and society in general.

The standards cover nine subjects: responsibility, competence, moral and legal standards, public statements, confidentiality, welfare of the consumer, professional relationships, utilization of assessment techniques, and pursuit of research activities.

The standards are of direct consequence to members of the American Psychological Association. These members may be brought before an ethical review board and expelled from the association if judged guilty of a serious ethical offense. An aggrieved client may bring charges against psychologists by contacting either the state associations or the American Psychological Association.

What if the practitioner is not a member of the American Psychological Association? In such cases, the aggrieved client is dependent upon state laws and regulations. In many states, such as Pennsylvania, the ethical standards of the American Psychological Association have been incorporated into the laws and regulations governing the practice of psychology.

Research Ethics

In addition to *Ethical Standards of Psychologists*, the American Psychological Association has issued a comprehensive ethical guide for researchers entitled *Ethical Principles in the Conduct of Research with Human Participants*. This publication, like *Ethical Standards of Psychologists*, emphasizes the responsibilities of the individual psychologist who conducts research. Ten principles with extensive discussion are presented.

The principles emphasize that the decision to conduct any research project should include a careful weighing of the potential benefits against the potential risks and costs. Another key concept is embodied in Principle 7, which discusses informed consent.

Principle 7: the ethical investigator protects participants from physical and mental discomfort, harm, and danger. If the risk of such consequences exists, the investigator is required to inform the participant of the fact, secure consent before proceeding and take all possible measures to minimize distress. A research procedure may not be used if it is likely to cause serious and lasting harm to the participants (APA, 1973, p. 61).

Keys to the implementation of this principle are the questions of competence and knowledge. In order for a research subject to agree to accept risks, the person must be mentally competent. A minor, a mentally retarded or senile person might not have the mental competence to weigh the risks and comprehend the undertaking. Psychologists are expected to be able to establish that subjects were competent or, if not, that their interests were represented by an independent advocate who was competent. Information must be provided to ensure that the competent person will have sufficient knowledge to weigh the risks of participation prudently.

Standards for Providers

Ethical questions are also discussed in another recent American Psychological Association publication, *Standards for Providers of Psychological Services*. The intent of this publication is to "improve the quality, effectiveness, and accessibility of psychology to all that require them" (APA, 1977b).

The standards specifically cover five types of psychological services: assessment, interventions (counseling, psychotherapy, and process consultation), consultation related to assessment or interventions, program development, and supervision of psychological services. Standards that apply to these services are titled providers, programs, accountability, and environment. The keystone to the standards is that psychological services should only be provided by a Ph.D.-level psychologist or someone under the direct supervision of such a professional psychologist.

In their present form, the standards cover only four specialities: clinical, counseling, industrial-organizational, and school psychology. Since community psychology is not included in the standards, their applicability to community psychology is ambiguous. As has been discussed, many of the activities of community psychology fall under one of the five types of service areas covered by the standards. It is suggested here that community psychology be added as a specialty to be covered by the standards and that these standards be written to allow more flexibility for those adding a new specialty.

Licensing

All fifty states and the District of Columbia have enacted laws at one time or another regulating the practice of psychology (see consideration of sunset legislation in chapter 1.) These laws provide either certification or licensing to regulate the use of the title *psychologist*, and to regulate the provision of psychological services. Most states require the doctoral degree for licensing or certification. Some states also permit the licensing of Master's-level psychologists when they have sufficient experience. The incorporation of the ethical standards of the American Psychological Association into many states' licensing regulations gives such standards the force of law.

Most state psychology licensing laws are ambiguous as to whether the activities of community psychologists are covered. A majority of the state laws specifically include direct clinical service and consultation. Most state laws also regulate the term *psychologist* and the use of psychological techniques. Virtually all state laws are based upon psychological interventions that existed ten or fifteen years ago. As we have seen from the historical analysis, community psychology in its present form was unknown when these laws were written. Some laws explicitly exempt social psychology from their regulations. Therefore, present-day community psychologists can claim precedent for their activities as being either licensed or not.

Impetus for revision of licensing laws invariably comes from within the profession itself. At the present time, the leadership of the Community Division of the American Psychological Association seems to be opposed to further modifications in state laws to include community psychology (APA, 1978a).

It is suggested that community psychology will leave itself open to exploitation by unqualified or unethical persons if it does not bring itself into the regulated mainstream of psychology. Licensing and related regulation is the only way to police the unethical or incompetent uses of community psychology and provides a mechanism for backing up ethical and professional standards with the force of law. It is also the best method to clarify in advance the perimeters along which allegations of malpractice would be judged.

Malpractice

Malpractice is damage to another person as a result of negligence (Van Hoose, 1977). There are four basic conditions that must be met for malpractice:

1. The establishment of a duty by the defendant to the plaintiff. For example, when a professional accepts fees for services, a duty to the client is established.

2. The establishment of negligence or improper action. This occurs when usual standards of practice are not allowed.

3. The establishment of a causal relationship between an accident and an injury.

4. The establishment of damage to person or persons.

Courts use the ethical and professional standards as criteria for judging negligence in dealing with any profession. Therefore, community psychologists should be prepared to defend their actions by these standards. This criteria would be used regardless of whether community psychology activities were included in either professional standards or licensing laws.

Checklist of Ethical Issues

The subject of ethical and legal standards is currently one of much discussion and of great fluidity. The professional and the lawyer are advised to keep current in their readings on the subject. For the near future, it is recommended that attention to ethical and legal issues for any intervention in community psychology be judged by the following critical issues:

1. Identification of the problem. How was the problem defined? Did a number of professionals with different perspectives have input into the definition? To what extent were the involved persons consulted? To whom was this a problem?

2. Selection of goals. Have diverse members of the community taken part in the selection of its goals? Are these goals selected from a number of alternatives? Have

the potential benefits and risks been discussed openly with the community? Whose interests do those goals serve? Are changes in goals to be made with broad-based community input?

3. Selection of the intervention methods. Do all the persons or their representatives understand the risks and benefits in the various intervention methods? Do these representatives have an input in the final choice of the intervention method? Has the community been given candid data both positive and negative about the effectiveness of the intervention method? Will community representatives have input into any changes in the methods?

4. Intrusion of intervention method. Are the intervention methods the least disruptive of present community patterns? Does the method provide for the maximum protection of individual and community privacy and require the least intrusion into that community?

5. Accountability. Has a comprehensive system of collecting data before, during, and after the intervention been established? Is ongoing evaluation of the effectiveness of the intervention built into the procedure? Have procedures been established for feedback of this data to interested professionals and community members?

6. Competence of person or persons conducting the psychological intervention. Are the persons who will carry out the intervention competent? Have they reviewed relevant research literature? Is adequate supervision provided for those persons who are not Ph.D.-level and/or licensed or certified psychologists?

7. Competence of the community. Is the community competent to make judgments in its best interest? If there is reason to doubt the mental or social competence of the clients, have provisions been made for community advocates to represent those clients or communities? (Iscoe, 1974, pp. 607-613).

8. Confidentiality. Will the confidentiality of data be protected? Have community representatives agreed on the form in which data will be released to the public? Have the sensitivities of individuals or groups that may appear in an unfavorable light been considered?

9. Right to terminate intervention. Have the community, its representatives, and the professionals been given adequate safeguards to allow them to terminate the intervention program? Have the general conditions for such termination been specified? Have plans also been provided for the eventual orderly termination of the intervention?

10. Outside review and generalization. Have plans for present outcome and evaluation data to professional peers been established? Is there a mechanism for input from concerned peers into the decision-making process?

11. Multiple loyalties. Have the obligations and loyalties of the professionals been clarified and made public? If the psychologists are to represent particular institutions or organizations, has the meaning of these obligations and potential implications been made known?

12. Other responsibilities. Have other potential ethical and legal issues been addressed? Will all the applicable ethical, professional, and legal standards be followed?

The above checklist has been adapted from the American Psychological Association *Ethical Standards* and from the book, *Ethical Issues in Behavior Modification* (Stolz, 1977, pp. 110-113). This checklist presents a format for asking questions but does not give answers.

In summary, it is recommended that community psychologists treat all interventions as research projects and that those protections provided by the *Ethical Guide for Research* should be provided for all subjects of all psychological interventions with special protections built in for incompetent, confined, powerless, or otherwise vulnerable communities.

LEGAL ISSUES IN THE PRACTICE OF COMMUNITY PSYCHOLOGY

A. When does community psychology activity qualify under licensing laws as "psychological practice" and when does it not?

Background

Laws licensing psychologists were written initially with a focus on traditional clinical/therapeutic activities and in many respects parallel medical licensing laws. Community psychologists usually work from something other than a medical model and their activities are somewhat different from traditional clinical psychology. These activities include research, evaluation, planning, community action, and consultation. Some states exclude some of these activities in their licensing laws while others include them. For example, Pennsylvania at one point in its statute exempts social psychology from the licensing requirements that might include research, planning, and community change, which are also community psychology activities.

Questions

1. Is there any case law in Pennsylvania or other states clarifying what qualifies as psychological practice?

2. Is community psychology licensed in Pennsylvania or other states?

3. What guidelines would practitioners follow to decide whether community psychology activities are covered by licensing laws?

4. Are practices of community psychologists covered under federal regulations such as the National Register of Health Care Providers in Psychology?

B. What potential risks do community psychologists have for malpractice and/or negligence suits?

Background

Community psychologists are not usually treating "patients" under traditional medical constraints, and have, therefore, not been the subject of malpractice suits. However, a potential for negligence and/or malpractice lies in research, evaluation, community change, and consultation.

Questions

1. Is there precedent for suing in the types of roles that community psychologists assume? (Researcher, evaluator, consultant, community change agent.) If so, what would some of the legal parameters of such suits be?

2. Is there case law which applies?

3. Is there professional insurance available to cover potential liabilities of community psychologists?

C. Is evaluation research done on agencies receiving public funds (federal, state, or county) in the public domain or can it be kept secret?

Background

Community psychologists often serve as evaluators of criminal justice, social welfare, and mental health agencies. These evaluations are usually required by some government funding source, or may be undertaken voluntarily. Let us consider agencies providing a service to the public, which are either a branch of government, or are subcontracted to perform a public service, and receive public funds.

Efforts are often made to keep evaluation reports from the public when they are unfavorable.

According to the ethical standards of the American Psychological Association, research is public — secret research is contrary to the scientific communication of knowledge. The assumption is, therefore, made by members of the association that all research is public unless specifically set up as confidential. (In contrast, therapeutic relationships are assumed to be confidential.) Psychologists are, therefore, unprepared to deal with agencies who, on receipt of an unfavorable evaluation, are told that they cannot write or talk about it to others.

Questions

1. Is there a general right to privacy when agencies contract for evaluations?

2. Do individuals working for agencies have the right to keep evaluation reports that may directly or indirectly criticize them secret?

3. To what extent can contracts be used to clarify the above issues for a particular evaluation?

4. What, if any, difference does public funding of the agency make? Does Pennsylvania's "Right to Know" statute apply? If so, are there exceptions or exclusions?

5. Can case law help to clarify the differences between a research (and

therefore public) situation, and a therapeutic or consultative (and therefore private) situation?

6. Do Department of Health, Education and Welfare, (Health and Human Services) regulations on informed consent in psychological research have any standing or application to the law on this subject?

BIBLIOGRAPHY

Alinsky, S. D. *Rules for radicals*. New York: Random House, 1972.

American Psychological Association, Division of Community Psychology. Executive committee report on licensing and accreditation. Newsletter, 1978a, 11(2), 4.

American Psychological Association. *Ethical principles in the conduct of research with human participants*. Washington, D.C.: American Psychological Association, 1973.

American Psychological Association. *Ethical standards of psychologists*. Washington, D.C.: American Psychological Association, 1977a.

American Psychological Association. *Graduate study in psychology*. Washington, D.C.: American Psychological Association, 1978b.

American Psychological Association. *Standards for providers of psychological services*. Washington, D.C.: American Psychological Association, 1977b.

Andrulis, D. P., Barton, A. K., and Aponte, J. F. Perspectives on the training experiences and the training needs of community psychologists. *American Journal of Community Psychology*, 1978, 6, 265-270.

Association for the Advancement of Psychology. *Advance*, 1978, 5 (2).

Barton, A. K., Andrulis, D. P., Grove, W. P., and Aponte, J. F. A look at community psychology training programs in the seventies. *American Journal of Community Psychology*, 1976, 4, 1-11.

Bennett, C. C., Anderson, L. S., Cooper, S., Hassol, L., Klein, D. C., and Rosenblum, C., eds. *Community psychology: A report of the Boston conference on the education of psychologists for community mental health*. Boston: Boston University Press, 1965.

Brown, S. W., Wienckowski, L. A., and Stolz, S. B. *Behavior modification: Perspective on a current issue*. Washington, D.C.: U.S. Department of Health, Education and Welfare, National Institute of Mental Health, 1975.

Caplan, G. *The theory and practice of mental health consultation*. New York: Basic Books, 1970.

Cook, P. E., ed. *Community psychology and community mental health: Introductory readings*. San Francisco: Holden-Day, 1970.

Cowen, E. L. Training clinical psychologists for community mental health functions: Description of a practicum experience. In I. Iscoe and C. D. Spielberger, eds. *Community psychology: Perspectives in training and research*. New York: Appleton-Century-Crofts, 1970.

Frederico, R. C. *The social welfare institution*. Lexington, Mass.: D. C. Heath, 1976.

Goldberg, F. J. An undergraduate training program in community psychology. *American Journal of Community Psychology*, 1976, 4, 327-337.

Heller, K., and Monahan, J. *Psychology and community change*. Homewood, Ill.: The Dorsey Press, 1977.

Iscoe, I. Community psychology and the competent community. *American Psychologist*, 1974, *29*, 607-613.

Iscoe, I. National training conference in community psychology. *American Psychologist*, 1975, *30*, 1194-1198.

Iscoe, I., and Spielberger, C. D. *Community psychology: Perspectives in training and research.* New York: Appleton-Century-Crofts, 1970.

Korman, M. National conference on levels and patterns of professional training in psychology: The major themes. *American Psychologist*, 1974, *29*, 441-449.

Lewin, K. *Field theory in social science.* New York: Harper & Row, 1951.

Mann, P. A. *Community psychology: Concepts and applications.* New York: The Free Press, 1978.

Murrell, S. A. *Community psychology and social systems: A conceptual framework and intervention guide.* New York: Behavioral Publications, 1973.

Newbrough, J. R., Rhoades, W. C., and Seeman, J. The development of community psychology training at George Peabody College. In I. Iscoe and C. D. Spielberger, eds. *Community psychology: Perspectives in training and research.* New York: Appleton-Century-Crofts, 1970.

Nietzel, M. T., Winett, R. A., MacDonald, M. L., and Davidson, W. S. *Behavioral approaches to community psychology.* New York: Pergamon Press, 1977.

Parad, H. J., and Rapoport, L. Advanced social work educational programs in community mental health. In S. E. Golann and C. Eisdorfer, eds. *Handbook of community mental health.* New York: Appleton-Century-Crofts, 1972.

Rappaport, J. *Community psychology: Values, research, and action.* New York: Holt, Rinehart & Winston, 1977.

Sarason, S. B. *The psychological sense of community: Prospects for a community psychologist.* San Francisco: Jossey-Bass, 1974.

Sarason, S. B., and Levin, M. Graduate education and the Yale psychoeducational clinic. In I. Iscoe and C. D. Spielberger, eds. *Community psychology: Perspectives in training and research.* New York: Appleton-Century-Crofts, 1970.

Singer, J. L., and Bard, M. The psychological foundations of a community-oriented clinical psychology training program. In I. Iscoe and C. D. Spielberger, eds. *Community psychology: Perspectives in training and research.* New York: Appleton-Century-Crofts, 1970.

Stein, D. Reflections on the community mental health program of Albert Einstein College of Medicine, Yeshiva University. In I. Iscoe and C. D. Spielberger, eds. *Community psychology: Perspectives in training and research.* New York: Appleton-Century-Crofts, 1970.

Stolz, S. *Ethical issues in behavior modification.* San Francisco: Jossey-Bass, 1978.

Turner, J. A., and Goodson, W. H., Jr. Behavioral technology applied to a community mental health center: A demonstration. *Journal of Community Psychology*, 1977, *5*, 209-224.

Van Hoose, W. H., and Kottler, J. A. *Ethical and legal issues in counseling and psychotherapy.* San Francisco: Jossey-Bass, 1977.

Witmer, L. Clinical psychology. *Psychological Clinic*, 1907, *1*, 1-9.

Wrightsman, L. *Social psychology.* Monterey, Calif.: Brooks/Cole Publishing Company, 1977.

Zax, M., and Specter, G. A. *An introduction to community psychology.* New York: John Wiley & Sons, Inc., 1974.

The Clinical
Neuropsychologist

HISTORICAL BACKGROUND

Of the various specialty areas within the field of psychology, clinical neuropsychology appears to be among the more recent to emerge. Yet the historical underpinnings for this field have existed since the latter half of the nineteenth century.

Present-day clinical neuropsychology integrates clinical psychology with physiological psychology and places specific emphasis upon human brain functioning. It also devotes significant attention to sensory and higher perceptual and motor functions.

The beginning of organized modern psychology is marked by substantial attention to the topics of sensation and perception. In the 1850s, Professor Wilhelm Wundt of the University of Leipzig in Germany came to the conclusion that the phenomenon of perception was more "psychological" than "physiological." He published *Beitrage Zur Theorie der Sinneswhrnehmung* (Contributions Toward a Theory of Correct Perception) in 1858. Although Wundt was initially trained as a physician, he later became an eminent psychologist and established the world's first psychology laboratory in Leipzig in 1879.

Wundt was able to attract other foremost scientists to his laboratory. These colleagues were mainly interested in sensory functions such as audition, vision, touch, taste, smell, and kinesthesis. The volume of scientific publications by Wundt and his colleagues was impressive. Among such scientists were Friedrich Kieosow, F. Angell, E. Tischer, C. Lourens, J. Merkel, and E. Luft. Friedrich Kieosow produced classical studies in the area of taste. F. Angell, E. Tischer, C. Lourens, J. Merkel, and E. Luft published psychological research in the area of audition. Research was also conducted on the psychophysics of light and retinal excitation, the psychophysics of color, peripheral vision, and color blindness.

In the early twentieth century, the anatomist Franz Joseph Gall began to expound his theories on the subject of phrenology. Phrenology, initially called craniology, represents one of the early attempts to understand brain behavior relations. Franz Gall postulated a relationship between skull configuration and specific behaviors. His thirty-seven "faculties" were divided into two main groups, affective and intellectual. According to Gall, each of the thirty-seven faculties resided in specific localities in the brain. He reasoned that specific underlying brain faculties could be located by palpation of contours and bumps of the skull.

Although many phrenological theories have been discredited (Boring, 1929; Flugel, 1964), neuropsychologists believe that phrenology has provided them with some important issues. Among such issues is the question of whether specific functions can be localized to specific brain locations. Another by-product of Gall's formulations was the engendering of a more critical and systematic approach to the assessment of brain-behavior relations.

The early twentieth century was marked by a significant increase in our knowledge of the human nervous system. Persons credited with this upsurge of knowledge were Francois Magendie, M. J. Flourens, Luige Rolando, Marshall Hall, and Sir Charles Bell. One of the more notable contributions in this realm was Bell's discovery of the distinction between sensory and motor nerves and the specificity of the sensory nerve impulse. He also studied the reciprocal innervation in extensor-flexor interaction in the same limb. Bell's significant research was published in his book *Nervous System of the Human Body* in 1930. Francois Magendie, the French physiologist, independently arrived at the same conclusion. The Bell-Magendie Law indicates that the motor nerves are situated in the ventral roots of the spinal cord, whereas the sensory nerves are situated in the dorsal roots and spinal ganglia. Bell's findings dispelled the then-prevailing notion that sensory and motor functions were performed by all nerves.

The reader will recognize the information just considered as recent history relating to nerve physiology and to attempts at gaining a more complete understanding of brain functioning. It is the author's opinion that both areas of investigation provide concrete historical underpinnings for what has now emerged as the field of clinical neuropsychology.

Alexander Romonovich Luria

There are many neuropsychologists who have contributed significantly to our understanding of brain-behavior relations. The bulk of consideration will be given to the work of Ward C. Halstead and Ralph M. Reitan. Any consideration of clinical neuropsychology would be incomplete, however, without at least alluding to the work of the late Alexander Romonovich Luria. Professor Luria, formerly of the Institute of Psychology at the University of Moscow, contributed significantly to this field. He provided insights into the field of aphasiology and offered many profound and practical suggestions for a unified theory of brain functioning (Luria, 1962, 1963, 1973). Professor Luria also devised a variety of clinical assessment instruments which some practitioners find helpful in assessing human brain functioning. Luria placed great emphasis upon qualitative, as opposed to quantitative, indices of brain functioning in his assessments. This is one of the major differences between his approach and that of Americans such as Halstead and Reitan. Golden, Hammeke, and Purisch (1978) have effectively quantified some of Luria's techniques and thus appear to have answered some of the criticisms of the neuropsychologists whose emphasis is upon quantification of information.

Ward C. Halstead

The late Ward C. Halstead was one of the major orchestrators of the present direction in clinical neuropsychology in the United States. His early dissatisfaction with the usual psychological techniques for the assessment of human brain functioning set the stage for extensive explorations into more adequate techniques. Dr. Halstead established the first laboratory devoted to the study of human brain-behavior relations at the University of Chicago in 1934. He initiated a series of systematic efforts to understand brain functioning better. In so doing, he devised procedures and techniques to differentiate brain-damaged from non-brain-damaged individuals. His empirical approach continues to be used by many contemporary clinical neuropsychologists. In his book *Brain and Intelligence* (1947), he presents many of his early insights and assessment techniques. Dr. Halstead's work in the area of assessment of brain functioning was continued and refined by Ralph M. Reitan. Dr. Reitan recognized the brain as the major organ of "adaptive behavior" and as a former student of Halstead's, emphasized the enormous complexity of the brain. As with Halstead, Reitan believed that an adequate assessment of brain functioning must include many and diverse abilities. In the currently employed Halstead Neuropsychological Test Battery, such abilities include: sensory, that is, touch, hearing and vision; motor, that is, gross and fine, psycho- and perceptual motor. In addition, the approach includes assessment of: tactuo-spatial problem solving, tactual memory, mental manipulative facility, nonverbal abstraction and conceptual reasoning, psychometric intelligence, the adequacy of language functioning, basic speech sounds (phonemic) discrimination, rhythm pattern discrimination, and an assessment of personality functioning as measured by personality screening techniques. In the Halstead approach to assessing brain functioning, there is a strong emphasis upon quantitating information obtained from tests. This is in contrast to Professor Luria's approach alluded to earlier. It should be repeated, however, that Golden has effected modifications in Luria's earlier approaches which allow for quantitative assessments (Golden, Hammeke, and Purisch, 1978). The Halstead approach is essentially empirical and places little emphasis, if any, upon theoretical models upon which to base brain functioning. Professor Luria, however, insisted that there be a unified theory of brain organization and functioning (Luria, 1973). Luria believed that such a theoretical base would not only add to our understanding of the organization and functioning of the brain, but also would facilitate the structuring of appropriate rehabilitation courses of action for the brain-compromised person.

Despite these divergent viewpoints, there is a healthy and growing international information exchange within the field. This is perhaps best exemplified in the international organization known as the International Neuropsychology Society. There will be a brief consideration of this organization later in this chapter.

TRAINING

Because of the relative infancy of neuropsychology, as it has become known today, many practitioners have not had the uniform specialized training that is associated with other established disciplines such as medicine, law, and dentistry. Many clinical neuropsychologists have obtained their skills by working with neurologically compromised patients in conjunction with neurological and neurosurgical specialists. They have attended workshops and studied neuroanatomy, neuropathology, and neurology on an individual basis. There is a clear need for the development of more formal training programs. The need is gradually being met by the increasing numbers of sources now offering training of various types to psychologists and students of neuroscience who reflect more than superficial interest in clinical neuropsychology (Sheer and Lubin, 1980).

Sheer and Lubin (1980) conducted a survey of a variety of types of training offered in clinical neuropsychology. The growing list attests to the gradual and essential growth of clinical neuropsychology as an emerged specialty with emerging basic training requirements. Results of this survey portrayed four general categories:

1. Training with other disciplines such as speech pathology and neurology. Training consists of lectures and rotations with systematic education sequences.

2. Pre- and postdoctoral internship sequences.

3. Formal training in neuropsychology leading to the Ph.D., in either clinical or physiological psychology or a related area. This education is supported by a one- or two-year postdoctoral fellowship focusing upon clinical neuropsychology. The latter would include clinical and research components. Several universities have instituted the approach that a student is admitted to a predoctoral program in a field such as neuroscience or clinical psychology with an emphasis on neuropsychology. Examples of such universities are University of Iowa, University of Wisconsin Medical School, University of Michigan Medical School, University of Arizona, University of Colorado Medical School, and University of South Dakota. Similar sequences

exist at the University of Ottawa, Canada, in a joint program with Carleton and McGill Universities.

4. Separate formal training programs in clinical neuropsychology, such as are offered at Cornell, University of Houston, Memphis State University, Boston University in conjunction with Boston VA Medical Center, Tufts and Clark Universities (Massachusetts), Temple University, City College of New York, New York University, University of Texas Medical School, Baylor University Medical School, University of Tennessee, and in Canada, at University of Windsor and Victoria.

In the past, at the University of Minnesota, three training models were conceptualized: Model I, incorporating neuropsychology training in the traditional clinical and counseling sequences; Model II, an interdepartmental program combining neuropsychology and the neurosciences department; and Model III, a coordinated curriculum leading to a combined Ph.D. Psy.D. degree.

The following institutions conduct internship training in clinical neuropsychology. However, financial support is not available in all cases. *

Source	Duration	Type
Eastern Pennsylvania Psychiatric Institute Henry Avenue and Abbotsford Road Philadelphia, Pa. 19129	1 year	Predoctoral
Lafayette Clinic 951 East Lafayette Detroit, Mich. 48207	1 and 2 years	Postdoctoral
Rush-Presbyterian St. Luke's Medical Center 1753 Congress Parkway, West Chicago, Ill. 60612	1 year	Pre- and postdoctoral
University of Colorado Medical Center 4206 East 9th Street Denver, Colo. 80202	Individualized	Postdoctoral
University of Oklahoma Health Sciences Center P.O. Box 26901 Oklahoma City, Okla. 73190	Individualized	Postdoctoral
University of Wisconsin Center for Health Sciences 600 North Highland Avenue Madison, Wis. 53792	Individualized	Pre- and postdoctoral

---

*The data in this list are from D. E. Sheer and B. Lubin, "Survey of training programs in clinical neuropsychology," *Journal of Clinical Psychology*, October 1980, *36* (4), 1035-1039. Used by permission of the authors.

Military and Veterans Administration internship training courses in clinical neuropsychology are available at the following institutions:*

Source	Duration	Type
U.S.A.F. Medical Center Department of Mental Health Milford Hall Lackland Air Force Base, Tex. 78232	1 year	Pre- and postdoctoral
U.S.A.F. Medical Center Wright-Patterson Air Force Base Dayton, Ohio 45322	Individualized	Predoctoral
Harry S. Truman Memorial VA Medical Center 800 Stadium Road Columbia, Mo. 65201	Individualized	Predoctoral Veterans Administration stipend
VA Medical Center 1670 Clairmont Road Decatur, Ga. 30033	1 year	Predoctoral Veterans Administration stipend
VA Medical Center 1030 Jefferson Avenue Memphis, Tenn. 38104	1 year	
VA Medical Center Brain Injury Rehabilitation Center Palo Alto, Calif. 93801	1 year	Predoctoral
VA Medical Center S.W. US Veterans Hospital Road Portland, Oreg. 97201	3-4 months rotation	Predoctoral
VA Medical Center West Haven, Conn. 06516	Individualized	Predoctoral

Most experienced neuropsychologists have had significant exposure to neurology, neuropathology, and to a variety of techniques of neuropsychological evaluation. Many have had exposure to the Halstead neuropsychology test procedures. A growing number of practicing clinical neuropsychologists have had their initial systematic exposure to the field by attending a 1-week workshop on human neuropsychology conducted by Ralph M. Reitan. Dr. Reitan and associates have been conducting these workshops for more than twenty years.

---

*The data in this list are from D. E. Sheer and B. Lubin, "Survey of training programs in clinical neuropsychology," *Journal of Clinical Psychology*, October 1980, *36* (4), 1035-1039. Used by permission of the authors.

The clinical neuropsychologist must possess a strong background in psychometric assessment in addition to having some knowledge of neuropathology as it impacts upon human brain functioning. The practitioner must have knowledge of behavior associated with a variety of types of brain pathology. This experience may be obtained by working closely with neurologists and neurosurgeons and by being exposed to patients who reflect varying types of neurological deficits.

PRACTICING CLINICAL NEUROPSYCHOLOGY

Institutional Settings

The clinical neuropsychologist in an institutional setting may be seen most frequently on a hospital neurological service, or working closely with such a service. The clinical neuropsychologist may be expected to make contributions in the area of differential diagnosis and assessment of assets and liabilities. Based upon residual abilities, the clinical neuropsychologist is in a position to assist in vocational counseling and planning.

An extremely important task for the clinical neuropsychologist is that of providing information as a basis for employing more serious neurological diagnostic procedures (Filskov and Goldstein, 1974). There is a positive relationship between accuracy of neurological diagnostic procedure and mortality risk. This relationship excludes the development within recent years of the technique of computerized tomography. Procedures such as physical-neurological examination, electroencephalography, and brain scan produce no risk to life. However, their accuracy as diagnostic procedures vis-à-vis occult cerebral pathology reflects serious limitations. Procedures such as cerebral angiography, cisternography, and pneumoencephalography all reflect accuracy levels significantly higher than those of electroencephalography, brain scan, and physical-neurological examination. Morbidity/mortality rates associated with these more accurate procedures, however, range from 2 to 6 percent (Filskov and Goldstein, 1974). The accuracy of neuropsychological assessment on variables such as laterality of dysfunction, hit rate (identification of brain pathology), and type of cerebral insult compares favorably with that of the more risky neurologic procedures (Filskov and Goldstein, 1974). In these latter procedures, the central nervous system is traumatized in some manner. For example, a major cerebral arterial network is penetrated to inject opaque fluid which will outline the network to be observed. Such a procedure carries with it the risk of causing a spasm of the traumatized blood vessel, or dislodging intravessel plaque (substances adhering to the inner lining of the blood vessel). Should such material obstruct a major vessel at a subsequent point, this could result in a major cerebrovascular event.

The clinical neuropsychologist is in a critical position to provide objective evidence of neuropsychologic improvement as the patient moves toward recovery. Initial neuropsychologic data may provide baseline information to which subsequent data may be compared, and thus neuropsychologic "movement" may be systematically charted.

The clinical neuropsychologist is in a position to assess recovery patterns associated with variables such as patient age, type of lesion, and lesion location. On the basis of this experiential background, the clinical neuropsychologist may offer important opinions as to the likelihood of further improvement in neuropsychologic functioning.

In the area of inservice training, the clinical neuropsychologist can be expected to provide educational experiences in the realm of brain-behavior relations. In teaching hospitals, clinical neuropsychologists are called upon to provide lectures to medical, psychiatry, and neurology residents; psychology graduate students; student nurses; and to a variety of other health service professionals.

In the area of research in human brain-behavior relations, the clinical neuropsychologist can provide expertise in research design and frequently can be expected to be a resource person to specialists from other disciplines. He or she may be expected to maintain meticulous data on patients in order to provide a more complete understanding of the effects of brain lesions of varying types and in varying situations on human behavior.

Children's Settings

In the area of childhood development and central nervous system disorders, medical and neurological diagnostic techniques reflect significant limitations. It is in this realm that the clinical neuropsychologist is in a position to make major contributions. Here the clinical neuropsychologist will confront many issues for which answers are not readily available. Too often the only evidence of abnormal brain integrity is "behavior dysfunction." Behavioral assessment is part of the clinical neuropsychologist's task. He or she may be expected to render opinions on the presence of cerebral dysfunction. Whether hyperkinetic phenomena are associated with neuropsychologic dysfunction will also frequently have to be addressed.

The clinical neuropsychologist will be expected to assess the child's strengths as well as weaknesses. In this regard, the clinical neuropsychologist may be expected to aid the school psychologist in prescriptive educational formulations for the individual child. In the area of developmental learning disabilities and reading disabilities, the clinical neuropsychologist will be expected to render expert opinions as to the possible impact of brain dysfunction upon the condition.

Private Practice

The independent practitioner's role is an ineluctable phenomenon in the field of psychology. The clear national trends in this direction are addressed in chapters 1 and 2. The clinical neuropsychologist in private practice may limit professional activities to adults or children, diagnosis, treatment and diagnosis, diagnosis and helping in devising appropriate prescriptive educational formulations, or diagnosis and vocational counseling-exploration. The private practitioner may frequently be called upon as a consultant to a neurologist, neurosurgeon, or psychiatrist who may have hospital privileges. Many psychiatrists are interested in obtaining neuropsychological assessments to help determine the differential contributions of organic versus emotional factors in altering patient behavior. The special knowledge and techniques possessed by the clinical neuropsychologist can alert the psychiatrist to organically determined behavioral deficits.

The clinical neuropsychologist can expect to be called upon to evaluate patients in various local hospitals and may expect to be afforded consultant privileges at these hospitals either on a formal or informal basis. It is conceivable that in the not-too-distant future, clinical neuropsychologists will extensively be granted formal hospital privileges.

Head injuries present a particularly vexing set of problems for the health service provider. In cases of what seem to be minor head insults, marked personality alterations have been observed (Jennett, 1976). Feelings of confusion are frequently reflected, and maintaining adaptive emotional control becomes a problem for many victims of head trauma. The clinical neuropsychologist is in a position to render helpful opinions as to etiology (based upon assessment of brain functioning) and appropriate forms of treatment. The private neurological practitioner working with the head trauma victim will be able to contribute significantly to the overall understanding of this phenomenon. By meticulous documentation of all aspects of head insult, including behavioral, personality, neuropsychologic as well as physical factors, better knowledge of prognostic indices may be obtained. In addition, vocational exploration may be initiated in conjunction with a counseling psychologist.

In private practice, referrals may be expected from other psychologists who have been requested to address the issue of brain dysfunction. Such psychologists may not be entirely satisfied with employing the usual psychological tests for "organicity." These tests (the more traditional, usual tests of "organicity") may have been administered with either equivocal or negative results, and the psychologist prefers to use more elaborate and sophisticated neuropsychological test procedures.

Referrals may also come from educational specialists. This is more likely to occur with children reflecting developmental disabilities such as learning and reading (dyslexia) problems. Neuropsychological evaluations of the child reflecting hyperkinesis and minimal brain dysfunction may also be required.

In the medical setting, such as a medical unit of a hospital, the clinical neuropsychologist might be expected to focus on more obvious medical

issues such as differential diagnosis, laterality of dysfunction, and generalized or bilateral cerebral dysfunction.

CONCEPTS OF STRUCTURE AND FUNCTION AND
IMPLICATIONS FOR CLINICAL NEUROPSYCHOLOGISTS

The clinical neuropsychologist is interested in both the structure and
function of the central nervous system with particular reference to the
human brain. The concepts of structure and function are extremely important because they may point to certain "apparent" ambiguities in neuropsychologic data. At the same time, more accurate assessment of these
concepts sets the stage for clarification of such apparent ambiguities. The
clinical neuropsychologist must address "the criterion problem" whenever
called upon to effect an assessment of brain functioning (neuropsychological evaluation). The criterion problem refers to the potential conflict
inherent in the use of medical data such as that derived from electroencephalography, brain biopsies, brain scan, and other structurally based
procedures to assess the validity of neuropsychological data. Where positive
neuropsychological data are not supported by medical data, the former are
often referred to as "false positive." Resolution of this "apparent conflict" in
this manner is at times simplistic.

Structure and function are distinct entities and should be recognized as
such. To assess the structural integrity of the central nervous system, the
physician may employ a variety of procedures. Such procedures may
include brain scans, computerized tomography, cerebral angiography, and
myelography, to mention a few. By training and tradition, the physician is
the appropriate professional to speak to the issue of structural integrity of
the central nervous system. By training and tradition, the psychologist has
always been concerned with the functional integrity (behavior) of the
person. The psychologist has a tradition of assessing human functions
through psychometric and behavioral procedures. Where the structural
integrity of the brain appears to be intact, as assessed by structurally oriented
assessment techniques, the psychologist may observe compromise via functionally oriented assessment techniques. The point needing emphasis is that
positive neuropsychological data must be viewed as just that, and the practitioner must not make the mistake of dismissing such findings simply
because they are not supported by structurally oriented techniques. Should
the practitioner make this mistake, the person being evaluated may end up
being the real victim. In the presence of occult brain pathology, structurally
oriented techniques at times produce "unremarkable" (negative) results.
Experienced neurologists and neuropsychologists are familiar with the
limitations of structurally oriented procedures. Such clinicians have also
been exposed to situations in which a positive neuropsychological profile
was the initial presentation of cerebral compromise which subsequently
manifested itself structurally. This psychologist contends that it is as inap-

propriate to use structurally oriented criteria as a basis for judging validity of functionally based data as it would be to use functionally oriented criteria as a basis for judging the validity of structurally based data. The following example of the latter phenomenon should lend appropriate perspective to the issue:

Mr. Doe is a 38-year-old gentleman who has been complaining of severe right-sided headaches of recent onset. The physical-neurological examination reflects a positive left-sided babinski reflex. His electroencephalogram is positive with a focus of abnormal electrical discharge over the right frontotemporal region of the brain. In addition, there is a completely negative neuropsychological evaluation. If we use the neuropsychological evaluation as criterion for the validity of the aforementioned positive structurally oriented test data, we would have to judge the positive data as invalid. In the cited example (an actual case), the error is obvious, that is, structurally positive data is just that. It is clear that health service providers must include such data in their future treatment regimens for this individual.

Until recent advances in computerized tomography, brain tumors were often not detectable by using the regular neurodiagnostic procedures until the tumor matured to certain structural dimensions (Brain, 1977). Neurologists and neurosurgeons are quick to acknowledge the limitations of many neurodiagnostic procedures. A major problem is the failure to indicate the presence of pathology where it, in fact, exists. This assumes critical proportions when one realizes that the issue of life and death may be involved. Often behavior deficits are the earliest indices of compromise to the central nervous system. An example of this is in the study of head trauma. Regular neurologic assessment not infrequently produces "essentially negative" results, whereas personality and other behavioral and neuropsychologic measures may reflect significant "post-traumatic" alterations. Such behavioral changes may be relatively permanent and structurally based referent may never be identified. The sensitivity of brain function assessments is perhaps well illustrated by the technique of sequential testing. For example, the clinical neuropsychologist obtains baseline information on an individual who has recently undergone an operation for excision of a brain tumor. Six months later, a second administration of the tests may reflect significant improvement in brain functioning, despite overall results remaining in the dysfunctional range. On structurally based parameters, changes indicating improvement in that time period may not have been apparent. Subsequent neuropsychologic testing can help the rehabilitation process by monitoring the rate of improvement of neuropsychologic functions. Such testing may also produce valuable information on the course and prognosis of similar insults to the brain. The following case illustrates the advantage of sequential neuropsychological testing:

This 22-year-old male was transferred to the receiving hospital with the diagnosis of cerebral contusion. He had been admitted to the referring hospital as an emergency after being involved in an automobile accident in which he sustained head injuries. His condition was reported to have been comatose with spastic quadriparesis. Skull x-rays and carotid arteriograms were performed; a subdural hematoma was suspected on the right side. Bilateral craniectomies were performed with evacuation of approximately 300 ml of blood from the right side. A tracheostomy had been performed prior to surgery. Incomplete records were received from the referring hospital, but apparently the patient showed progressive improvement following surgical intervention. The patient noted some difficulty in walking due to weakness in the lower extremities and poor coordination. He would feel lightheaded and weak on sitting up for a while but these symptoms would subside on lying down. The electroencephalogram was abnormal because of slowing on the right frontocentral temporal and parietal areas; similar slowing was also noted in the left frontocentral area; occasional right mid-temporal sharp waves and mild generalized paroxysmal slow waves were also seen. The diagnosis was acute subdural hematoma.

Transfer to the current hospital was requested for the purpose of rehabilitation, physiotherapy, and medical evaluation. At the time of admission, he was well oriented and cooperative. Scars from the recent craniectomies in both temporoparietal areas were noted. There was a slightly temporal deviation of the left eyeball; pupils were equal and reacted normally to light; fundi were not remarkable. Blood pressure readings were within normal limits. Heart and lung findings were negative. Neurologic evaluation was essentially normal except for slight unsteadiness. The serologic test was non-reactive; the results of routine tests on blood, urine, and chemistries were within normal limits. At this time the patient appeared to have full physical and mental recovery from a medical standpoint and seemed to be very alert, rational, and logical. He had regained his strength, no longer noting weakness of legs as he had previously. Coordination had returned to normal; no vertigo, visual disturbances, or other symptoms were noted. In addition, he had regained approximately twenty-five pounds. He was given a regular discharge to the present hospital following a period of approximately two months hospitalization.

Prior to his injury, this patient was a college student and he expressed a strong desire to return to college. The first neuropsychological evaluation was conducted at the receiving hospital approximately two months following the automobile accident. That neuropsychological profile reflected greatest deficits in tasks calling for conceptual and abstract thinking. Also, marked deficits were observed in psychometric I.Q. which included a seventeen-point performance I.Q. disparity when compared with verbal. Marked motor deficits on the left body side were observed, as well as some evidence of bilateral visual imperception. As a result of this neuropsychological testing, the patient was not considered an appropriate candidate for college at this time. At the time of discharge, it was the medical opinion that he would be able to return to college. A six-month follow-up neuropsychological evaluation was arranged.

Seven months later, the patient returned for the second neuropsychological evaluation. At that time, he continued to indicate a strong interest in returning to college. In the second evaluation it was noted that in the area of abstraction and conceptual thinking, significant improvement had occurred, since he was now functioning in the realm characteristic of college students. However, with respect to psychometric I.Q. functioning, his previous Dull-Normal IQ. had improved to the Average range. Some mild weakness continued to be noted on the left body side in the upper extremity; however, visual imperception had disappeared. The overall neuropsychological profile had shown improvement. He was told of the generalized improvement; however, he was also counseled that before undertaking college, he would do well to allow a little more time to pass to permit more complete cognitive recovery. This suggestion was based upon the improved but still questionable psychometric I.Q. values (for college purposes) registered at the time of this evaluation. The character and patterning of the I.Q.'s suggested a higher level of recovery was likely to occur. He was given another appointment for six months subsequent to the present evaluation. At that time, the gains he had made in nonverbal abstraction-conceptual thinking were maintained. In addition, the psychometric I.Q. had improved to the Bright-Normal range. This patient, although reflecting auditory and visual extinction on the left body side, was counseled that he might consider returning to college at this time. He was further counseled that should he return, he should consider starting out on a part-time basis and gradually increase to full-time. The patient did return to college; however, we have heard no more from him subsequently.

The foregoing example reflects the contributions that neuropsychologists can make in the area of diagnosis, as well as recovery of functioning and the interface of such functioning with vocational counseling.

The next case illustrates the very important point that cognitive-psychological deficits often are the most devastating sequelae to brain trauma. The case also points to the fact that recovery of primary sensory and motor functions often bears little or no relation to recovery of cognitive-neuropsychological functions:

Approximately twenty-seven months prior to evaluation, this attractive, neatly attired, well-oriented young lady was struck by an automobile and sustained severe head trauma. She underwent immediate treatment at a local hospital. Prior to the accident, she was gainfully employed on a full-time basis and was contemplating furthering her education. Premorbid academic results suggested higher than average capabilities. A neuropsychological evaluation was requested to assess the degree of brain dysfunction. The patient had made significant positive strides in physical improvement, such as strength, sensory, and motor functioning. Despite the foregoing, the manifest cognitive deficits at home and in the rehabilitation process were quite severe. There was question of the possible etiology of the cognitive deficits, in view of the improved motor and sensory functioning.

Medical specialists suggested that there may be underlying emotional factors etiologicaly related to the lag of neuropsychological recovery behind overall physical recovery. The complete neuropsychological testing reflected moderate to severely impaired adaptive abilities depending upon organic brain functioning. Such impairment was noted across all neuropsychological abilities tested and provided unequivocal evidence of compromised brain functioning. On the basis of the type of injury this patient sustained, the character and pattern of the neuropsychological profile would have been highly predictable. In conclusion, emotional factors will certainly be involved in the overall head trauma recovery process. It is important, however, to realize that, in this case, although such factors may complicate the neuropsychological recovery process, the basic etiology remains the traumatic insult. In the present case, this is particularly apparent since there was overwhelming evidence to support the view that the head trauma was etiologically primary with respect to cognitive deficits continually manifested.

It is vitally important that rehabilitation personnel be continually aware of the fact that recovery of neuropsychological and cognitive functions often occurs at vastly different rates than does recovery of sensory, motor, and other medical-psychological indices of recovery.

Computerized anatomical tomography is a highly sophisticated neuro-diagnostic procedure that significantly improves neurodiagnostic capability. This technique demonstrates minute alterations in organ density and is capable of portraying intraorgan abnormalities, for example, tumors and other structural anomalies. This technique represents a major advance in medical science. Research assessing relative accuracy of computerized tomography and clinical neuropsychology data is proceeding on issues ranging from assessing brains of schizophrenics, to accuracy of "hit rate" among organics. Investigators should not be surprised, however, to find a less than one-to-one correlation between the two sources of information. Despite the advances represented by computerized tomography, the technique still represents a "structural assessment." The structure-function dichotomy continues to exist with its attendant problems associated with predicting one from measures based upon the other. Such problems will continue until knowledge represented by structure and function assessment techniques achieve perfection, at which point one might expect complete convergence of data emerging from the two sources, a phenomenon not expected in the near future.

THE INTERNATIONAL NEUROPSYCHOLOGY SOCIETY (INS)

The International Neuropsychology Society (INS) is the one organization that reflects the breadth and diversification in clinical neuropsychology. This organization conducted its first organizational meeting on September

5, 1965, in Chicago at the annual convention of the American Psychological Association. Aaron Smith of the University of Nebraska Medical School and Ray Dennerel of the Michigan Epilepsy Center in Detroit initiated the meeting. The impetus for this gathering was the presentation and discussion of a research study in brain functioning. The study had been conducted by Dr. Smith. Approximately fifty professionals attended. A steering committee was formulated to decide future directions for the society, and a newsletter was started.

In February 1973, the first annual convention was held in New Orleans, Louisiana. Since then annual conventions have been held. The membership as of March 1982 was approximately 1600. In this organization, membership is broad based and is comprised of representatives from medicine, speech pathology, biology, anatomy, psychology, physiology, and other disciplines.

The INS represents a forum for the exchange and sharing of information relevant to neuroscience. At annual conventions, an assembly of neuroscientists from different countries convenes to conduct and participate in workshops, as well as to hear presentations of research relevant to brain-behavior relations.*

CREDENTIALING

Credentialing is the single most significant issue facing clinical neuropsychologists today. As with any emerging discipline, establishing credentialing standards must be meticulously addressed. While trying to speak to the issue of such standards, the clinical neuropsychologist is confronted with many problems and questions. The following are in the writer's opinion critical questions to be addressed:

1. Which organization should be concerned with credentialing the clinical neuropsychologist practitioner? Should it be the American Psychological Association or the International Neuropsychological Society?

2. Should credentialing be done by the American Board of Examiners for Professional Psychology?

3. Should credentialing lie within the province of state professional organizations?

4. Should credentialing be predicated upon a specified period of postdoctoral education?

5. Should training that leads to providing a basis for credentialing be in conjunction with an institution providing prescribed sets of experiences?

---

*The author wishes to extend sincere thanks to Aaron Smith, Ph.D., Professor and Director, Neuropsychology Laboratory, University of Michigan Speech and Hearing Sciences Department, for providing this information.

6. Should partial credit be given for predoctoral training?

7. Should a grandfather clause be accepted to allow for clinical neuropsychologist practitioners already practicing in the field?

In the past twenty years, the author has observed continued growth and expansion in the field of clinical neuropsychology. More graduate psychology programs are incorporating facets of clinical neuropsychology into elective course offerings. More interest is being shown in the neuropsychological approach to diagnosis, as well as to the neuropsychology of the intact central nervous system.

To this author the positive future of clinical neuropsychology is obvious. The time for the establishment of uniform educational and experiential standards is now. Responsible representatives of the field should unite in their efforts to guarantee a rightful place for clinical neuropsychology among the existing more established health service professions. The International Neuropsychology Society could represent a first step in this direction.

MAJOR LEGAL ISSUES FACING THE
CLINICAL NEUROPSYCHOLOGIST

Neuropsychological test results of head trauma at times point to subtle deficits in function that are not always observed in medical examinations and laboratory studies.

Background

The psychologist assesses the brain in terms of observable behavior. If behavior associated with abnormal brain functioning is observed, the psychologist infers brain damage.

As mentioned earlier, the problem with many medical tests and procedures is that pathology is often not observable structurally until the pathological process has "matured" to certain structural dimensions. In short, the psychologist assesses function, the physician assesses structure via laboratory studies and other procedures. There is an obvious need for input from both disciplines.

Questions

In the instance of a child whose brain is still developing, the effects of head trauma on neuropsychological functioning may be significant. Depending upon the severity of brain injury, as well as age of the child, it is conceivable that the head injury may have significant bearing on the future development of the child's cognitive capacity and direction.

1. What is the legal status of positive neuropsychological information as opposed to negative medical findings?

2. Is it possible that the clinical neuropsychologist may be held liable if medical evidence of impairment is lacking while neuropsychological test evidence of pathology is observed and reported?

Background

Among many private hospitals throughout the United States, there is a hesitancy to afford psychologists professional privileges of any sort on a formal basis. In the past, the Joint Commission for the Accreditation of Hospitals (JCAH) has limited professional privileges to members of the "medical staff." Until recently medical staff membership has been limited to licensed physicians and dentists (JCAH, 1979). In the JCAH monograph, *Medical Staff Bylaws* (1978), there is an allusion to the fact that *"in some states other professionals such as podiatrists and clinical psychologists if qualified, are permitted by law to be members of the medical staff"* (italics added). Although one might interpret this as extending the concept of privileges beyond a narrower previous stipulation, it is a significant distance from a clear positive affirmation of privilege status for health service professionals other than licensed physicians and dentists. The tangible result of this less-than-clear-cut affirmation has been hesitancy on the part of many private hospitals to grant formal privileges to nonmedical and nondental health service professionals, specifically psychologists. With respect to the practicing neuropsychologist, some private hospitals allow limited privileges on an informal basis. At times, the fear of jeopardizing accreditation status has proven to be the basis for the hesitancy to grant the neuropsychologist privileges on a more formal basis.

Questions

1. Under such an informal arrangement with regard to privileges, what is the potential and actual liability incurred by the neuropsychologist who, while evaluating a hospitalized patient, encounters a patient experiencing cardiac arrest?

2. What is the potential and actual liability incurred by the neuropsychologist if the patient is seized by an event, during an evaluation, which culminates in death?

3. From a legal perspective, should the neuropsychologist not agree to such an informal arrangement?

BIBLIOGRAPHY

Boring, E. G. *A history of experimental psychology.* New York: Appleton-Century-Crofts, 1929.

Brain, R. *Diseases of the nervous system.* London: Oxford University Press, 8th ed., 1977.

Brain, R. *Speech disorders.* London: Butterworth Press, 1964.

Filskov, S. B., and Goldstein, S. G. Diagnostic validity of the Halstead-Reitan neuropsychological battery. *Journal of Consulting and Clinical Psychology*, 1974, *42*, 382-388.

Flourens, M. J. P. *Recherches expérimentales sur les propriétés et les fonctions du système nerveux dans les animaux vertébrés*. Paris: Crevot, 1824.

Flugel, J. C. *A hundred years of psychology, 1833-1933*. New York: Basic Books, 1964.

Franz, S. I. On the functions of the cerebrum: The frontal lobes in relation to the production and retention of simple sensory-motor habits. *American Journal of Physiology*, 1902 *8*, 1-22.

Fritsch, G., and Hitzig, E. Ueber die elektrische erregbrakeit des grosshirns. *Archives of Anatomy and Physiology*, 1870, *1*, 300-332.

Golden, C. J., Hammeke, T. A., and Purisch, A D. Diagnostic validity of a standardized neuropsychological battery derived from Luria's neuropsychological tests. *Journal of Consulting and Clinical Psychology*, 1978, *46*, 1258-1265.

Goodglass, H. Examination of purposeful movement. In H. G. Burr, ed. *The aphasic adult: Evaluation and rehabilitation*. University of Virginia, Charlottesville: Wayside, 1964, 103-110.

Goodglass, H. Linguistic changes in aphasic speech. In H. G. Burr, ed. *The aphasic adult: Evaluation and rehabilitation*. University of Virginia, Charlottesville: Wayside, 1964, 35-42.

Goodglass, H. Studies of the grammar of aphasics. In S. Rosenberg and J. Koplin, eds. *Developments in applied psycholinguistics research*. New York: Macmillan, 1968.

Goodglass, H., and Berko, J. A grammatism and inflectional morphology in English. *Journal of Speech and Hearing Research*, 1960, *3*, 257-267.

Goodglass, H., and Kaplan, E. Disturbance of gesture and pantomime in aphasia. *Brain*, 1963, *86*, 703-720.

Goodglass, H., and Quadfasel, F. A. Language laterality in left-handed aphasics. *Brain*, 1954, *77*, 521-548.

Halstead, W. C. *Brain and intelligence*. Chicago: University of Chicago Press, 1947.

Harlow, H. F., and Bromer, J. A. Acquisition of new responses during inactivation of the motor, premotor, and somesthetic cortex in the monkey. *Journal of General Psychology*, 1942, *26*, 299-313.

Head, H. *Aphasia and kindred disorders of speech*. New York: Macmillan, 1926, 2 vols.

Jennett, B. Assessment of the severity of head injury. *Journal of Neurology, Neurosurgery and Psychiatry*, 1976, *39*, 647-655.

Joint Commission for the Accreditation of Hospitals. *Accreditation Manual for Hospitals*. Chicago: Joint Commission for the Accreditation of Hospitals, 1972.

Joint Commission for the Accreditation of Hospitals. *Medical staff bylaws*. Chicago: Joint Commission for the Accreditation of Hospitals, 1978.

Lashley, K. S. *Brain mechanisms and intelligence*. Chicago: University of Chicago Press, 1929.

Lezak, M. D. *Neuropsychological assessment*. London: Oxford University Press, 1976.

Luria, A. R. *The working brain*. New York: Basic Books, 1973.

Luria, A. R. *Higher cortical functions of man*. Moscow: Moscow University Press, 1962. New York: Basic Books, (English translation).

Luria, A. R. *Human brain and mental processes*. Moscow: Academy of Pedagogical Sciences Press, 1963, New York: Harper & Row (English translation).

Luria, A. R., and Rapaport, M. Y. Regional symptoms of disturbances of higher cortical functions in intracerebral tumors of left hemisphere. *Questions of Neurosurgery*, 1962, *4*.

Luria, A. R., and Skorodumova, A. V. Right fixed hemianopsia. In *Collection in memoriam of S. V. Kravkov*. Moscow: 1947.

Misiak, Henry K., and Sexton, Virginia Staudt. *History of psychology*. New York: Grune & Stratton, 1966.

Reitan, R. M. Manual for the administration of the Halstead-Reitan neuropsychology battery. Unpublished report, Indianapolis, Ind.: University of Indiana Medical Center, 1959.

Reitan, R. M., and Davidson, L. *Clinical neuropsychology: Current status and applications*. New York: Halstead Press, 1974.

Sheer, D. E., and Lubin, B. Survey of training programs in clinical neuropsychology. *Journal of Clinical Psychology*, 1980, *36*, 1035-1039.

Small L. *Neuropsychodiagnosis in psychotherapy*. New York: Brunner/Mazel, 1973.

Stichbury, J. C. Assessment of disability following severe head injury. *Physiotherapy*, 1975, *61*, 268-272.

Teuber, H. L. Effects of brain wounds implicating right or left hemisphere in man: Hemisphere differences and hemisphere interaction in vision, audition, and somesthesis. In V. D. Mountcastle, ed. *Interhemispheric relations and cerebral dominance*. Baltimore: Johns Hopkins Press, 1962, 132-157.

Teuber, H. L., Battersby, W. S., and Bender, M. B. Performance of complex visual tasks after cerebral lesions. *Journal of Nervous and Mental Diseases*, 1951, *114*, 413-429.

Weisenberg, T. H., and McBride, K. E. *Aphasia: A clinical and psychological study*. London: Oxford University Press, 1935.

Wolman, B. B. *Handbook of clinical psychology*. New York: McGraw Hill, 1965, 653-681.

REFERENCE NOTES

Va. Academy of Clinical Psychologists and Resnick v. Blue Shield of S. Va., Blue Shield of SW Va. & Neuropsychiatric Society of Va., Inc. U.S. Court of Appeals, 4th Circuit. No. 79-1345. Argued, 2-5-80. Decided, 6-16-80.

The Psychologist in the Employee Assistance Program Consortium

INTRODUCTION

Traditionally, psychologists have been employed in industry in what can be viewed as three broad categories: personnel psychology, engineering psychology, and organizational psychology. Personnel psychology is generally concerned with the assessment and prediction of employee performance, and the design of training programs as they relate to job performance and methods for evaluation of these programs. Personnel psychology was and continues to be plagued with issues concerning the assessment procedures themselves and the individual conducting these procedures. These issues affect the actual assessment of an employee's performance and contaminate any prediction of future performance. Personnel psychology is not necessarily concerned with the needs of the employee, as such, but more with management's requirements.

Engineering psychology focuses on the evaluation of job design, emphasizing equipment and the work environment. The purpose is to increase work performance and the employee's satisfaction with his or her job. This psychology uses a "one-way" approach — how to utilize an employee effectively through the correct design of equipment and environment.

Organizational psychology deals with the nature and design of industrial organizations and their effects on employee motivation and attitudes. Group processes and leadership in the work setting are also areas that are studied. Unlike personnel and engineering psychology, organizational psychology is probably the one traditional area that closely approaches a description of the roles of a psychologist in an employee assistance program. In organizational psychology, employees and their attitudes, wishes, and desires are recognized as affecting the work environment.

These three areas of industrial psychology have provided some impressive information relative to cost effectiveness, safety, and employee motivation and attitudes. While these remain active and valid issues for concern, it has become increasingly apparent that areas outside of those traditionally studied can also have an effect on employees. Employee assistance programs address these areas, the personal problems of employees.

The definitions and objectives of employee assistance programs are as diverse as the professional backgrounds of the individuals who direct them. As a psychologist who directed an employee assistance program consortium, I define an employee assistance program as a psychological service to employees that provides diagnostic, evaluative, referral, and/or treatment services in seven broad problem areas: psychological/emotional, marital/family, alcohol and other drugs, job-related, financial, legal, and medical. The overall goal is to provide these services to employees of consortium members at an employee's request. It is not necessary that the employee's work performance be such that he or she is forced to use the service. This is an important distinction. There are those employee assistance programs whose primary goal is that of building a service via supervisor-referred employees (clients). In such a program, significant pressure is placed on the supervisor to detect the troubled employee. A program designed to encourage self-referrals will maintain a higher usage rate than one built on supervisor referrals. It is this author's experience that employees will readily use a confidential employee assistance service, irrespective of the problem, when it is advertised and perceived as a benefit.

Historically, the psychologist in industry functioned in a management support position. Research, methods of evaluation, assessment, and placement were performed without much attention to the needs or desires of employees. The psychologist in the employee assistance program must satisfy the needs of management and labor in order to ensure the maximum overall benefits resulting from such a service. The psychologist must believe that what is good for management is good for labor and vice versa in order to maintain an effective service-oriented program. Recent formations of Labor-Management Participation Teams within the steel industry (Bethlehem Steel Corporation) attest to the philosophy that labor and management must and can be aligned. The psychologist who directs an employee assistance program with this in mind will have incorporated a key ingredient into the formula necessary for a successful employee assistance program.

Over the last thirty-five years, psychology, as a profession, has witnessed significant development in the area of specialization and application. At one time, the U.S. Army and the Veterans Administration's hospital system were probably the most likely employers of psychologists. Today, the number of specialties within the profession, and consequent employment opportunities, seems to be continually expanding. The employee assistance program in business and industry is one of these emerging specialties.

Employee assistance programs are extremely diverse in design and function. Some predetermining factors in their design are as follows: the companies themselves, the work settings, the relationships between labor and management within each company, the differences in services available in each community, and the qualifications of the staff of these programs. The common denominator, however, is that of providing an opportunity for the employee (and the spouse and dependents, if desired) to receive services for problems that may or may not have affected the employee's job perform-ance.

Here, discussion will focus on the consortium approach to employee assistance programs and the roles of the psychologist. A consortium is defined as two or more companies that purchase diagnostic, evaluative, referral, and/or treatment services from a common provider. Business and industries with small to moderate (50-500) employee populations utilize this approach most frequently since they may also elect to join a consortium for a variety of reasons. These reasons might range from cost effectiveness to increased ease with which services are used outside of the work setting.

In order to understand fully our current purpose, it is necessary to exam-ine the historical background that facilitated the growth and development of employee assistance programs.

The efforts of Alcoholics Anonymous (AA) in industry in the early 1940s are seen as the foundation from which employee assistance programs ulti-mately developed. The concern was to save the job of the alcoholic em-ployee by convincing the employee to join the AA fellowship. AA believed that business and industry could play an important role, not only in hiring a recovered person, but also in identifying an employee with an alcohol prob-lem and encouraging him or her to seek help. Supervisors were trained to identify such an employee by looking for symptoms, such as bloodshot eyes, hand tremors, and the smell of alcohol — that is, the alcoholic who could be identified by almost anyone because the problem was so advanced.

Unfortunately, this method brought several problems with it. The super-vising employee with an alcohol problem was never identified because it was he or she who was "diagnosing" other employees. If an upper-level management employee had the problem, this middle-management "diagnos-tician" was certainly not about to suggest that his or her employer had such a problem. Furthermore, employees were aware that supervisors were "looking" for certain signs and symptoms, and the alcoholic employee was careful not to exhibit any of them while on the job.

Since alcoholic people are quite adept at "conning" others with excuses, apologies, and "bad luck" stories, once identified, the problem employee could convince the supervisor that alcohol was actually not the problem. Thus, the employee obtained sympathy for the "problems that were driving him or her to drink."

A final problem with this identification approach revolved around the certainty with which the supervisor could "diagnose" the alcoholic. Because of the embarrassment, not to mention the legal complications in which the supervisor could become involved, the problem often reached the chronic stage before identification. Then, the supervisor often conferred with the personnel department, upper-level management, and/or the medical department, compromising confidentiality and resulting in the delivery of an ultimatum to the employee. Even in confronting an employee with an alcohol problem, the supervisor was no match for those skillful in developing excuses for drinking.

The methods for diagnosing the alcoholic employee in industry became more sophisticated after the founding of the National Council on Alcoholism (NCA) in 1944. With the formulation of NCA's Department of Labor and Management Services in 1963, national attention was drawn to the issue of the alcoholic employee in business and industry. One of the most important concepts introduced was a method for the early identification of alcoholism by focusing on job performance. Further, labor and management were brought together in an attempt to develop and administer employee alcoholism programs at the local, state, and national levels. NCA also established a working relationship with the AFL-CIO Department of Community Services. Despite the continued denial of such problems by both employees and management in some areas, these activities created a national consciousness concerning alcoholism in the work place. They were among the first coordinated efforts aimed at educating not only labor and management, but also health care professionals, educators, and the general population.

Under the Department of Health, Education, and Welfare (now Health and Human Services), the National Institute on Alcohol Abuse and Alcoholism (NIAAA) became actively involved in the issues revolving around the alcoholic in the work place. In the early 1970s, NIAAA trained certain individuals from across the United States to work with industry (management and labor) in an attempt to alleviate the problem of industrial alcohol abuse. This initial involvement by NIAAA is considered the direct forerunner of "broadbrush" employee assistance programs. Alcohol was not the only issue — it was considered one of many problem areas that could affect the job performance of employees.

With the emergence of the broadbrush philosophy came the need for individuals with the necessary experience and education to see the client and determine his or her needs, and also to become involved in the design, publicity, marketing, and direction of the employee assistance program.

DESIGN OF AN EMPLOYEE ASSISTANCE PROGRAM

The type of program that is designed and consequently offered for use by employees and their families depends, to a large extent, on the qualifications of the individuals who are seeing these people. The more experienced and qualified these individuals are in handling clients with a wide variety of problems, the more professional the service that can be offered to companies and their employees. Essentially, this means that the psychologist, by the very nature of his or her profession's educational standards and experience in dealing with clients, has much to contribute to such a program.

The psychologist can facilitate a determination of the scope of services that will be offered, for example: the kinds of crisis situations that are appropriate for the staff to handle; whether or not the program will evaluate, diagnose, and refer; the possibility of a provision for treatment services; and the choice to extend services to spouses and dependents of employees. These are all options of program design, controlled by the education and experience of the staff of the program. Attractiveness to business and industry will, in large part, be determined by not only what is offered, but who is offering it. Therefore, if business and industry are expected to support such a service philosophically and financially, it is necessary to be capable of offering more than a service that merely shuffles clients (employees) through offices.

To a degree, successful marketing of the program is a direct function of program design. An adequate definition of program services (design) is necessary not only for successful marketing (that is, management understands what is being offered), but also in order that clients have a cogent overview of services.

The concept of staff qualifications determining, in large part, program design is important in the marketing approach, since the design is the core of that approach. Great success has been found when the marketing presentations are conducted by those individuals (psychologists) who are providing the services, insofar as they are the services. In discussing the employee assistance program with top management, the psychologist is quite capable of discussing the kinds of services being offered, the kinds of problems encountered with clients, and the success rates with regard to motivating clients to participate in treatment and/or which require some sort of action to resolve the problems. As an integral part of the services being offered, the psychologist defines the services, explains how they are offered, and how they work.

Approaches to the top management of business and industry must be solidly based in "the product" (that is, what the services are), in addition to the actual cost and potential cost-effectiveness. There appears to be a commonly held philosophy that management is primarily concerned with saving money and will only be interested in an employee assistance program that can document this. Actually, cost and cost-effectiveness are somewhat secondary issues. This is especially true as it pertains to consortiums. As the group grows, costs are absorbed over a larger base (number of member companies). The costs associated with providing the services are not a direct function of the total number of employees represented. From personal experience, two psychologists can handle a total employee count of 15,000 to 20,000 with an expected annual penetration rate of 10 percent. This means that approximately 2,000 employees and/or family members will use the service in any one year. Management well understands that the consortium model is cost-effective and the result is that they focus more on the services provided to employees, rather than on justifying the service from the overall, real and predicted cost and/or cost-effective perspective. Once top management accepts the value of such a "benefit" to its employees, middle management, union officers, and supervisors are introduced to the service. It is extremely important for these individuals to understand the service and pass on the information to employees under their direction. Acceptance, as a benefit, and use of the service by the employee will be greatly enhanced by this understanding and resultant word-of-mouth from these management levels.

The employee's familiarity with the service and passing that information on to others are probably the best methods of publicizing employee assistance programs. Some standard publicity techniques that can be utilized are brochures, posters, and articles or reminders in in-house newsletters. Several of the newer techniques consist of closed-circuit television tapes, membership cards, payroll stuffers, presentations to full union membership meetings, and, in some instances, presentations to employee assemblies.

It appears that the key to an employee's understanding that he or she can use the service confidentially and without management intervention lies in two areas: (1) as many people as possible within the company understanding what the service is all about and the ease with which it can be used; and (2) in the amount of publicity given the service by the company and management personnel. This entails not only continually reminding the employee of the availability of services, but also, if the program is offered to the spouse and dependents, informing and reminding them at regular intervals of the services. This could mean sending publicity materials to the home, along with a letter explaining what the program is all about, the services available, how it can be used, confidentiality, etc. The availability for utilization of an employee assistance program by family members can be very important to the success of the program. To the employee, it could mean the resolution of a problem at home that might have eventually affected the work performance record of that employee. In marketing the program, a company that is a prospective consortium member could see this aspect of the program as an important "plus" that could avoid a number of problems, not just for the employee, but also for the company in terms of time, money, and morale.

The methods of publicity used in each company that is a member of the consortium depends on the wishes of the individual company and those methods that the employee assistance program has found to be most attractive to employees and their families. The size of each company and the philosophy of management also determines what can be effectively utilized. The company itself might devise its own methods for publicizing the availability of services either along with or apart from the publicity that the program offers.

It can be seen from this discussion that there are many roles in which the psychologist can function in the development and operation of an employee assistance program consortium. We have discussed the roles and requirements of the areas of marketing and publicity, areas that might be foreign to many psychologists in their everyday activities. However, the roles of diagnostician, referral source, and treatment provider are not so unfamiliar.

As had been emphasized, the diagnostician *is* the service. It may be said, then, that this role of diagnostician is the most important role of the psychologist in the employee assistance program. As diagnostician, the psychologist can combine the interview and psychometric techniques, when necessary, in order to determine the problem. This is especially necessary when there is evidence that obtaining a differential diagnosis is in order.

At this point, the decision is made to treat, refer, or resolve the problem. The decision to treat is based on several criteria: the psychologist's knowledge of his or her own expertise in relation to the problems of each individual employee; the nature of the problem of the employee; the wishes of the employee (client); cost factors; and the availability of time.

Generally speaking, the factor that most severely limits the direct treatment of an employee (client) is time. In the consortium model, the majority of the psychologist's time is usually spent in performing initial interviews and evaluations; however, a full treatment component could be developed.

The decision to refer the employee is based on the aforementioned criteria, along with the knowledge and availability of appropriate public and private community treatment resources. Awareness of these local resources is essential when considering the possibility of a treatment component in the design of the employee assistance program. The lack of community treatment resources can force the employee assistance program consortium to incorporate this component into its design.

The employees (clients) may be referred into the program in one of three ways: self-referred, management-directed, or management-forced. As a self-referral, the employee contacts the program on his or her own to obtain services. Management is not aware of this particular employee's use of services. In this instance, the problem is at such a stage that work performance usually has not yet been affected.

In the case of a directed-referral, it is *suggested* by management that the employee contact the program for services. Usually, work performance, absenteeism, or lateness is at such a stage that, if left unchecked, the employee will most likely become a forced-referral.

At the point of forced-referral, the employee is informed by management (usually the personnel administrator) that some positive action must be taken toward improving work performance as defined by those standards expected of each employee. If those standards are not met, the employee is also informed that he or she will face termination. It is very important that management does not focus attention on whether or not any personal problem exists or what that problem might be, but focuses only on job performance and attendance. However, inherent in the concept of forced-referral is the philosophy that some personal problem is the cause of performance deterioration, and the employee is usually given time to resolve the matter. If the employee assistance program director is contacted about services for this employee, it then becomes the responsibility of the program's psychologist to determine if a personal problem exists that is the cause, either in whole or in part, of the employee's poor record. Any action taken by management with respect to either termination or continued employment, however, is based solely on the work performance record. A release of confidential information is secured at the forced-referral level when the employee (client) requests that the company be given any information that the employee specifies. Most employee assistance programs see very few employees (clients) under these stringent conditions.

Assuming that a self-referred employee (client) is motivated to resolve the problem, the job of the psychologist is much easier. The energy and attention of both the client and the psychologist can be directed at resolution of the problem and/or appropriate referrals for treatment. In a forced-referral situation, the energy and attention of the psychologist must also be given to appropriate interview and psychometric techniques and to motivating the client to attend to the problem. This in no way implies that *all* self-referred clients possess the necessary knowledge, insight, or motivation to solve their problems but, generally speaking, the psychologist's job is much less troublesome in dealing with such clients. It may be noteworthy at this time to point out that the majority of clients from a well-publicized, management- and union-endorsed employee assistance program will be seen on a self-referred basis.

Broadbrush employee assistance programs can be directed by a variety of professionals and paraprofessionals. Programs exist that are directed by business-oriented individuals, social workers, physicians, personnel workers, and psychologists. It has been found that the psychologist can function very effectively as director of an employee assistance program. In this role, the psychologist, with assistance from other well-qualified (educated and experienced) individuals, can participate in all areas of the program or can operate alone in any one or combination of roles. In whatever capacity the psychologist wishes to operate, as director, he or she wears many hats and performs many duties, including overseeing the staff and general administration of the program. However, in order to direct the staff and the activities of the program effectively, the director must be sufficiently familiar with all aspects. Depending on the past experience of the psychologist, he or she might need to spend considerable time in certain areas in order to gain the necessary experience and knowledge in those areas of deficiency.

Psychologists are spending an increasing amount of time in positions that are administrative as well as clinical, positions not so different from "middle" or "top" management in business and industry. Effective direction of an employee assistance program is as crucial to their success as the leadership within the companies that are members of the consortium.

As director of an employee assistance program, psychologists must be able not only to combine successfully their clinical and administrative duties, but also to distinguish successfully between the two functions when necessary. It would be highly inappropriate for psychologists to relate to other staff members as clients; however, these professionals would not be realizing their fullest potential if those characteristics that comprise an effective psychologist (perceptiveness, understanding, etc.) were not used. Psychologists can exercise their professional knowledge when adjusting to the administrative responsibilities of defining the design, objectives, and goals necessary for the growth and success of employee assistance programs.

As director, the psychologist represents the employee assistance program itself, the services it offers, the staff, the design, the objectives and goals, and even the consortium members, to a certain extent. The planning, structure, and direction of the program are on the shoulders of the director/ psychologist. He or she must be able to manage effectively the program and its staff and activities, if the program is to succeed.

PROFESSIONAL NOTES

Along with the continued expansion of psychology into more diverse areas of specialization and application is an obvious parallel expansion in the professional issues concerning psychologists. Within the past ten years, numerous issues have been identified and defined. Some of these include: patient rights (right to treatment in its least restrictive form), right to due process and informed consent, rights of minors, state licensing laws, advertising by psychologists, third-party payments, the Professional Standards Review Committee, health systems agencies, the Presidential Commission on Mental Health, and national health insurance. These are vital, and only some of the more recent issues with which the psychologist, working in any professional setting, should be familiar. Psychologists in employee assistance programs may find themselves concerned with these issues more as they apply to the professional/personal interests than in the daily operation of an employee assistance program.

Some of the more traditional issues, such as confidentiality, require more awareness and vigilance of potentially detrimental situations because of the unique relationships that exist between management, the employee (client), and the psychologist of an employee assistance program. Often, a concurrent relationship exists between the psychologist and the employee (client) and the psychologist and management. The psychologist might be providing services other than those to employees (clients). While seeing employees (clients), the psychologist might be performing duties in educating and training supervisors relative to motivating employees to use the employee assistance services, providing management services such as stress seminars, and communicating employee usage rates to key individuals within the company. These are all situations that place the psychologist director of an employee assistance program in a more complex position than that of a psychologist in a traditional clinical setting. The psychologist is often presented with unsolicited information concerning employees (who might or might not be clients) simply because he or she is available to management for other purposes. It is extremely important for the psychologist to stress continually the confidentiality of services. In some instances, the employee (client) should be forewarned that the psychologist might be at the employee's work place on occasion. Educating the employee (client) about the roles the psychologist plays with regard to the company is often worth the energy expended in terms of allaying any fears the client might have when seeing the psychologist in the work place. Regardless of the relationships that exist, the psychologist must impress upon the employee (client) that he or she is the "holder" of the privilege. Simply, this means that the employee (client) determines what and to whom confidential information is released.

Section 504 of the National Rehabilitation Act of 1973 states that: "No otherwise qualified handicapped individual in the United States . . . shall, solely by reason of his handicap, be excluded from the participation in, be denied the benefits of, or be subjected to discrimination under any program or activity receiving federal financial assistance" (Section 504, 1977, p. 1). Among other afflictions, Section 504 addresses the rights of those individuals with an alcohol and/or drug addiction or emotional illness. These individuals are considered to be handicapped, and employers cannot use these handicaps as a basis for not hiring or promoting them. This means that the handicap might have to be accommodated in terms of accessibility, but only to a reasonable degree. This degree is determined by the size and type of business or industry and the cost involved. Particularly relevant to addictions is the regulation that an employer does not need to change the standards concerning performance or behavior when poor work performance or disruptive behavior is the result of an employee's addiction.

Federal legislation (S. 2515) has, and will, create unique circumstances for employee assistance programs. A bill, presented by Senators Hathaway and Williams in February 1978, required government contractors (those having contracts in excess of $2,500), "to establish and operate alcohol abuse and alcoholism programs and services, or otherwise arrange for referral to such services, and for other purposes" (Hathaway and Williams, 1978). This bill was referred to the Committees on Human Resources and Government Affairs by unanimous consent.

There also appears to be a climate among labor management that is conducive to the development of employee assistance programs. The philosophy that personal problems deserve the same time and attention as those of a medical nature is one that is gradually becoming more commonly held. The following case study exemplifies the dual (emotional and medical) nature of the causes of problems not infrequently encountered by the employee assistance psychologist:

S. J. (age 30) and his wife were referred by his supervisor for marriage counseling. According to the supervisor, S. J. had complained to him that his (S. J.'s) wife was seeing another man and that this was affecting his work performance. The supervisor confirmed that S. J. had, over several months, been late, repeatedly absent, and unable to concentrate while on the job.

During the initial interview, S. J.'s wife defined what she considered to be the real issues. These were S. J.'s explosive personality (temper), his physical abuse of her, and his constant threats of physical harm directed toward their two children (ages 6 and 7).

S. J. stated that his main problem was recurring headaches (weekly). These headaches began in the back of his head and spread across the top ending just above his eyes. He described the pain as almost unbearable. It was at these times that he was abusive and capable of exploding over minor issues. S. J. claimed no memory for events during the attacks. Further interviewing revealed that S. J. had been unconscious for approximately two to three minutes (at age 13) due to falling and striking the back of his head. He began experiencing headaches about six months after this accident with increasing frequency and pain.

With this information, this author administered the finger oscillation test (Reitan, 1959) and the grip strength test (Jamar Hand Dynamometer). The test results reflected Fields' motor reversal phenomenon (Fields, 1979) and, when combined with the reported symptoms, suggested that S. J. may have been experiencing some form of seizure activity. The data and history were seen as sufficient justification for referral to a neurologist. A subsequent electroencephalograph reflected a seizure pattern. Before a complete regimen of treatment for the seizure disorder could be initiated, the client committed suicide.

It is the norm rather than the exception that the psychologist in the employee assistance program is exposed to a diversity of problems. In this position, the psychologist is often the first health professional that the employee has seen with regard to specific symptoms and/or problems. The above case illustrates problems, marital and family, complicated by neurological dysfunction. It is imperative that the psychologist have a broad range of experiences and skills in the areas of diagnostics and treatment. Through this expertise, services to employer and employee are expanded, and continued growth of the consortium is enhanced.

Psychologists in employee assistance programs find that they are involved in the education of top management in order to gain support for the concept of allowing employees a vehicle, as well as time, necessary to resolve problems of a personal nature. Of course, there are those who would deny that a specific employee population needs such a service — a reminder of the early denials by some industries of alcohol problems within its work force.

Pending federal legislation and a developing belief in the need for employee assistance services seem to have been, in part, a natural outgrowth of Section 504. These are more than just regulations concerning discrimination in the hiring and termination of handicapped persons; they have led to indications that business and industry are willing to provide services for all employees in order to prevent personal problems from interfering with job performance.

Again, it is not only a matter of providing these benefits to the employee whose job has already been adversely affected. The employee assistance program is beneficial to employees, regardless of their performance, and is ultimately beneficial to the stability of the company itself. A sound employee assistance program, in effect, reduces turnover and its related costs and, practically speaking, helps to create a better work environment.

BIBLIOGRAPHY

Conversations with Geriann C. Lioi, Staff Counseling Psychologist, INROADS employee assistance program consortium, Reading, Pa., 1979.

Fields, F. R. J. A motor reversal phenomenon in individuals with medically documented cerebral electrophysiological disturbances. *Clinical Neuropsychology,* 1979, *1*(2) 48-50.

Hathaway, W. D., and Williams, H. *Senate bill 2515.* 95th Congress: 2d session, United States Senate, February 6, 1978.

Levinson, D., and Klerman, G. L. In retrospect: The clinician-executive. In S. Feldman, ed. *Administration in mental health.* Rockville, Md.: National Institute of Mental Health, 1972a.

Levinson, D., and Klerman, G. L. In retrospect: The clinician-executive revisited. In S. Feldman, ed. *Administration in mental health.* Rockville, Md.: National Institute of Mental Health, 1972b.

Martin, A. R. *An approach to supervisory training for North Carolina occupational program's employee assistance programs.* Washington, D.C.: Department of Human Resources, Division of Mental Health Services, Alcohol and Drug Abuse Services, 1976.

Mayer, A. J., and Simons, P. E. Management: Company shrink. *Newsweek,* October 24, 1977, *90*(17), 96.

National Council on Alcoholism. NCA-pioneered labor-management programs. *NCA Bulletin*, 1974, 1(1).

Reitan, R. M. Manual for the administration of the Halstead-Reitan Neuropsychology Battery. Unpublished report, 1959. Bloomington, Ind.: University of Indiana Medical Center.

Rights of alcoholics. *The Almacan*, 1977, 7(8).

Schlenger, W. E., Hallan, J. B., and Hayward, B. J. *Characteristics of selected occupational programs*. Raleigh, N.C.: Human Ecology Institute, 1976.

Section 504, Rehabilitation Act of 1973 fact sheet. Washington, D.C.: United States Department of Health, Education, and Welfare, Office of the Secretary, Office for Civil Rights, 1977.

Wrich, J. T. *The employee assistance program*. Center City, Minn.: Hazelden, 1974.

9   G. THOMAS GATES

A Judge Views Psychology

A. INTRODUCTION

Law and psychology are similar in that both deal with human activities. Behavioral control is the ultimate end product of each profession. Nonetheless, the imagery of a "Cold War," as described by Professor Sheldon Glueck,[1] between lawyers and psychologists is but recently emerging from the thaw stage.[2] Perhaps the distrust on the part of the legal profession is rooted in the fact that psychology, as a separate discipline, is in its infancy when compared to the historical role of the law and lawyers in the control of human behavior. A likely cause for the slow development of a rapport is a distrust based upon a mutual lack of knowledge. Such a mutual distrust is inherent in any undertaking that approaches the same goal with totally dissimilar methods.

Interdisciplinary Disputes

In many ways jurisprudence has been out of cadence with the advanced state of psychology. The most discordant sounds in law are the quaint, unscientific terms ascribed to various forms of mental illness. *Lunacy, insanity, idiocy, incompetency,* and *diminished capacity* are but a few examples of the language found in the case law and statutory law of the United States. The courts have engaged in complex and confounded rationalization of such simple terms as *shall* as being directory or mandatory; *reasonable* in terms of standards; *obscenity* to whom and under what circumstances. Yet relatively little time is devoted to bringing psychological and legal terms into harmony.

The role of a psychologist as an expert witness in the law gives rise to another point of stress between the professions. Lawyers are accustomed to seeking out facts and applying those facts to the accepted law. Expert witnesses are employed in the law by reason of necessity. Opinion evidence is considered as a very low grade form of evidence since it is subjective and dependent upon the adoption of one or more of the disputed facts in any given case. While attorneys may placidly accept a physician's diagnosis as a fact, when it is nothing more than opinion, they rebel with vigor at a psychologist's opinion as to a matter in litigation.

Interdisciplinary disputes will continue until there is a cordiality based upon an understanding of the mutually exclusive roles each profession bears to the other. Understanding, in this context, is neither to approve nor disapprove, but merely to comprehend, to provide an adequate foundation for the act of judgment. Interdisciplinary bliss between psychology and the law should not be expected unless one is willing to accept the assumption that all scholarly roads lead to Rome. There is profit in the adage that a boiling pot makes good broth.

Psychology and Its Relationship to the Legal Enterprise

Frustration, irritation, confusion, and ultimately anger are the only foreseeable outcomes of a lack of understanding between lawyers and psychologists. A psychologist has much to contribute to the law if the contribution is understandingly made. The psychologist must understand that, unlike a science, the law is based upon common experience, commonly accepted beliefs, and by generally adopted attitudes as reflected by statutory enactment. Unlike science, basic legal precedents accepted and acknowledged today may be abrogated completely tomorrow. For example, it has long been rooted in our law that the government was immune from lawsuits instituted by individuals to vindicate wrongs visited upon individuals by government agents. This principle of sovereign immunity has long been accepted by the courts as the law of the land, while many of the justices of those courts candidly acknowledge that the doctrine has no valid historical base and its current application is indefensible.

Some courts in various states have abrogated the doctrine by judicial fiat,[3] while other courts continue to follow the precedent, suggesting that its abolition is a legislative function. The point is that even basic, long-recognized legal principles known to many to be unacceptable in today's society are followed by some courts and overruled by others, demonstrating that the law is not like a scientific fact. It has been established scientifically and for a long time that an apple will always fall down from a tree. We cannot accept the legal fact that sovereign immunity will be with us tomorrow. Perhaps it can best be said that the law lags science because it is attuned to public rather than scientific opinion.

Collaborative Efforts Between Law and Social Sciences

Psychologists possess a wealth of skills, techniques, and information about human behavior which affords a fertile resource to be employed by an imaginative, practicing attorney. Collaboration between a psychologist and a practicing attorney is profitable to both either in the in-court or out-of-court setting.

The in-court aspect ordinarily casts the psychologist in the role of an expert witness who, where allowable, renders an opinion about a matter under judicial scrutiny. In recent times, legal counsel has engaged the services of psychologists to assist in the jury selection process and in the cross-examination of witnesses.

The association of Trial Lawyers of America has recently prepared a substantial text *Psychology and Persuasion in the Courtroom* for use at a trial lawyers' seminar. The text probes the subjects of semantics, body language, juror interaction, the use of gestures, manipulation of space in the courtroom, and other psychological techniques based on reported experiments.

The out-of-court setting is that least employed by lawyers. It serves little purpose at this point to speculate why lawyers do not avail themselves of the psychological skills available to them other than, perhaps, the apathy already referred to. However, effective preventative law procedures dictate psychological counseling as a wise course to follow in such matters as drafting of wills and executing instruments that may be the subject of future attack on the grounds of incompetence or undue influence. While both are legal concepts, they are ultimately opinions, the value of which depends upon the factual basis of the person rendering the opinion.

Attorneys would serve their clients well if they suggested to their clients that they take a standard psychological examination at or about the time they execute wills or other instruments that may be the subject of later attack. There are a number of widely recognized and frequently employed psychological tests for the determination of intelligence, emotional stability, perception, and distortion in thinking and ideation. With this type of evidence obtained contemporaneously with the legal act, it is not difficult to project the outcome of any attack on the validity of the instrument. Any contrary evidence would be of little probative value since it would, of necessity, be of later construction and an act of retroactive judgment, which would be of little value when weighed against the currency of the instrument drafted in consultation with a psychologist.

In the field of domestic relations, a long-neglected area of the law, psychological consultation by an attorney is of inestimable value. The fields of child development and family relationships have long been a specialty of psychologists. The employment of a psychologist by an attorney might well result in reconciliation or, upon its failure, the suggestion of desirable adjustments in the family relationships in the event of a divorce.

As an ancillary service to courts, psychologists have proven of inestimable value. Some courts routinely require psychological testing and evaluation of all children entering the juvenile court system. Many courts require psychological evaluation as a part of the pre-sentence reports prepared to assist judges in selecting sentencing alternatives.[4] Structured outpatient psychotherapy is frequently a condition imposed by courts in imposing probationary sentences. Trial judges are frequently called upon to render an awesome decision in child custody cases. It is not uncommon for judges to insist upon independent home studies and psychological evaluations of the contestants in custody cases. A psychological evaluation of the child or children who are the subject of a custody dispute is also welcomed by the enlightened trial court.

Litigation of issues that will have an impact on the general public are frequently instituted with the view of having the case ultimately reviewed by the court either in the jurisdiction or in the United States Supreme Court. On the trial level, the employment of social psychologists for the purpose of testifying as to test results and trends forms a basis for later argument before appellate courts. These higher courts turn a deaf ear on arguments based upon so-called general understandings without any factual basis upon which the argument is based. A recent Judicature review notes that the United States Supreme Court "has been placing increased reliance on data generated by social scientists."[5]

Lawyers have, for a long time, recognized and acknowledged the need for expert witnesses in a variety of aspects of litigation. While judges and lawyers have made frequent use of doctors and psychiatrists, the psychiatrist's nonmedical counterpart, the psychologist, has largely remained untapped as a potential source of valid legal aid. Despite the fact that psychologists have qualified in most courts as expert witnesses and in some courts have been found to be more qualified on a particular aspect of the case than psychiatrists, we still see reticence on the part of attorneys to engage this more available or accessible, and doubtlessly less expensive, source of expertise.

Professions of Words

Unquestionably, much of the uncomfortableness that exists between the various professions results from word use. Without an understanding of the terminology employed by each discipline, confusion and misunderstanding is inevitable. Mr. Justice Holmes wrote, "A word is not a crystal, transparent and unchanged, it is the skin of a living thought and may vary greatly in color and content according to the circumstances and the time in which it is used."[6]

While the legal profession is as guilty as any in the use of code words or expressions foreign to others, it also recognizes that words differ in meaning depending upon the context in which the words are used, as well as the place and manner of use.

A *bench* means different things depending on whether you are speaking to a cobbler, carpenter, or surveyor. A *ribbon* means one thing in ladies apparel and quite another to a secretary talking about her typewriter. A *dog* does not bark for a machinist; it is a tool.

Admittedly, it is a formidable task for lawyers to understand and grasp fully psychological terminology. Likewise, it is understandable that psychologists, as well as others, are totally at sea in attempting to understand complex legal phraseology and the Latin terms and expressions so frequently employed. However, I suggest this is the root of discord between the disciplines and it must be understood and conquered before significant progress will be made in the field.

Translation of Legal Concepts of Mental Capacity

Both case law and statutory law in the United States contain a wide variety of definitions for the same terms. Often the definition of the term employed will depend upon the context of the case in which it is employed. For example, in criminal law, we frequently find the terms *insanity, diminished capacity, irresistible impulse, lunacy*, and *incompetency*.

The general test of responsibility for crime in most states is commonly known as the "McNaughton Rule."[7] In general, it may be stated as the capacity, or lack of capacity, to understand the nature and consequences of the act charged and the ability to distinguish between right and wrong in respect to such act. In a majority of jurisdictions, knowledge of right and wrong is the exclusive test of criminal responsibility.[8] In determining whether an accused has the capacity to distinguish between right and wrong, the inquiry must be addressed to the individual's capacity in respect to the particular act involved, and not to his or her capacity in the abstract.[9] When the McNaughton test is met, want of a capacity is a complete defense and a jury is justified in returning a verdict of not guilty by reason of insanity, even though they found as a fact that the accused committed the particular criminal act under scrutiny.[10]

In other criminal cases, including in some jurisdictions the crime of murder, the diminished capacity test is employed. When this test is applied, insanity may reduce the degree of the offense under circumstances in which the crime is divided into degrees. If a particular intent is a necessary element of the greater degree, and a mental defect, while insufficient to excuse commission of the crime, may be considered in determining whether or not one possesses the capacity to entertain the deliberate and premeditated design requisite to the higher degree of the offense, the mental test of diminished capacity operates to reduce the grade of the offense.[11]

Still other jurisdictions make use of the so-called irresistible impulse test. The courts hold that an impulse is irresistible and may constitute a defense to a crime if it is produced by, and grew out of, some mental disease affecting the volition, as distinguished from the perceptive powers, so that the person affected, while able to understand the nature and consequences of his or her act, and to perceive that it is wrong, is unable, because of such mental disease, to resist the impulse to do it.[12]

The American Law Institute has provided what has been characterized as a restatement of the McNaughton test in language consonant with current legal and psychological thought. It has been adopted by every federal circuit except the first, and by fifteen states. The test is that a person is not responsible for criminal conduct if, at the time of such conduct, as a result of mental disease or defect, he or she lacks substantial capacity either to appreciate the criminality of the conduct or to conform his or her conduct to the requirements of law.[13]

Incompetency for the purpose of standing trial is yet another legal test frequently encountered. Unlike a civil case where an incompetent may be forced to trial with a guardian appointed to represent his or her interests, a criminal defendant who is incompetent cannot be tried at all. This test of incompetency comprehends a mental disease of such a nature as to interfere substantially with the defendant's ability to understand the nature of the proceedings and to cooperate intelligently with counsel in the trial of the case. If this pretrial finding is made, the actual trial is postponed until the accused becomes competent. In many cases, the incompetency prevails for such a long period of time that once competency is restored, the person cannot be tried because the necessary witnesses are either dead or their whereabouts are unknown.

On the civil side of law, a number of so-called insanity tests are employed. For example, persons may become so incompetent, as a result of mental illness, that they are unable to manage their own affairs. Thus, a guardian may be appointed if there is such an essential privation of reasoning facilities, or such mental impairment as to render the subject incapable of understanding and acting with discretion in the ordinary affairs of life.[14] The magic phrase, often repeated in the law, is that a person is incompetent if the illness would render him or her susceptible to becoming the victim of designing persons.

Testamentary capacity is another area of the law requiring the application of a different test of mental illness. Testamentary capacity consists of a mentality and memory insufficient to understand the nature and purpose of the transaction, to comprehend generally the nature, situation, or extent of the property owned, and to recollect the testator's relationship to the objects of the bounty and to those who naturally would have some claim to his or her remembrance and to understand the manner and effect of the desired disposition of the estate.[15] Thus, an individual lacking testamentary capacity is incapable of making a will and case books abound with lawsuits attacking the validity of wills on the basis that, at the time the will was drawn and signed, the testator lacked testamentary capacity. If the will is successfully attacked, then the estate of the descendant who lacked testamentary capacity passes to the statutory heirs.

It is interesting to note that, in considering testamentary capacity, many courts note that no particular degree of mentality constitutes a standard for testamentary capacity, so that its existence must be determined largely from the facts and circumstances of each case. A higher order of intelligence, or an absolutely sound mind in all respects, is not required. Nor does mental weakness in itself disqualify an individual from writing a will. One may lack testamentary capacity without being insane when measured by other legal standards of insanity, diminished capacity, irresistible impulse, incompetency, or mental illness generally.[16]

Most, if not all states, provide for the involuntary commitment to a mental institution of individuals suffering from mental illness. The fact that a person is of unsound mind is not, standing alone, sufficient to justify a commitment. Although statutes differ, the general rule is that a person may be committed if he or she is so mentally unsound as to make it reasonably probable that if allowed to remain at large he or she would, by reason of such mental condition, endanger life, person, or property or become a menace to the safety of the public.[17]

Some states, such as Pennsylvania, responding to peculiar current situations, have provided extremely strict statutory standards for commitment. In Pennsylvania, for example, the standard to be employed in all involuntary commitments, both civil and criminal, provides that a person may not be committed unless he or she is "severely mentally disabled." The statute defines individuals as severely mentally disabled when as a result of mental illness, their capacity to exercise self-control, judgment, and discretion in the conduct of their affairs and social relations or to care for their own personal needs is so lessened that they pose a clear and present danger of harm to others or to themselves. The key phrase is the existence of "clear and present danger." The statute then refines the expression by providing that clear and present danger to others must be shown by establishing that, within thirty days, the person has inflicted or attempted to inflict serious bodily harm on another and that there is a reasonable probability that such conduct will be repeated. Continuing, the statute provides that clear and present danger to himself or herself shall be shown by establishing, within the past thirty days, that the person acted in such a manner as to evidence that, without care, he or she would be unable to satisfy the need for nourishment, personal or medical care, shelter, or self-protection and safety and that there is a reasonable probability that death, serious bodily injury, or serious physical debilitation would ensue within thirty days unless involuntarily committed for the purpose of receiving adequate treatment. Clear and present danger to the individual may also be known when the person has attempted suicide and there is a reasonable probability of suicide unless committed and treated. Finally, clear and present danger to the individual may also be shown when the person has severely mutilated himself or herself or attempted to do so and that there is a reasonable probability of mutilation unless involuntarily committed and adequately treated.[18]

In the field of domestic relations, and for the purpose of marriage and divorce, the law has assigned another standard for mental illness. As a general rule, mental illness arising after marriage is not grounds for divorce unless made so by statute.[19] Where such grounds do exist, however, the terms usually require that the insane spouse must have been confined to a proper institution for the time specified and, sometimes, a commission is appointed by the court in which the divorce is pending to determine if the spouse is insane.[20] Other statutes only require a mental condition such that the person requires supervision of the kind given by a hospital for the insane, although the patient is harmless enough to be placed outside the hospital in a private home but under hospital outpatient supervision.[21]

On the other hand, mental illness at the time of the marriage may not only be grounds for divorce but it may supply an independent basis for decreeing an annulment. Thus, a person of unsound mind at the time of marriage is considered by many courts as incapable of agreeing to the marriage vows and the marriage is void. In this context, unsound mind is usually tested by the capacity of the person to understand the special nature of the contract of marriage and the duties and responsibilities it entails. This test is not a precise one and must be determined from the facts and circumstances of each case.[22]

In the area of civil law generally, a person may lack contractual capacity so that the person bound by the terms of a contract may avoid his or her responsibility upon establishing one of a number of mental conditions containing quaint legal labels. At common law, lunacy[23] was used to describe the state when one's loss of reality contact via sickness, grief, or other forms of insanity is separated by lucid intervals. Basically, it is described as periodical insanity. Although today the term and the distinction are pretty much discarded, a so-called lunatic was considered as incapable of entering into legally binding contractual relations.[24]

A more advanced decay and feebleness of the intellectual capacities has been termed *imbecility*.[25] It too allows persons so afflicted to avoid the legal consequences of their acts. Mania, delusions, senile dementia, excessive use of intoxicants, or the excessive use of narcotics may cause mental impairment to such a degree that the beneficent law permits such individuals to avoid the consequences of their civil acts.[26]

The matter that usually brings lawyers and psychologists or psychiatrists into confrontation is the fact that psychology, in the main, addresses the cause, and the cause is not a defense — only the result.

B. LICENSURE

Validity of Legislation Regulating Licensure

State legislatures frequently require the obtaining of a license before a person is permitted to act in any particular field. The licensure statutes can roughly be divided into three categories. The first category is the licensure requirements that are designed primarily as revenue raisers, for example, dog licenses, hunting licenses, and automobile registration permits. The second category of licensure requirements is to protect the public by only issuing licenses to qualified people to act in certain fields, for example, medical doctors, optometrists, osteopaths, accountants, lawyers, and barbers. The third category is the result of a combination of revenue-raising motives and the protection of the public. The primary example of this is an automobile operator's permit.

The constitutionality of the licensing requirements has been upheld by most courts when the purposes of licensure and the scope of the licensure statutes meet constitutional standards.

Constitutional Basis

State governments are permitted to regulate constitutionally fields of activity that have a direct effect on the public health, welfare, and safety. This power, generally referred to as the state's police power, is the constitutional basis for allowing states to make regulations for the protection of the health and welfare of its citizens, and it forms the basis for the promulgation of rules and the licensing certification of practitioners of psychology. [1]

Legislation in these areas will be sustained if it appears reasonably related to the exercise of such power and is free from discrimination or arbitrariness. [2] Some statutes have been challenged, with varying degrees of success, on the ground that the licensure requirements result in the taking of property without due process of law. [3]

A Florida court struck down the statutory licensure scheme for practitioners of psychology because the licensing board was given entirely too broad discretion in issuing licenses or certificates. [4] For example, the court saw unconstitutionality in the requirement that all applicants must have either a degree of Doctor of Philosophy with a major in psychology, such degree to be conferred by a university approved by the board, or an equivalent degree "in the field of psychology." The board was empowered to determine what would constitute such a degree. In brief, the real basis was that the statutory scheme failed to establish the standards to be applied and, in effect, delegated the application of the statute without sufficient limitations on the discretion of the board.

A New York statute providing for the certification of individuals representing themselves as psychologists was held to be constitutional in that it spelled out, in detail, requirements for certification that appeared to be reasonably related to the public health and welfare. [5]

Scope of Regulations

The licensing of practicing psychologists is not the product of uniform statutory law. Nonetheless, the more recently adopted statutes do seem to have common features. Generally, the act itself is supervised by a board of psychologist examiners. The administrator is ordinarily the commissioner of professional and occupational affairs of the state, which is the same bureau that supervises the licensing and certification of all professions and occupations in the state.

The practice of psychology itself is ordinarily defined. A typical definition is the "holding oneself out to the public by any title or description of services incorporating the words 'psychological,' 'psychologist' or 'psychology' and under such description offers to render to the public for remuneration any of the covered psychological services."[6] A sampling of the services include the application of established principles of learning, motivation, perception, thinking, and emotional relationships to problems of personality evaluation, group relations, and behavior adjustment. The applications of the principles include, but usually are not restricted to counseling and the use of psychological methods with persons or groups with adjustment problems in the areas of work, family, school, and personal relationships. The services also covered include the measuring and testing of personality, intelligence, aptitude, and emotions, and offering services as a psychological consultant.

A typical statute then creates a board of psychologist examiners and requires an applicant who is qualified to take and pass an examination before receiving a certificate of licensure. The basic requirement for qualification is that the applicant be a graduate of an accredited college or university holding a degree of Doctor of Philosophy or a Doctor of Education in Psychology plus two years of postdoctorate experience acceptable to the board. Other statutes additionally allow an applicant to be licensed if he or she is a graduate of an accredited college or university and holds a doctorate degree in a field related to psychology, providing the individual's experience and training are acceptable to the board as being equivalent to two years' postdoctorate experience. In addition, a few states allow the licensing of a graduate of an accredited college or university holding a Master's Degree in Psychology or other behavioral sciences plus four years of experience provided his or her education and experience are acceptable to the board as being equivalent to that of two years' postdoctorate experience. [7]

Sanctions

Most statutes render it unlawful for any person to engage in the practice of psychology, as defined by the statute, or to offer or even attempt to do so, unless the individual is first licensed under the provisions of the act. Violators may usually be punished by fines or imprisonment or may be the subject of an injunction proceeding prohibiting the individual from the unlawful practice of psychology under penalty of the contempt powers of the court to imprison a violator of the prohibitive injunction.

The above is a general description of acceptable statutory licensure schemes, but an individual must consult the particular statute in the state in which he or she intends to practice. Although all but three states and the District of Columbia have statutory licensure or certification schemes, they are not uniform and they are rich in variety and diversity.

C. LEGAL AND ETHICAL INTERFACE

Ethics

Most professional groups maintain professional coherence by the adoption and observation of a body of moral principles or values that govern the conduct of the members of the profession. Thus, the American Medical Association has adopted an extensive code of ethics. The American Bar Association has promulgated a Code of Professional Responsibility articulating canons, ethical considerations, and disciplinary rules for the conduct of lawyers. Most states have adopted the American Bar Association's Code of Professional Responsibility by order of the ultimate appellate court of the state.

While the ethical considerations are rich in diversity, there is a common denominator and that is the requirement of confidentiality. The ethical requirement of confidentiality is imposed upon the profession by the various codes of responsibility, and an overwhelming majority of state jurisdictions compel confidentiality in certain areas by statutory law. In other jurisdictions, and under some circumstances, in the absence of a statute, courts have found an independent constitutional basis for requiring confidentiality and prohibiting disclosure where certain relationships exist.

Confidential Communications Privilege

In virtually every jurisdiction in the United States, communications arising out of or in the course of a relationship between a psychologist and a patient are privileged and inadmissible in judicial or quasi-judicial proceedings. The privilege usually exists only on behalf of the patient, and usually it only applies to confidential communications made during the course of treatment of the patient.[1] A few states have adopted statutes that enlarge the scope of coverage to include all communications between the psychologist and his or her patient. The general purpose of the privilege is to assure the patient that disclosure of intimate details to the psychologist will not be revealed to the rest of the world, thereby aiding treatment by a more complete disclosure of information on the patient's part.[2]

Generally speaking, there was no such privilege recognized at the common law.[3] However, as we have noted before, most states have adopted statutes prohibiting disclosure under certain circumstances. A few states recognize the existence of such a privilege even in the absence of a statute on the basis of either the United States Constitution or the state's constitutional guarantee of the right of privacy.[4] A few jurisdictions have upheld the privilege based upon the American Medical Association's Code of Ethics, Section 9.[5]

In measuring the extent of coverage of the statutory privilege, the courts attempt to reconcile the public policy of discouraging the disclosure of intimate details related by the patient in order to aid in his or her treatment with furthering the administration of justice through the use of all relevant evidence.[6] Thus, a trial judge held a psychologist in contempt for refusing to release records of inpatient treatment of a juvenile delinquent's mother because the trial judge thought such records would be of value in determining a proper disposition of the case. It was thought that if the mother could provide a proper home and supervision for the juvenile, probation into the mother's custody was the appropriate disposition. However, the psychologist chose to exercise what he thought was a statutory right on his part. On appeal to the ultimate appellate court, it was decided that the statute did not cover the psychologist, but the court, nonetheless, concluded that an individual's right to privacy in preventing the disclosure of information revealed in the context of a psychotherapist-patient relationship had deeper roots than the statutory privilege. Thus, the court found a constitutional basis in the Bill of Rights which would entitle the psychologist-patient to refuse to release the confidential records.[7]

In some jurisdictions, by statute, the privilege is limited to protecting communications made in the course of treatment, or in some cases, during diagnosis. As an alternative, other statutes protect communications necessary to enable the psychologist to treat the patient.[8]

Generally, the statutory schemes have in common that the communication must have been made during the course of the professional relationship.[9] Further, the communication must also have been confidential. Conversely, other courts have refused to apply the privilege if disclosure of the information would not embarrass the patient or if the information could have been gained without the benefit of any professional knowledge.[10] Many courts refuse to extend the privilege to marital proceedings involving child custody.[11]

Frequently, statutory schemes limit psychologist-patient privileges. The most common limitation is the so-called patient-litigant exception, which excludes the privilege if the patient puts his or her mental competency or condition in issue. This exception is also invoked if the patient presents evidence of his or her mental condition, such as calling the psychologist as a witness to testify on the patient's behalf.[12]

Criminal proceedings usually occasion another series of statutory exceptions. Some allow disclosure of communications in all criminal proceedings, while others only remove the privilege if the patient raises a defense of insanity.[13] A few statutes specifically provide for disclosure of otherwise confidential communications if they are made to a court-appointed psychologist when the party's mental condition is an issue.[14]

While the statute governs the right to assert the privilege, it generally is only exercisable by the patient and in the patient's interest.[15] A few statutes allow psychologists to assert the privilege also, but never for their own interests.[16] A patient's legal representative, such as a guardian or the representative of a deceased patient, can also assert the privilege, in some statutory schemes, if the interests of the estate and the representative are not adverse.[17] Without such a right, no one can prevent disclosure, no matter how injurious to the patient or others.[18] Of course, like any privilege, it can be waived. An express waiver must be voluntary by the patient, however.[19] The courts usually will allow a deceased party's representative to waive the privilege if the communications are confidential or embarrassing, and unless suicide was involved.[20] Waiver, of course, may be implied if the patient introduces the issue of his or her mental health, claims mental injury, alleges treatment by a psychologist, or claims insanity.[21] If the patient introduces testimony concerning the psychologist-patient communications, the privilege is considered as being waived.[22] Also, if during the course of trial, counsel for the patient fails to object to the psychological evidence, the privilege is waived.[23]

The majority of statutes provide that the privilege can be waived only by the patient or his or her legal representative in most cases. If the patient is incompetent, then the waiver can only be made by his or her committee, guardian ad litem, or other protecting party.[24]

D. MENTAL HEALTH PROCEDURES

The law recognizes that committing mentally ill patients to institutions, either voluntarily or involuntarily, constitutes a substantial deprivation of liberty. At the same time, the courts recognize that families frequently, and sometimes callously, use mental institutions as a dumping ground for mentally ill family members and children.[1] The legislative response to these conditions is the enactment of mental health procedures acts which attempt to avoid the evils and assure individuals that their liberty will not be curtailed without some semblance of due process.

Due Process

The constitutional requirement of due process in the United States does not mandate that the state enact any specific form of proceedings to determine the mental competency of a citizen. However, once the state undertakes to enact a body of law governing mental health procedures, due process requires that the proceedings conform to the enabling statute.[2]

Due process of law basically requires that a person whose sanity is in question be accorded the same protection as a defendant in a criminal proceeding.[3] The subject must receive notice if he or she is to be bound by the adjudication[4] and especially if there is a chance of commitment.[5] Notice consists of the time and place for the hearing, and usually it must be given within a reasonable time before the hearing is to take place in order to enable the subject to seek counsel.[6] Some statutory schemes require that notice be given to at least some of the subject's close relatives as well.[7]

Notice is not constitutionally required if holding the hearing in the subject's presence might be injurious to his or her health, provided that a licensed physician or other professional examines the subject and a relative has the opportunity to contest the proceeding.[8] The notice requirements are not as strict if the subject is already in custody and being represented by legal counsel.[9]

The courts are divided over the issue of the ability to waive the notice requirement. Some say subjects waive their right if they request commitment or the appointment of a guardian.[10] Others say it is waived if the subject[11] or his or her attorney[12] actually appears at the hearing. A few courts maintain that an incompetent can never waive the constitutional right to due process notice.[13]

The second requirement of due process is the right of the subject to have a hearing[14] which, in most cases, is more in the form of an inquisition rather than a trial.[15] However, the subject does have the right to appear at the hearing[16] and to defend herself or himself.[17] He or she has the right to legal counsel,[18] either private[19] or court appointed, if the subject is indigent.[20] The individual may elect to testify on his or her own behalf,[21] but it is not unconstitutional for the petitioner to call the subject as a witness.[22] The subject has the right to produce rebuttal evidence[23] and to examine witnesses,[24] although in practice this is rarely done except in unusual cases.

There is authority, under the common law, for the right of the subject to a jury trial in an insanity proceeding.[25] Since property rights are no longer affected by an insanity adjudication under modern law,[26] due process does not require a jury trial.[27] Thus, it has been held that it is constitutionally permissible for a state to dispense expressly with jury trials in insanity proceedings[28] and to replace them with a commission or hearing officers.[29] Some jurisdictions, however, have extended state constitutional guarantees of trial by jury to insanity proceedings.[30]

If a person is to be committed, the minimum due process requirement is a finding that the subject must be dangerous to himself or herself or others.[31] Again we find state statutes rich in their diversity in the definition of committable mental illness, but these minimum requirements will pass constitutional muster.[32]

The nature and duration of the commitment must, in order to satisfy due process, bear some reasonable relation to the purpose for which the individual is committed. Differing standards apply to persons charged with crimes but not yet tried or convicted. Most statutory schemes compel a disposition where commitment is indicated in the least restrictive facility consistent with the subject's condition.[33]

Equal Protection

The focus of the equal protection analysis in mental health procedures centers on the rights afforded a person charged with a crime versus civil insanity proceedings. The general rule is that a criminal defendant whose sanity is in question, even if charges have merely been filed,[34] must be given the same procedural safeguards guaranteed to noncriminals.[35] Such safeguards include proper examination by a licensed professional, a hearing upon notice, periodic review of the need for continued commitment, and trial by jury, if allowed in that jurisdiction.[36] The same requirements must be expended for criminals who may be civilly committed at the expiration of their penal sentence.[37]

It has been held to be a denial of the United States constitutional requirement of equal protection to commit a criminal defendant on an insanity finding based on a different standard than a civilly committed person.[38] However, it is not unconstitutional to deny a jury trial in civil commitment proceedings, and allow one in criminal commitments,[39] since there is no fundamental right to such a trial in the former case.[40]

Commitment Proceedings

A commitment hearing is a judicial proceeding that is civil in nature.[41] Jurisdiction is determined by statute, and can be conferred on special courts[42] or on a county insanity board.[43] In the absence of any designation, the local court of equity has jurisdiction over incompetents.[44]

Ordinarily, an action for commitment is commenced by petition or complaint filed by a relative, friend, guardian, jail warden, or any other person, even by the individual.[45] Notice of the commitment hearing is generally a constitutional requirement, as we noted herein.[46] Before commitment, the subject is, of course, entitled to all procedural due process rights described here before.

A commitment that fails to comply with the statutory or constitutional requirements is illegal, and any restraint thereunder is void.[47] Individuals who have been wrongfully committed may seek to be discharged, provided they are sane when they seek their remedy.[48] Furthermore, they may be entitled to bring a tort action for malicious prosecution,[49] false imprisonment,[50] or for a remedy under the Federal Civil Rights Act.[51]

E. GENERAL LAW AFFECTING THE PRACTICE OF PSYCHOLOGY

For our purposes, law can be generally considered in two categories, contract and tort. Contract law has no particular significance to practicing psychologists, for it is basically the same law applicable to all citizens. Practitioners will be faced with the law of sales with respect to purchasing office equipment and supplies. Psychologists must be familiar with employment laws for they are bound, as any other employer, by the vast body of laws governing employees' rights, statutory duties imposed upon all employers with respect to unemployment compensation, withholding tax duties, and a vast variety of other regulatory employment statutes.

Of course, a practicing psychologist must be familiar with the licensure procedures in the jurisdiction in which he or she intends to practice. A few states are experimenting with the concept of maintaining professional competency, and there is much to be said in favor of these innovations, even though professional resistance is strong.

Particular attention must, of course, be given to the matter of fees and fee structures. Oral agreements with respect to fees are, of course, enforceable. However, in the absence of an oral or written agreement concerning the fee arrangement between psychologist and client, he is entitled to recover only the reasonable, prevailing fee for the services rendered. Since this frequently entails unwanted litigation, a practitioner would be well counseled to always have a fee understanding with the patient before undertaking any professional services.

Of considerably more interest and concern to practicing psychologists is the area of tort liability. Whenever an individual has been injured or damaged as a result of the conduct of another, the law allows a remedy to the injured party. The object of the law is to restore the injured party to his or her original condition and ordinarily the only way that can be accomplished is by the award and payment of money damages. Certain types of liability insurance are available to practitioners to protect against financial loss when it is determined that the practitioner is liable for money damages to a patient. Statutes in some states require a practitioner to purchase and maintain liability insurance in schemes that are somewhat analogous to those involving persons seeking licenses to operate motor vehicles.

Negligence — Malpractice

Perhaps there is no word in the English language that engenders more fear among professionals than the term *malpractice*. While it is most frequently thought of in association with medical doctors, in law it extends to lawyers themselves, nurses, hospitals, beauticians, teachers, and any other professional. However the term is understood by laymen, malpractice is nothing more than a particular form of negligence resulting in damages to another.

When we speak of malpractice, we are talking of a form of negligence that consists of not applying the degree of care and skill by a professional[1] which the profession in general ordinarily employs under similar circumstances.[2] Although it is generally stated that malpractice arises because of negligence,[3] it is not necessarily limited to acts of negligence.[4] Malpractice may result from the lack of skill or neglect to apply possessed skill,[5] or from willful, negligent or ignorant practices.[6]

Psychiatrists, doctors treating mental illnesses, and the directors of mental hospitals have been held liable in various ways that can be similarly applied to practicing psychologists. One way is through a failure to advise the patient of any dangers that may result from a course of treatment,[7] unless such disclosure could prove harmful to the patient.[8] The corollary to this phase of litigation is the doctrine of informed consent. The guiding principles are that when a patient is mentally and physically able to consult about his or her condition, in the absence of an emergency, the consent of the patient is a prerequisite to treatment and it is necessary that the patient be advised of alternate methods of treatment available and the inherent dangers and possibilities of success of such alternatives. The philosophy behind the theory of informed consent is that patients have the right and responsibility to determine whether they want to risk the suggested course of treatment. If a patient's decision is to be a knowing and intelligent one, he or she must understand the risks involved.[9]

Another application of the negligence of malpractice concept of tort liability involves the commitment proceedings. While some courts have accorded a privilege to psychiatrists and doctors in such actions,[10] other courts do not recognize the immunity and apply the usual standard of care to a psychiatrist, psychologist, or physician certifying insanity.[11] Courts have not hesitated to find malpractice when a psychiatrist prematurely discharges a hospitalized mental patient.[12] Lately, courts have also been inclined to find malpractice when a psychotherapist becomes involved with "social" treatment rather than professional treatment.[13] Thus, in *"Chapman" v. McCabe*, (U.S. District Court, E.d. Pa., No. 76-342, Sept. 16, 1977), a malpractice in the amount of six hundred sixty-five thousand dollars ($665,000) was awarded against an osteopath, who had no formal psychiatric training, who undertook to treat a female patient by having sexual relations with her during office sessions in order to "fill her emptiness."

It should be noted that the liability for malpractice lies in a tort action, even though the relationship of the parties is a contractual one. This arises out of the nature of the physician-patient relationship.[14] Thus, it has been held to be irrelevant that the treatment or services were rendered gratuitously or at the request of a third party.[15]

There can be no liability unless the plaintiff establishes a duty on the part of the defendant owing to the person treated.[16] The common law rule is that a medical practitioner is liable for injury to a patient resulting from the practitioner's want of requisite knowledge and skill, the omission of reasonable care and diligence, or the failure to exercise his or her best judgment.[17]

With regard to the standard of care, it has been defined as that of reasonable and ordinary care, skill, and diligence as physicians or psychologists in good standing in the same neighborhood, in the same general line of practice, ordinarily have and exercise in like cases.[18] This standard is not the average merit among the range of worst to best practitioners, but the reasonable average skill among ordinarily good ones.[19] In this regard, malpractice differs from ordinary negligence since that standard of care applies to ordinary, reasonable, prudent men and women and not to professional proficiency.

The standard is somewhat more flexible than it seems at first, since other factors are taken into account to determine if the practitioner has performed with the requisite ability, skill, and care. These factors include the principles of the particular school of practice,[20] the stage of the field's knowledge and science at the time of treatment,[21] custom and usage,[22] and the locality or place of practice.[23] A recent Arizona Court of Appeals case indicates a trend to recognize that a national standard of care may exist for doctors treating traumatic injuries. It would seem logical that where there exists a minimum national standard of care in any given profession, the locality rule should be abandoned and the national standard applied.[24]

Additionally, in order to recover for malpractice, the plaintiff must establish a causal or proximate connection between the practitioner's want of skill or care and the injury giving rise to the action.[25] A mere lack of skill or care on the practitioner's part will not result in liability, even for nominal damages, if there is no injury to the plaintiff.[26] Nor is a practitioner liable for a lack of success or poor result of the treatment, or even for injurious consequences, unless the plaintiff can show the requisite want of due care or skill.[27]

The doctrine of res ipsa loquitur or, in other words, strict or absolute liability, does not apply in malpractice cases, including those involving treatment of mental diseases. In plain words, a practitioner is not an insurer of the desired result.[28]

The practitioner may have a defense to a malpractice suit if the patient was contributorily negligent or assumed the risk.[29] Negligence on the patient's part is not a bar to recovery if the negligence did not contribute proximately to the injury caused by the defendant's malpractice.[30] It appears that a patient's refusal to submit to treatment suggested by the defendant does not constitute an assumption of the risk that such refusal might ultimately result in greater injury to the patient than would otherwise be occasioned because of the defendant's malpractice.[31]

In brief, the injury must be foreseeable and avoidable by the exercise of reasonable and ordinary care that psychologists in good standing in the community would ordinarily possess. Generally, a psychologist is not required to foresee that the patient will be negligent and proximately contribute to the undesired result.

Ordinarily, plaintiffs can only recover compensation to reimburse them for the usual and ordinary pecuniary losses.[32] A defendant is only liable for his or her malpractice, and not the original illness or problem, nor for any aggravation of the injury by others.[33]

Defamation

As a general rule of law, imputations of insanity or impaired mental faculties,[34] of intellectual weaknesses,[35] or of mental retardation[36] are held to be defamatory per se and actionable without proof of any special damages when published of a private person.[37] Oral imputations of such mental disease or mental illness are called slander and are usually actionable without proof of special damage if spoken with reference to the person's business, employment, occupation, office, or profession.[38] However, for statements made about "public figures," a plaintiff must prove actual malice in uttering the falsities on the defendant's part in order to recover damages.[39]

Such statements by physicians or professionals in related fields, such as psychologists,[40] are generally considered to be privileged and, thus, nonactionable, although the existence of the privilege is determined by the general rules of defamation actions.[41] The privileged communication or statement is one which, except for the occasion on which or the circumstances under which it is made, would be defamatory and actionable.[42] In analyzing a psychologist's liability, it must first be decided if the publication is privileged. If it is not, then liability for defamation is determined in the same manner as that of any other person.[43] Even if the communication is not privileged, a psychologist may have other defenses to the defamatory communication, such as consent[44] on the patient's part or the truth of the statement.[45]

Another problem that arises in this area is the psychologist's liability for disclosure of professional communications made by a patient to him or her and which are protected by the psychologist-patient confidential privilege referred to above. Such an action could be based on either the breach of the psychologist-patient relationship or a defamation action.[46] Whichever course is pursued, the courts have said that the responsibility of the doctor to keep confidences may be outweighed by a higher duty to give out information which, even though defamatory, is of sufficiently important interest to protect disclosure.[47] In essence, a breach of psychologist-patient privilege against disclosure of confidential communications may be accorded a qualified privilege against liability for defamation.[48]

Thus, a qualified privilege is granted to communications that are made, in good faith, on any subject matter in which the person communicating has an interest or a duty to a person having a corresponding interest or a duty.[49] The essential elements are good faith, an interest to be upheld, a statement limited in its scope to this interest, a proper occasion, and publication in a proper manner and to proper parties only.[50] In the absence of proof of actual malice or ill-will, a plaintiff cannot recover damages if the statement is protected by a qualified privilege.[51]

The rules regarding qualified privilege have been held to apply to medical practitioners employed privately[52] and to those employed by state schools[53]

or mental hospitals,[54] including psychologists.[55] The defamatory statements of a physician employed to report on the fitness of an employee or
applicant for employment have been held to be conditionally privileged
also.[56] This would seem to be applicable to psychologists making similar
psychological evaluations of employees for a common employer.

It must be noted that defamatory statements made in compelled testimony, pleadings, interrogatories, or other judicial proceedings are absolutely privileged if material to the inquiry and are not impertinent or scan-
dalous, as such.[57] Malice is irrelevant to absolute privilege, in effect making
a civil remedy nearly impossible.[58] To make the defense of absolute privilege
available, the statement must be made on privilege occasion,[59] which for a
psychologist will probably be in connection with an allegation of mental
disorder in an affidavit, certificate, or testimony.

Some courts have granted the protection of absolute privilege to statements made in lunacy[60] or commitment proceedings,[61] and to judicial proceedings, such as affidavits,[62] testimony,[63] and workmen's compensation
hearings.[64] There is an absolute privilege for reports of public officers to
their superiors, such as an examination report of an inmate to the head of
the prison.[65] Similarly, there is an absolute privilege for communications
from one psychologist to another or from one physician to another if necessary and pertinent to the treatment being rendered.[66]

False Imprisonment

A person is liable for damages resulting from false imprisonment for
conduct in connection with insanity proceedings if it appears that he was
causally responsible for the unlawful arrest or confinement of the plaintiff
and if the person cannot claim immunity.[67] While liability for false imprisonment, in most sanity proceedings, is barred if the detention or commitment was executed in a lawful manner[68] or in accordance with statutory
mental health commitment proceeding acts, most physicians who are involved in them are usually held not liable on the basis that they were privileged or immune from such liability.[69]

Two theories in support of immunity from false imprisonment are advanced. One is that since court-appointed physicians are, in effect, judicial
officers, they are entitled to the protection of judicial immunity for any
involvement they may have.[70] Another theory is that physicians are expert
witnesses and are thus immune on the theory of absolute privilege for testimony relevant to judicial inquiry.[71]

There have been reported cases of physicians being held liable for false
imprisonment when they failed to examine the patient but gave evidence as
to the patient's insanity anyway.[72] Liability can still be imposed on physicians even if the entire proceedings were void, if the physician never, in fact,
examined the patient.[73] An interview with others, even family, has been
considered by some courts as no examination at all and can result in liabil-

ity.[74] Furthermore, reliance on previous examinations by other professionals may affect liability.[75]

There is usually no liability for false imprisonment if the examination was merely inadequate or erroneous.[76] This principle has been applied in circumstances where, although there was no real examination, it was determined to be the best possible evaluation under the circumstances,[77] and even where the examination was superficial[78] or negligent.[79] In other cases, the courts have overlooked erroneous or inadequate examinations if the doctor was unbiased[80] or only involved as a witness in the commitment proceedings.[81]

Emotional Distress

The term *emotional distress* really covers two different concepts. Emotional distress can be the basis of a tort action in itself; it can also be viewed as an element of damages in an action based on a breach of duty one person owes another.

As a general rule of law, there is no liability for an action based on negligence where the resulting damage is merely mental or emotional disturbance.[82] This rule generally applies where there is no bodily impact,[83] although some jurisdictions have departed from the impact rule.[84] Thus, where no resulting injury to the person or the body of the plaintiff occurs, in those jurisdictions embracing the impact rule, there can be no recovery.[85] The majority of courts have allowed recovery for emotional distress in the absence of physical injury where the defendant visited it intentionally or where the wrongful act was willful, wanton, or malicious.[86] Some courts require insult, abuse, inhumanity, or extreme or outrageous conduct resulting in "severe emotional distress."[87]

Perhaps of more concern to the practicing psychologist is emotional distress as an element of damages. In some instances, a plaintiff who is suing for a breach of some right, other than the interest in emotional tranquility, may recover for mental distress resulting from that breach. Examples of this are mental distress flowing from trespass to real estate, intentional trespass to personal property, and breaches of contract where such damage was within the contemplation of the parties or the breach results in damage or personal injury.[88] Damages for mental anguish have been awarded where a physician breached a contract for medical services which resulted in physical injury to the plaintiff.[89] In an action for personal injuries, the plaintiff may recover from mental anguish that accompanies such injury.[90]

Awards for mental distress may include compensation for insult, indignity, and humiliation.[91] However, such awards are usually based upon a wrongful act causing mental distress when the act was performed intentionally, maliciously, or wantonly.[92] Courts generally have not allowed recovery for emotional distress where it was alleged that the injury arose from a physician's willful or negligent making of a wrong diagnosis, wrong treatment, or unspecified error.[93] Some courts have allowed recovery, however, where the physician breached a contract for services,[94] including delay in rendering treatment and failure to perform a specific treatment.[95]

NOTES

A.

1. S. Glueck, *Law and Psychiatry: Cold War or Entente Cordiale?* (Baltimore: Johns Hopkins University Press, 1962).

2. *Commonwealth v. Walzack*, 468 Pa. 210 (1976).

3. *Mayle v. Pennsylvania Department of Highways*, Pa. Supreme, 388 A.2d 709 (1978).

4. Pennsylvania Rules of Criminal Procedures, Rule 1403 Aids in Imposing Sentence, "B" Psychiatric or Diagnostic Examinations.

5. Judicature, September 1978: *Furhman v. Georgia*, 408 U.S. 238 (1972); *Smith v. Organization of Foster Families*, 53 L.ed 2d 25.

6. *Towne v. Eisner*, 245 U.S. 418 (1918).

7. *Dusky v. U.S.*, 271 F.2d 385 (C.A. Mo.); *People v. Nash*, 338 P.2d 416, 52 C.2d 36; *Castro v. People*, 346 P.2d 1020.

8. *Leland v. State of Oregon*, 72 S.Ct. 1002, 343 U.S. 790, 96 L.Ed. 1302.

9. *Spurlock v. State*, 368 S.W.2d 299, 212 Ten. 132; *State v. Hairston*, 23 S.E.2d 385, 222 N.C. 455.

10. *U.S. v. Trujillo*, 497 F.2d 408 (C.A.N.M.).

11. *State v. Podilla*, 347 P.2d 312, 66 N.M. 289; *Battalino v. People*, 199 P.2d 897, 118 Colo. 587.

12. *U.S. v. Ettorre*, 387 F. Supp. 582 (D.C. Pa.); *People v. Luther* 232 N.W.2d 184, 394 Mich. 619.

13. *People v. Drew*, C.A. Supreme Ct. Vol. 47 U.S. Law Week p. 2249.

14. *In re Guardianship of Hyde*, 176 N.W.2d 234, 185 Neb. 428; *In re Cass' Guardianship*, 54 N.W.2d 68, 155 Neb. 792; *In re Guardianship of Bogan*, 441 P.2d 972; Doll v. Doll 156 So.2d 275.

15. *Taylor v. U.S.*, 113 F. Supp. 143 (D.C. Ark.); *In re Lingenfleter's Estate*, 241 P.2d 990, 38 Cal. 2d 571; *Wallhauser v. Rummel*, 96 A.2d 289, 25 N.J. Super. 358.

16. *Callaway v. Blankenbaker*, 141 S.W.2d 810, 346 Mo. 383; *In re Behrend's Will*, 290 N.W. 78, 227 Iowa 1099.

17. *U.S. v. Yviyak*, 392 F. Supp. 532 (D.C. N.Y.); *In re L.L.*, 144 Cal. Rptr. 11, 39 C.A. 3d 205.

18. Pennsylvania Mental Health Procedures Act, 1976, P.L. 817, No. 143 (50 P.S. Sec.7502).

19. *Shelton v. Shelton*, 74 S.E.2d 5, 209 Ga. 454; *Savre v. Savre*, 42 N.W.2d 642, 77 N.D. 242.

20. *Finklestein v. Finklestein*, 198 P.2d 98, 88 C.A.2d 4; *Jacobs v. Jacobs*, 76 A.2d 742, 6 Terry (Del.) 544.

21. *Dodrer v. Dodrer*, 37 A.2d 919, 183 Md. 413.

22. *Del la Montanya v. De la Montanya*, 281 P. 825, 131 Or. 23; *Ertel v. Ertel*, 40 N.E.2d 85, 313 Ill. App. 326.

23. *Commonwealth v. Haskell*, 2 Brewst. (Pa.) 496; *In re Anderson*, 132 N.C. 243, 40 S.E. 649.

24. *Smith v. Hickenbottom*, 57 Iowa 733, 11 N.W. 644, 667.

25. *In re Vanauken*, 10 N.J. Eq. 186, 195.

26. *Matter of Gannon*, 21 N.Y.S. 960, 2 Misc. 329, 333, affd. 35 N.E. 207, 139 N.Y. 654; *Dibble v. Currier*, 83 S.E. 949, 950, 142 Ga. 855, Ann. Cas. 1916C1; *Rush v. Megee*, 36 Ind. 69, 80; *Davis v. Denny*, 50 A. 1037, 94 Md. 390, 393.

B.

1. 82 C.J.S. Statutes S9 et seq.

2. 81 A.L.R, 2d 791.

3. 53 C.J.S. Licenses, Sec.17.

4. *Husband v. Cassel*, (1961, Fla.) 130 So.2d 69.

5. *National Psychological Association v. University of New York*, S. N.Y.2d 197, app. dismd. 365 U.S. 298.

6. Pennsylvania Act of 1972, March 23, P.L. 136 No. 52 Sec. 2.

7. Id. Sec.6.

C.

1. 44 A.L.R.3d 24, 41-46, Sec. 3 (b-g).

2. 44 A.L.R.3d 24, 41, Sec. 3(b); *Taylor v. U.S.* 95, App. D.C. 373, 222 F.2d 398 (1955). *McCormick on Evidence*, Second Edition (West Publishing Co., St. Paul), P. 213, N.9.

3. *Franklin v. State*, 8 Md.App. 134, 258 A.2d 767 (1969); *Ritt v. Ritt*, 98 N.J. Super. 590, 238 A.2d 196 (1967) reversed 52 N.J. 177, 244 A.2d, 497; *State v. Genna*, 163 La. 701, 112 So. 655, cert. denied 275 U.S. 522, 72 L.Ed. 405, 48 S. Ct. 22 (167).

4. *State v. Evans*, 104 Ariz. 434, 454 P.2d 976 (1969); *Binxer v. Ruvell*, Civ. Docket No. 52-3-25-35, Cir. Ct. Cook County, Ill. (1952).

5. *Ritt v. Ritt*, 98 N.J. Super. 590, 238 A.2d 196 (1967), reversed 52 N.J. 177, 244 A.2d 497; *Re: Cathey*, 55 Cal. 2d. 679, 12 Cal. Rptr. 762, 361 P.2d 426 (1961).

6. 44 A.L.R. 3d. 24, 34-35, Sec. 2(a), 46-47, Sec. 4(a).

7. *In re: "B", Appeal of Dr. Loren Roth*, Pa. Supreme Ct., No. 150 March Term 1977 (10/5/78).

8. 44 A.L.R. 3d 47, Sec. 4(b).

9. *Bogan v. Arkansas First National Bank*, 249 Ark. 840, 462 S.W.2d. 203 (1971); *State v. Jensen*, 286 Minn. 65, 174 N.W.2d. 226 (1970); *Kendall v. Gore Properties, Inc.*, 98 App. D.C. 378, 236 F.2d 673 (1956); *Mulvena v. Alexander*, 278 Mich. 265, 270 N.W. 291 (1936).

10. *Koonce v. State*, Okla. Crim., 456 P.2d 549 (1968); *Milans v. State*, 44 Misc. 2d. 290, 253 N.Y.S. 2d 662 (1964); *Price v. Price*, Mo. App., 311 S.W. 2d 341 (1958); *State v. Murphy*, 205 Iowa 1130, 217 N.W. 225 (1928).

11. *D. V. D.*, 108 N.J. Super. 149, 260 A.2d 255 (1969); *Baker v. Baker*, 92 Idaho 204, 440 P.2d 137 (1968).

12. *Bremer v. State*, 18 Md. App. 291, 307 A.2d 503 (1973); *People v. Goldbach*, 27 Cal. App. 3d. 563, 103 Cal. Rptr. 800 (1972); *Re: Lifschutz*, 2 Cal. 3d. 415, 85 Cal. Rptr. 829, 467 P.2d 557 (1970); *Eder v. Caslin*, 281 App. Div. 456, 120 N.Y.S. 2d 165 (1953); *Ballard v. Pacific Greyhound Lines*, 28 Cal. 2d 357, 170 P.2d 465 (1970).

13. *People v. Sigal*, 235 Cal. App. 2d 449, 45 Cal. Rptr. 481 (1965); *People v. Butly*, 38 App. Div. 2d 10, 326 N.Y.S. 2d 512; *Edmonds v. U.S.*, 104 App. D.C. 144, 260 F.2d 474 (1958); *People v. Hopkins*, 44 Cal. App. 3d. 699, 119 Cal. Rptr. 61 (1975); *People v. Goldbach*, 27 Cal App. 3d. 563, 103 Cal. Rptr. 800 (1972); *U.S. v. Carr*, 141 App. D.C. 229, 437 F.2d 662 (1970), cert. denied, 401 U.S. 920, 27 L.Ed. 823, 91 S. Ct. 907; *Catoe v. U.S.*, 76 App. D.C.292, 131 F.2d 16 (1942).

14. *Mastromino v. Director, Patuxent Institution*, 243 Md. 704, 221 A.2d. 910 (1966); *People v. Spencer*, 60 Cal. 2d 64, 31 Cal. Rptr. 782, 383, p.2d 134, cert. denied 377 U.S. 1007, 12 L.Ed. 2d 1055, 84 S. Ct. 1294 (1963).

15. *Wills v. Wills*, 215 Ga. 556, 111 S.E. 2d. 355 (1959); *Re: Warrington*, 303 N.Y. 129, 100 N.E. 2d 170 (1951).

16. *Re: Lifschutz*, 2 Cal. 3d 415, 85 Cal. Rptr. 829, 467 P.2d 557 (1970); *Felber v. Foote*, 321 F. Supp. 85 (D.C. Conn., 1970).

17. *Kendall v. Gore Properties*, 98 App. D.C. 378, 236 F.2d 673 (1956); *Kinbacker v. Schneider*, 194 Mis. 969, 89 N.Y.S. 2d. 350 (1949); *Hill v. Farmers Mutual Farm Insurance Co.*, 104 Mont. 471, 67 P.2d 831 (1937).

18. *Hampton v. Hampton*, 241 Or. 277, 405 P.2d 549 (1965); *State v. Case*, 253 N.C. 130, 116 S.E. 2d. 429 (1960), cert. denied, 365 U.S. 830, 5 L.Ed.2d. 707, 81 S.Ct. 717.

19. *Newell v. Newell*, 146 Cal. App. 2d. 166, 303 P.2d 839 (1956); *Re: Application of Tanharm*, 1 Misc. 2d. 264, 144 N.Y.S. 2d 401 (1955); *Roberts v. Superior Court of Butte Co.*, 9 Cal. 3d 330, 107 Cal. Rptr. 309, 408 P.2d 308 (1973).

20. *Tinney v. Neilson's Flowers, Inc.*, 61 Misc. 2d 717, 305 N.Y.S. 2d. 712 (1969), affirmed 35 App. Div. 2d. 532, 314 N.Y.S. 2d. 161; *Eder v. Caslin*, 281 App. Div. 456, 120 N.Y.S. 2d. 165 (1953); *Stiles v. Clifton Springs Sanitorium Co.*, 74 F. Supp. 907 (D.C. N.Y., 1947).

21. *Butler v. State, Miss.*, 245 So.2d 605 (1971); *People v. Givans*, 83 Ill. App. 2d. 423, 223 N.E.2d. 123 (1967); *Harter v. State*, 260 Iowa 605, 149 N.W.2d. 827 (1967); *Davis v. State*, 246 Ark. 838, 440 S.W.2d 244 (1969); cert. denied 403 U.S. 954, 29 L.Ed. 2d 865, 91 S.Ct. 2273; *Fahey v. U.S.*, 18 FRD. 231 (D.C. N.Y., 1955); *Mancinelli v. Texas Eastern Transmission Corp.*, 34 App. Div. 2d 535, 308 N.Y.S. 2d. 882 (1970); *Neese v. Neese*, 1 N.C. App. 426, 161 S.E. 2d. 841 (1968); *State v. Swinburne*, Mo., 324 S.W.2d 746 (1959); *State v. Cochran*, 356 Mo. 778, 203 S.W. 2d. 707 (1947).

22. *Davis v. Davis*, 1 App. Div. 2d 675, 146 N.Y.S. 2d 630 (1955); *Hardman v. State*, 89 Okla. Crim. 160, 205 P.2d 1175 (1949).

23. *State v. Vennard*, 159 Conn. 385, 270 A.2d 837 (1970) cert. denied 400 U.S. 1011, 27 L.Ed. 2d, 625, 91 S.Ct. 576; *Harter v. State*, 260 Iowa 605, 149 N.W. 2d. 827 (1967).

24. *Gaertner v. State*, 24 Mich. App. 503, 180 N.W.2d. 308 (1970), affirmed 385 Mich. 49, 187 N.W.2d, 429; *Kendall v. Gore Properties Inc.*, 98 App. D.C. 378, 236 F.2d. 673 (1956); *Kossar v. State*, 13 Mis. 2d 941, 179 N.Y.S. 2d. 71.

D.

1. *Goldy v. Beal*, Civil Action 75-791, M.D. Pa. 1976.

2. *Simon v. Kraft*, 182 U.S. 427, 45 L.Ed. 1165, 21 S.Ct. 836 (1900); *Colby v. Jackson*, 12 N.H. 526; *Appeal of Meurer*, 119 Pa. 115, 12 A. 868 (1888); *Re: Keene*,

Fla App. D.4, 343 So. 2d 916 (1977); *In Re: Helman*, 288 F.2d 159, 109 U.S. App. D.C. 375 (1961).

3. *Bartley v. Kremens*, 402 F. Supp. 1039 (D.C. Pa., 1975); *Lynch v. Baxley*, 386 F. Supp. 378 (D.C. Ala., 1974).

4. *Re: Moyhihan*, 332 Mo. 1022, 625 W.2d 410 (1933); *Re: Gannon*, 16 R.I. 537, 18 A. 159; *Re: Lambert*, 134 Cal. 626, 66 P. 851 (1901).

5. *Mass v. State*, Tex. Civ. App., 539 S.W. 2d. 936 (1976); *Doremus v. Farrell*, 407 F. Supp. 509 (D.C. Neb., 1975), *Trapnell v. Smith*, 131 Ga. App. 254, 205 S.E. 2d 875 (1974).

6. *Rehrer v. Weeks*, Fla. App. 106 So. 2d 865 (1958), *McGee v. Hayes*, 127 Cal. 336, 59 P. 767 (1899); *Behrensmeyer v. Kreitz*, 135 Ill. 591, 26 N.E. 704 (1891).

7. *In Re: Giandomenico*, 70 Pa. D. & C. 278 (C.P. Phila Co., 1950); *Re: Brookes Estate*, 24 Pa. Super. 430 (1904); *Evans v. Johnson*, 39 W. Va. 299, 19 S.E. 623 (1894).

8. *Arthurs v. Johnson*, Ky., 280 S.W.2d 504 (1955); *Chavannes v. Priestley*, 80 Iowa 316, 45 N.W. 766 (1890).

9. *State ex rel. Bevan v. Williams*, 316 Mo. 665, 291 S.W. 481 (1927).

10. *Clinton v. Twin State Oil Co.*, 34 F.2d 948 (D.C. Okla., 1929).

11. *Cook v. Dougherty*, 32 F. 2d 839, 59 App. D.C. 39 (1929); *Story v. Story*, 200 S.W.2d 146, 304 Ky. 100 (1947); *Martin v. Motsinger*, 130 Ind. 555, 30 N.E. 523 (1892); *Crow v. Meyersieck*, 88 Mo. 411.

12. *Martin v. Motsinger*, 130 Ind. 555, 30 N.E. 523 (1892); *Re: Vanuken*, 10 N.J. Eq. 186.

13. *Snyder v. Superior Court in and for San Diego County*, 206 Cal. 346, 274 P. 337; *State ex rel. Terry v. Holtkamp*, 330 Mo. 608, 51 S.W. 2d 13; *Re: Winnet*, 112 Okla. 43, 239 P. 603; *Bootman's National Bank v. Wurdeman*, 344 Mo. 573, 127 S.W. 2d. 438.

14. *Lynch v. Baxley*, 386 F. Supp. 378 (D.C. Ala., 1974); *Stamus v. Leonhardt*, 414 F. Supp. 439 (D.C. Iowa, 1976).

15. *Johnson v. Nelms*, 171 Tenn. 54, 100 S.W. 2d 921; *In Re: Dunn*, 239 N.C. 378, 79 S.E. 2d. 921; *State v. Linderholm*, 84 Kan. 603, 114 P. 857.

16. *Stamus v. Leonhardt*, 414 F. Supp. 439 (D.C. Iowa, 1976); *Greene v. State*, Tex. Civ. App. 537 S.W. 2d 100.

17. *State ex rel. Anderson v. U.S. Veterans Hospital*, 268 Minn. 213, 128 N.W.2d 710 (1964); *Re: Lambert*, 134 Cal. 626, 66 P. 851 (1901); *Glasco v. Brassard*, 94 Idaho 162, 483 P.2d 924.

18. *Heyford v. Parker*, 396 F.2d 393 C.A. Wyo., (1968); *Re: Beverly*, Fla., 342 So.2d. 481.

19. *Matter of Calcione*, Misc. 378 N.Y.S. 2d 581.

20. *Minnesota ex rel. Anderson v. Probate Ct.*, 309 U.S. 270, 84 L.Ed. 744, 60 S. Ct. 523 (1940); *Blevins v. Cook*, 66 N.M. 381, 348 P.2d 742.

21. *Re: Slamey*, 77 Ohio L. Abs. 189, 146 N.E.2d 466 (1957); *Re: Waite's Guardianship*, 14 Cal. 2d 727, 97 P.2d 238; *Ryman's Case*, 139 Pa. Super. 212, 11 A.2d. 677 (1940).

22. *People ex rel. Keith v. Keith*, 38 Ill. 2d. 405, 231 N.E.2d 387; *Re: Coburn* 165 Cal. 202, 131 P. 352; *Cogan v. Cogan*, 202 Mass. 58, 88 N.E. 662.

23. *State v. Dickman*, 175 Mo. App. 543, 157 S.W. 1012.

24. *State ex rel. Anderson v. U.S. Veterans Hospital,* 268 Minn. 213, 128 N.W.2d 710 (1964); *Whealton v. Whealton,* Fla. App., 184 So.2d. 228.

25. *Phillips v. Moore,* 100 U.S. 208, 25 L.Ed. 603 (1879); *Shumway v. Shumway,* 2 Vt. 339; 50 C.J.S. Juries. Sec. 68.

26. *Reynolds v. Reynolds,* 181 Tenn. 206, 180 S.W.2d, 894; *Re: Lemack's Estate,* 207 S.C. 137, 35 S.E. 2d, 34; *Smith v. Smith,* 254 Ala. 404, 48 So.2d 546; *Hughes v. Jones,* 116 N.Y. 67, 20 N.E. 446.

27. *Montana Co. v. St. Louis Mining and Mill Co.,* 152 U.S. 160, 38 L.Ed. 398, 14 S.Ct. 506 (1894); *Ward v. Booth,* 197 F.2d 963 (C.A. Hawaii, 1952), *Application of Garland,* 286 App. Div. 704, 146 N.Y.S. 2d 830; *People v. Studdard* 51 Ill. 2d. 190, 281 N.E.2d. 678.

28. *Re: Perham,* 104 N.H. 276, 184 A.2d 449.

29. *Commonwealth v. Bruno,* 435 Pa. 200, 255 A.2d 519 (1969), cert. granted 398 U.S. 937, 26 L.Ed. 2d 268, 90 S.Ct. 1847, cert. dismissed, 400 U.S. 350, 27 L.Ed. 2d. 433, 91 S.Ct. 479; *White v. White,* 108 Tex. 570, 196 S.W. 508, mod., Tex. Civil App., 183 S.W. 369.

30. *State v. Walker,* 13 Wash. App. 545, 536 P.2d 657; *DeHart v. Condit,* 51 N.J. Eq. 611, 28 A.603.

31. *Doremus v. Farrell,* 407 F. Supp. 509 (D.C. Neb., 1975); *O'Connor v. Donaldson,* 422 U.S. 563, 45 L.Ed.2d. 396, 95 S.Ct. 2486 (1974), on remand, 519 F.2d. 59 (C.A. Fla., 1975).

32. *In Re: Rogers,* 19 Cal.3d. 655, 139 Cal. Rptr. 861, 566 P.2d 997.

33. Pennsylvania Mental Health Procedures Act, 1976, P.L. 811, No. 143.

34. *Jackson v. Indiana,* 406 U.S. 715, 32 L.Ed.2d. 435, 92 S.Ct. 1845 (1971).

35. *U.S. ex rel Schuster v. Herold,* 410 F.2d 1071 (C.A. N.Y., 1969), cert. denied 396 U.S. 847, 24 L.Ed.2d. 96, 90 S.Ct. 81; *Baxstrom v. Herold,* 383 U.S. 107, 15 L.Ed.2d. 620, 86 S.Ct. 760 (1965).

36. Ibid.; Section on Due Process, supra.

37. *Baxstrom v. Herold,* 383 U.S. 107, 15 L.Ed.2d. 620, 86 S.Ct. 760 (1965).

38. *Jackson v. Indiana,* 406 U.S. 715, 32 L.Ed.2d. 435, 92 S.Ct. 1845 (1971).

39. *Re: Jones,* Fla., 339 So.2d 1117.

40. *State ex rel. Anderson v. U.S. Veterans Hospital,* 268 Minn. 213, 128 N.W.2d 710 (1964); *People ex rel. Keith v. Keith,* 38 Ill. 2d. 405, 231 N.E. 2d. 387.

41. *Davey v. Owen,* 133 Ohio St. 96, 12 N.E.2d 144 (1937).

42. *Application of MacCurdy,* 51 N.Y.S. 2d 673, 268 App. Div. 954; *Bean v. Los Angeles County,* 60 Cal. Rptr. 804, 252 C.A. 2d.754; *State ex rel. Rickey v. Superior Ct, for King Co.,* 59 Wash. 2d. 872, 371 P.2d 51; *Clark v. State ex rel. Rubin,* Fla. App., 122 So. 2d. 809.

43. *Prochaska v. Brinegar,* 251 Iowa 834, 102 N.W.2d. 870; *Ex Parte Gilbert,* 71 Okla. Cr. 268, Ill. P.2d 205.

44. *Strunk v. Strunk,* Ky., 445 S.W. 2d 145; *State v. King Co. Superior Ct.,* 101 Wash. 81, 172 P. 257.

45. *Mellville v. Sabbatino,* 30 Conn. Sup. 886, 313 A.2d 886; *Bronough v. Harding Hospital, Inc.,* 12 Ohio App. 2d. 110, 231 N.E. 2d 487; *Ferry v. Ferry,* 94 N.H. 595, 59 A.2d 151; *Commonwealth v. Stecula,* 63 Pa. D. & C. 94, 35 Del. Co. 138 (1948); *In Re: M. J. E.,* 118 Cal. Rptr. 398, 43 C.A. 3d. 792; *Geary v. Adkins,* 110 Ga. App. 529, 139 S.E. 2d 135; *Kalpakis v. Kalpakis,* 221 La. 739, 60 So. 2d. 217; *In Re: Bryant,* 214 La. 573, 38 So. 2d. 245; *State ex rel. Davey v. Owen,* 133

Ohio St. 96, 12 N.E. 2d. 144 (1937); *Gillboy and Schmidt,* "Voluntary" Hospitalization of the Mentally Ill, 66 N.W.L. Rev 429.

46. *Bell v. Wayne Co. General Hospital at Eloise,* 384 F. Supp. 1085 (D.C. Mich); *Lynch v. Baxley,* 386 F. Supp. 378 (D.C. Ala., 1974); *In Re: Barnard,* 455 F. 2d 1370, 147 U.S. App. D.C. 302.

47. *In Re: Burchans,* 53 Cal. Rptr. 409, 65 C.2d. 233, 418 P.2d. 1 (1966); *In Re: Curry,* 452 F. 2d 1360, 147 U.S. App. D.C. 28, app. after remand, 470 F.2d 368, 152 U.S. App. D.C. 220; *Stamus v. Leonhardt,* 414 F. Supp. 439 (D.C. Iowa 1976); *Suzuki v. Quisenberry,* 411 F. Supp. 113 (D.C. Hawaii).

25. *Kolesar v. U.S.,* 198 F. Supp. 517 (D.C. Fla.); *Wintersteen v. Semler,* 197 Or. 101 Wash. 81, 172 P. 257.

49. *Straka v. Voyles,* 69 Utah 123, 252 P. 677; 52 Am. Jur. 2d., Malicious Prosecution, Sec. 17.

50. *Mulberry v. Fuellhart,* 203 Pa. 573. 53 A. 504 (1902); 32 Am. Jur. 2d. False Imprisonment, Sec. 75; *Colby v. Jackson,* 12 N.H. 526.

51. 16 A.L.R. Fed. 440.

E.

1. *Mitchell v. Robinson,* Mo., 334 S.W. 2d 11, *Stone v. Proctor,* 259 N.C. 633, 131 S.E. 2d 297, *Di Giovanni v. Pessel,* 104 N.J. Super. 550, 250 A.2d. 756.

2. *Finley v. U.S.,* 314 F. Supp. 905 (D.C. Ohio); *Johnson v. Meyers,* 118 Ga. App. 773, 116 S.E.2d. 739.

3. *Shehee v. Aetna Casualty and Surety Co.,* 122 F. Supp. 1 (D.C. La.).

4. *Siirila v. Barrios,* 58 Mich. App. 721, 228 N.W.2d 801, affd. 398 Mich. 576,248 N.W.2d. 171; *Jones v. Furnell,* Ky., 406 S.W. 2d 154.

5. *Hill v. Steward,* Miss., 209 So. 2d 809; *Gunter v. Whitener,* Mo. App. 75 S.W. 2d. 588.

6. *Maddox v. Neptune,* 175 Kans. 465, 264 P.2d 1073; *In Re: Rosenkrans,* 84 N.J. Eq., 232, 94 A.42.

7. *Mitchell v. Robinson,* Mo., 334 S.W. 2d. 11 (1960).

8. *Lester v. Aetna Casualty and Surety Co.,* 240 F.2d 676 (C.A. La., 1957), cert. denied 354 U.S. 923, 1 L.Ed. 2d 1437, 77 S. Ct. 1383.

9. *Fernandez v. Baruch,* 52 N.J. 127, 244 A.2d 109; *Dunham v. Wright,* 423 F.2d 940 (3rd Cir. 1970); *Morgan v. State,* 65 Misc. 2d. 978, 319 N.Y.S. 2d. 151; *O'Neil v. State,* 66 Misc. 2d 936, 323 N.Y.S. 2d. 56; *Whitree v. State,* 56 Misc. 2d. 693, 290 N.Y.S. 2d. 486; *Dimitrijenic v. Chicago Wesley Memorial Hospital,* 92 Ill. App. 2d. 251, 236 N.E.2d 309; *Aiken v. Clary,* Mo., 396 S.W.2d. 668.

10. *Dunbar v. Greelaw,* 152 Mo. 270, 128 A.2d 218 (1956); *Mezullo v. Maletz,* 331 Mass. 233, 118 N.E. 2d 356 (1954).

11. *Di Giovanni v. Pessel,* 104 N.J. Super, 550, 250 A.2d 756; *Kleber v. Stevens,* 39 Misc. 2d. 712, 241 N.Y.S. 2d. 497.

12. *Hicks v. U.S.,* 357 F. Supp. 434 (D.C.D.C.); *Christy v. Saliterman,* Minn., 179 N.W.2d 288.

13. *Zipkin v. Freeman,* Mo., 436 S.W. 2d 753.

14. *Brown v. Moore,* 247 F.2d 711 (C.A. Pa., 1957), cert. den. 355 U.S. 882, 2 L.Ed. 112, 78 S. Ct. 148; *National Savings Bank v. Ward,* 100 U.S. 195, 25 L.Ed. 621; *Kogan v. Comstock,* 270 F.2d 839 (C.A. La.).

15. *Di Giovanni v. Pessel,* 104 N.J. Super. 550, 250 A.2d 756; *Voss v. Bridwell,*

188 Kan. 643 364 P.2d 955; *Rule v. Cheeseman*, 181 Kan. 957, 317 P.2d 743; *National Savings Bank v. Ward*, 100 U.S. 195, 25 L.Ed. 621; *Kozan v. Comstock*, 270 F.2d 839 (C.A. La.).

16. *Miller v. West*, 165 Md. 245, 167 A. 696 (1933).

17. *Wilson v. Huntgate*, Mo., 434 S.W. 2d 590; *Rickens v. Everhart*, 284 N.C. 95, 199 S.E. 2d 440; *Duprey v. Shane*, 39 Col. 2d.781, 249 P.2d 8; *Merriman v. Toothaker*, 9 Wash. App. 810, 515 P.2d 409; *Lake v. Baccus*, 59 Ga. App. 656, 2 S.E.2d 121, *Guest v. Greedin*, 257 F.2d (C.A.S.C.); *Custodio v. Barrer*, 289 Kay, 395, 158 S.W. 2d 609.

18. *Helling v. Carey*, 83 Wash. 2d 514, 519 P.2d 981; *Brown v. U.S.*, 419 F.2d 337 (C.A. Mo.); *Belshaw v. Feinstein*, 65 Cal. Rptr. 788, 258 C.A. 2d 711; *Hendry v. U.S.*, 418 F.2d 774 (C.A. N.Y.); *Mason v. Hall*, 72 Ga. App. 867, 35 S.E. 2d 478.

19. *Scrano v. Schnoor*, 158 Cal. App. 2d 612, 323 P. 2d 178; *Carbone v. Warburton*, 22 N.J. Super. 5, 91 A.2d 518, affd. 11 N.J. 418, 94 A.2d 680.

20. *Thompson v. Lillekie*, 273 F.2d 376 (C.A. Minn.); *Peterson v. Carter*, 182 F. Supp. 393 (D.C. Wis.); *Natanson v. Kline*, 186 Kan. 393, 350 P. 2d 1083, Clarified op. and reh. den. 187 Kan. 186, 354 P.2d 670.

21. *Bryant v. Rankin*, 332 F. Supp. 319 (D.C. Iowa), affmd. C.A.: 468 F. 2d 510; *Incollingo v. Ewing*, 444 Pa. 263, 299, 282 A.2d 206; *Tomer v. American Home Products Corp.*, 170 Conn, 681, 368 A.2d 35.

22. *Campbell v. U.S.*, 325 F. Supp. 207 (D.C. Fla.); *Becker v. Eisenstadt*, 60 N.J. Super. 240, 158 A.2d 706; *Perkins v. Park View Hospital*, 61 Ten App. 458, 456 S.W. 2d 276.

23. *Almli v. Updegraff*, 447 P.2d 586, 8 Ariz. App. 494; *Trogun v. Fruchtman*, 58 Wis. 2d 569, 207 N.W.2d 297.

24. *Pollard v. Goldsmith*, Ariz. Ct. of App., Div. One, Dept. B, No. 1, CA-Civ. 3447 (1977).

25. *Kolesar v. U.S.*, 198 F. Supp. 517 (D.C. Fla.); *Wintersteen v. Semler*, 197 Or. 601, 255 P. 2d 138; *Schrib v. Seidenberg*, App., 80 N.M. 573, 458 P.2d 825.

26. *Erving v. Goode*, 78 F. 442 (C.C. Ohio); *Craig v. Chambers*, 17 Ohio St. 253; *McBride v. Roy*, 177 Okla. 233, 58 P.2d 886.

27. *Harrigan v. U.S.*, 408 F. Supp. 177 (D.C. Pa.); *Curry v. Corn*, 277 N.Y.S. 2d 470, 52 Misc. 2d 1035; *Evans v. Bernhard*, 23 Ariz. App. 413, 533 P. 2d 721; *Stundon v. Stodnik*, Wyo. 469 P. 2d 16; *Starr v. Fregosi*, 370 F.2d 15 (C.A. Ga.); *LaPoint v. Shirley*, 409 F. Supp. 118 (D.C. Tex.); *Pegram v. Sisco*, 406 F. Supp. 776 (D.C. Ark.) affd. C.A. 547 F.2d 1172; *Coleman v. Garrison*, Del. Super., 327 A.2d 757, affd. 349 A.2d 8.

28. *Johnston v. Rodis*, 151 F. Supp. 345 (D.C. D.C., 1957).

29. *Levett v. Etkind*, 158 Conn. 567, 265 A.2d 70; *Rochester v. Katalan*, Del. Super., 320 A.2d 704; *Amdur v. Zim Israel Nav. Co.*, 310 F. Supp. 1033 (D.C. N.Y.).

30. *Bird v. Pritchard*, 33 Ohio App. 2d, 62 Ohio Ops. 3d. 96, 291 N.E. 2d 769; *Los Alamos Medical Center v. Coe*, 58 N.M. 686, 275 P.2d 175.

31. *Dodds v. Stellar*, 77 Cal. App. 2d 411, 175 P.2d 607.

32. *Elliott v. U.S.*, 329 F. Supp. 621 (D.C. Me.); *Ison v. McFall*, 55 Tenn. App. 326, 400 S.W. 2d 243; *Bridgewater v. Boyles*, Ohio App., 107 N.E. 2d. 641.

33. *Bockman v. Butler*, 226 Ark. 159, 288 S.W.2d 597; *Knutsen v. Brown*, 93 N.J. Super. 522, 226 A.2d 460 affd. 232 A.2d 833, 96 N.J. Super. 229; *Mundt v. Alta*

Bates Hospital, 35 Cal. Rptr. 848, 223 C.A.2d 413; *Corbett v. Clarke*, 187 Va. 222, 46 S.E. 2d 327.

34. *Alpar v. Weyerhauser Co.*, 20 N.C. App. 340, 201 S.E.2d 503, cert. den. 285 N.C. 85, 203 S.E. 2d 57; *Kenny v. Hatfield*, 351 Mich. 498, 88 N.W. 2d 535; *Stewart v. Ging*, 64 N.M. 270, 327 P.2d 333; *Cowper v. Vannier*, 20 Ill. App. 2d 499, 156 N.E. 2d 761 (1959).

35. *Dawkins v. Billingsley*, 69 Okla. 259, 172 P. 69 (1918).

36. *Braver v. Globe Newspaper Co.*, 351 Mass. 53, 217 N.E.2d 736 (1966).

37. *Mussachio v. Maida*, 137 N.Y.S. 2d 131 (Sup., 1954); *Wemple v. Delano*, 187 Misc. 710, 65 N.Y.S. 2d 322 (1946); *Totten v. Sun Printing and Publishing Association*, 109 F. 289 (C.C.N.Y., 1901).

38. *Barry v. Baugh*, Ill Ga. App. 813, 143 S.E. 2d 489 (1965); *Mussachio v. Maida*, 137 N.Y.S. 2d 131 (1954).

39. *New York Times Co. v. Sullivan*, 376 U.S. 254, 11 L.Ed.2d 686, 84 S.Ct. 710 (1964).

40. *Inverson v. Frandsen*, 237 F. 2d 898 (C.A. Utah, 1956).

41. *Simonsen v. Swenson*, 104 Neb. 224, 177 N.W. 831.

42. *Zeinfeld v. Hayes Freight Lines, Inc.*, 41 Ill. 3d 345, 243 N.E.2d 217; *Stice v. Beacon Newspaper Corp.*, 185 Kan. 61, 340 P.2d 396.

43. *Berry v. Moench*, 8 Utah 2d 191, 331 P.2d 814 (1958).

44. *Brice v. Curtis*, 38 App. C.D., 304, 38 L.R.A.-N.S. 69, Ann. Cas. 1913C 1070 (1912); *Washington Anapolis Hotel Co. v. Riddle*, 83 App. D.C. 288, 171 F. 2d 732 (1948).

45. *Casano v. WDSU-TV, Inc.*, 464 F.2d 3 (C.A. Miss.); *Madison v. Bolton*, 234 La. 997, 102 So. 2d. 433; *Griffin v. Opinion Rub. Co.*, 114 Mont. 502, 138 P.2d 580. Restatement, Torts Sec. 582.

46. *Munzer v. Blaisdell*, 183 Mis. 773, 49 N.Y.S. 2d 915, affd. without op. 269 App. Div. 970, 58 N.Y.S. 2d 359 (1944).

47. *Berry v. Moench*, 8 Utah 2d 191, 331 P.2d 814 (1958).

48. *Simonsen v. Swenson*, 104 Neb. 224, 178 N.W. 831 (1920).

49. *Kenny v. Cleary*, 47 App. Div. 2d 531, 363 N.Y.S. 2d 606; *Kroger Grocery and Baking Co. v. Yount*, 66 F.2d 700 (C.A.8); *Madison v. Bolton*, 234 La. 997, 102 So. 2d 433.

51. *Campbell v. Jewish Committee for Personal Service*, 125 Cal. App. 2d. 771, 271 P.2d 185 (1954).

50. *Berry v. Moench*, 8 Utah 2d 191, 331 P.2d 814 (1958); *Shoemaker v. Friedberg*, 80 Cal. App. 2d 911, 183 P.2d 318 (1947).

52. *Beatty v. Boston*, 13 Ohio L. Abs. 481 (App., 1932); *Barry v. Moench*, 8 Utah 2d 191, 331, P.2d 814 (1958).

53. *Kenny v. Gurley*, 208 Ala. 623, 95 So. 34 (1923).

54. *Collins v. Oklahoma State Hospital*, 76 Okla. 229, 184 P.946 (1916); *Iverson v. Frandsen*, 237 F.2d 898 (C.A. Utah, 1956); *Smith v. DiCora*, 42 App. Div. 2d 791, 346 N.Y.S. 2d. 546.

55. *Iverson v. Frandsen*, 237 F.2d 898 (C.A. Utah, 1956).

56. *Leonard v. Wilson*, 150 Fla. 503, 8 So. 2d 12 (1942); *New York and P.R.S.S. Co. v. Garcia*, 16 F.2d 734 (C.A. Puerto Rico, 1926).

57. *Smith v. Hatch*, 271 Cal. App. 2d 39, 76 Cal. Rptr. 350.

58. *Pacific Employers Insurance Co. v. Adams*, 196 Okla. 597, 168 P.2d 105;

Lamb v. Fedderwitz, 68 Ga. App. 233, 22 S.E.2d 657, affd. 195 Ga. 691, 25 S.E. 2d 414.

59. *Alexandria Gazette Corp. v. West*, 198 Va. 154, 93 S.E. 2d 274.

60. *Gilpin v. Tack*, 256 F. Supp. 562 (D.C. Ark.); *Jarman v. Offutt*, 239 N.C. 468, 80 S.E. 2d 248 (1954); *Dunbar v. Greenlaw*, 152 Me. 270, 128 A.wd 218 (1956).

61. *O'Bar v. Feist*, 292 Ala. 440, 296 So.2d 152; *Bailey v. McGill*, 247 N.C. 286, 100 S.E.2d. 860 (1957).

62. *Hager v. Major*, 353 Mo. 1166, 186 S.W.2d 564 (1945); *Noll v. Kerby*, 258 App. Div. 840, 15 N.Y.S. 2d 665 (1939).

63. *Corcoran v. Jerrel*, 185 Iowa 532, 170 N.W. 776 (1919).

64. *Mickens v. Davis*, 132 Kan. 49, 294 P. 896 (1931).

65. *Taylor v. Flotfeltz*, 201 F.2d 51 (C.A. Ky., 1952).

66. *Barry v. Moench*, 8 Utah 2d 191, 331 P.2d 814 (1958); *Thornburg v. Long*, 178 N.C. 589, 101 S.E. 99 (1919).

67. *White v. Padgett*, 475 F.2d 79 (C.A. Fla.), cert. den. 414 U.S. 861, 38 L.Ed. 2d. 112, 94 S.Ct. 78; *Washer v. Slater*, 67 App. Div. 385, 73 N.Y.S. 425; *Troutman v. State*, 273 App. Div. 619, 79 N.Y.S. 2d 709.

68. *Beaumont v. Segal*, Mass., 283 N.E.2d 858; *Pate v. Stevens*, Tex., Civ. App., 257 S.W. 2d 763 (1953) error dismissed; *Fowle v. Fowle*, 263 N.C. 724, 140 S.E.2d 398 (1965).

69. *Sukforth v. Thegen*, Me., 256 A.2d 162; *Young v. State*, 40 App. Div. 2d. 730, 336 N.Y.S. 2d 470.

70. *Barlett v. Weimer*, 268 F.2d 860 (C.A. Ind., 1959), cert. den. 361 U.S. 938, 4 L.Ed. 2d. 358, 80 S. Ct; 380; *Baer v. Smith*, 68 Cal. App. 2d 716, 157 P.2d 646 (1945); *Beckham v. Cline*, 151 Fla. 481, 10 So. 2d. 419 (1942).

71. *Bromund v. Holt*, 24 Wis. 2d 336, 129 N.W.2d 149 (1964); *Hurley v. Towne*, 155 Me. 433, 156 A.2d 377 (1959).

72. *DiGiovanni v. Pessel*, 55 N.J. 188, 260 A.2d 510; *White v. Padgett*, 475 F.2d 79 (C.A. Fla.), cert. den. 414 U.S. 861, 38 L.Ed.2d. 112, 94 S.Ct. 78; *Delatte v. Genovesse*, La.App., 228 So. 2d 252; *Sukeforth v. Thegen*, Me., 256 A.2d 162.

73. *Crouch v. Cameron*, Ky., 414 S.W. 2d 408 (1967).

74. *O'Rourke v. O'Rourke*, 227 La. 262, 79 So.2d 87 (1955).

75. *Walder v. Manahan*, 21 N.J. Misc. 1, 29 A.2d 395 (1942).

76. *Bangs v. State*, 41 App. Div. 2d 988, 343 N.Y.S. 2d-976; *Christiansen v. Weston*, 36 Ariz. 200, 284 P. 149 (1930).

77. *Christopher v. Henry*, 284 Ky. 127, 143 S.W.2d 1069 (1940).

78. *Bailey v. McGill*, 247 N.C. 286, 100 S.E. 2d 860 (1957).

79. *Niven v. Boland*, 177 Mass. 11, 58 N.E. 282 (1900).

80. *Ussery v. Haynes*, 344 Mo. 530, 127 S.W.2d 410 (1939).

81. *Ingo v. Koch*, 127 F.2d 667 (C.A. N.Y., 1942); *Brady v. Collon*, 68 R.I. 299, 27 A.2d 311 (1942).

82. *Knaub v. Gotwalt*, 422 Pa. 267, 220 A.2d 646; *Beaty v. Buckeye Fabric Finishing Co.*, 179 F. Supp. 688 (D.C. Ark.); *Kaufman v. Western Union Telegraph Co.*, 224 F.2d 723 (C.A. Tex.), cert. den. 350 U.S. 947, 100 L.Ed. 825, 76 S. Ct. 321.

83. *Preece v. Baur*, 143 F. Supp. 804 (D.C. Idaho); *Falsone v. Busch*, 45 N.J. 559, 214 A.2d 12.

84. *Neiderman v. Brodsky*, 436 Pa. 401 (1970).

85. *Ver Hagen v. Gibbons*, 47 Wis. 2d 220, 177 N.W.2d 83; *Knierim v. Izzo*, 22 Ill. 2d 73, 174 N.E.2d 157.

86. *Southern Express Co. v. Bryers*, 240 U.S. 612, 60 L.Ed. 825, 36 S.Ct. 410; *Smith v. Gowdy*, 196 Ky. 281, 244 S.W. 678; Restatement, Torts, 2d., Sec. 436A; *Krooz v. Ray* (A.D.), 382 N.Y.S. 2d 823; *Justus v. Atchinson*, 19 Cal. 3d 564, 139 Cal. Rptr. 97, 565 P.2d 122; *Comstock v. Wilson*, 257 N.Y. 231, 177 N.E. 431; *Clack v. Thomason*, 57 Ga. App. 253, 195 S.E. 218; *Ewing v. Pittsburgh C.C. & St. Louis R. Co.*, 147 Pa. 40, 23 A. 340; *Newby v. Alto Rivera Apts.*, 60 Cal. App, 3d. 288, 13 Cal. Rptr. 547; *Alcorn v. Anbro Engineering, Inc.*, 2 Cal. 3d 493, 86 Cal. Rptr. 88, 468 P.2d 216.

87. *U.S. v. Hambleton*, 185 F.2d 564 (C.A. Wash.); *Stafford v. Seward*, Tex. Civ. App., 295 S.W.2d 665, dismd, agr.; *Smith v. Aldridge*, Mo., 356 S.W.2d 532; *Murphy v. Tacoma*, 60 Wash. 2d 603, 374 P.2d 976; *Kuzma v. Millinery Workers Union*, 27 N.J.Super. 579, 99 A.2d 833; *Morse v. Duncan*, 14 F. 396 (C.C. Miss.); *Trigg v. St. Louis, K.C. & N.R. Co.*, 74 Mo. 147; *Sappington v. Atlanta & W.P.R. Co.*, 127 Ga. 178, 56 S.E. 311; *Langworthy v. Pulitzer Publishing Co.*, Mo., 368 S.W. 2d 385; *Morse v. Duncan*, 14 F. 396 (C.C. Miss.); *Rockhill v. Pollard*, 259 Or. 54, 485 P.2d 28.

88. *Bentley v. Industrial Fire Protection Co.*, La. App., 338 So. 2d 1177; *Wright v. Husband*, 193 Ark., 347, 99 S.W. 2d 583; *Valley Development Co. v. Weeks*, 147 Colo. 591, 364 P.2d 730; *Western Union Telegraph Co. v. Weeks*, 100 Fla. 495., 129 So. 743; *Eckenrode v. Life of America Insurance Co.*, 470 F.2d 1 (C.A. Ill.); *Gruenberg v. Aetna Ins. Co.*, 9 Cal. 3d 566, 108 Cal. Rptr. 480, 510 P.2d 1032.

89. *Hood v. Moffett*, 109 Miss. 757, 69 So. 664.

90. *DiMare v. Crisci*, 58 Cal. 2d 292, 23 Cal. Rptr. 772, 373 P.2d 860; *Green v. Floe*, 28 Wash. 2d 620, 183 P.2d 771.

91. Restatement, Torts, Sec. 905 comment d.; *Powers v. Motors Security Co.*, La. App., 168 So. 2d 922, writ refused 247 La. 257, 170 So. 2d 511.

92. *McKinley v. Chicago and N.W.R. Co.*, 44 Iowa 314, affd. 99 U.S. 147, 25 L.Ed. 272; *Browning v. Slenderella Systems of Seattle*, 54 Wash. 2d 440, 341 P.2d 859; *Erwin v. Milligan*, 188 Ark. 658, 67 S.W. 2d 592.

93. *Hood v. Moffett*, 109 Miss. 757, 69 So. 664; *Norton v. Hamilton*, 92 Ga. App. 727, 89 S.E. 2d 809.

94. *Sullivan v. O'Connor*, Mass., 296 N.E.2d 183 (1973).

95. *O'Brien v. Stoner*, 443 F.2d 1013 (1972); *Graham v. Roberts*, 441 F.2d 995, 142 U.S. App. D.C. 305 (1970); *Norton v. Hamilton*, 92 Ga. App. 727, 89 S.E. 2d 309; *Bishop v. Byrne*, 265 F. Supp. 460 (D.C. W. Va., 1967).

A Jurist's Legal Opinion Regarding Practical Legal Issues Facing the Psychologist Practitioner

CLINICAL PSYCHOLOGY

T. N. Tumilty

Q. What is the greatest liability threat to the clinical psychologist and what can the practitioner do to best avoid it?

A. A clinical psychologist is a professional, an expert in the art of treating patients suffering from mental disease or disorder. As a professional, he or she is held to the same standard of care that the law employs to adjudge doctors in medical matters, attorneys in legal matters, and dentists in dental matters. The law imposes liability on all individuals, experts and non-experts, for harm caused to others. The harm or injury must result from negligence or from the failure to act when the law imposes a duty upon a person to act. Quite naturally, the standard of conduct imposed upon a professional or expert is different from and greater than that imposed upon a nonprofessional, nonexpert layman.

The standard of care imposed by the law upon clinical psychologists is that they must possess that skill and learning commonly possessed by members of the profession in good standing; and they will be liable if harm results because they do not have those skills.* Negligence of a clinical psychologist would be the greatest exposure to legal liability. Omitting to do something that a member of the profession in good standing, guided by professional consideration, would ordinarily do, or doing something that such a professional would not do, results in liability.

It would be anticipated that the act of omission would present more potential exposure to liability than would the act of commission. Thus, the

---

Johnson v. Cole, Minn., 300 N.W. 791 (1941).

failure to advise a patient of any dangers that may result from a prescribed course of treatment would be the area of prime concern to a clinical psychologist.

The answer to the conjunctive question is rather obvious. A clinical psychologist should avoid the sometimes tempting urge to experiment when traditional forms of treatment appear to produce no results. While a psychologist does not have to be in total agreement with the members of his or her professional specialty to be freed from negligence, there must exist at least a school of thought in the area since the law recognizes that each discipline in a professional society entertains diverse opinions. Nonetheless, a clinical psychologist would be liable if he or she fails to ascertain a full operational fact basis upon which the course of treatment is planned and that the treatment itself is embraced by equally skilled and learned members of the profession.

What we have just said is directed at avoiding liability. The answer to the question of avoiding the consequences of liability is somewhat more complex. Recognition must be made of the fact that we live in a litigious society and no amount of caution can dispel the possibility of being sued. Everybody is subject to being sued, but only those found by a competent tribunal to be legally liable for the consequences of their conduct can be successfully sued. True, the distinction is fine but of some consequence. The stigma of being sued has greatly diminished in the eyes of the general public. We are an urban and sophisticated society. Nevertheless, the results of a successful suit can be financially devastating. In order to avoid the consequence of a liability suit, the clinical psychologist, as well as any other professional, is well advised to shield himself or herself from fiscal disaster by purchasing malpractice insurance. Such insurance policies impose a duty on the part of the insurance carrier to defend even the most frivolous lawsuits against the insured professional. The legal costs and expenses of such a defense would be well worth the premium invested.

Q.   What are the primary factors the clinical psychologist should keep in mind when testifying as an expert witness so that the testimony will be most effective?

A.   Ordinarily, witnesses in court proceedings are prohibited from giving opinion testimony. The law reasons that an opinion is only that; it creates no fact. It is what someone thinks about something and the thought may be precisely accurate or totally inaccurate, and yet represent the honest conviction of the person who expresses it. It is because of this that opinion evidence, where admissible, is considered of low grade and not entitled to much weight when contradicted by positive testimony as to actual facts.

In a very real sense, all testimony given by any witnesses as to what they observed with their senses is opinion evidence, since one testifies to the reaction of his or her senses to a stimulus. Nonetheless, in a legal sense, the line of demarcation between those matters considered to be fact and those considered to be opinions is frequently so indistinct that the question of admitting any given testimony is reposed to the sound discretion of the trial judge. The judge is guided solely by a resolution in his or her own mind of the simple question: is an opinion necessary to aid the jury in arriving at fair and just verdict? Necessity, then, is the mother of expert opinion testimony.

With this in mind, it also must be understood that laymen tend to give considerably more weight to the testimony of expert witnesses than the testimony of a lay witness. By reason of the education, experience, and expertise of the witness, an expert's testimony has great impact upon a jury. Consequently, it would seem that the American Psychological Association Ethical Standard (1.22-22) is more agreeable to the law. Generally, this principle provides that, when psychologists testify as expert witnesses, they should only make such statements as they are qualified to make on the basis of professional training and experience, and which they can substantiate by evidence that would be acceptable to recognized specialists in the same field. They should be prepared to state their opinion with reasonable certainty, shared by like professionals of similar training and experience. Where applicable, a clinical psychologist should acknowledge that, on a particular point in issue, there may be at least two "schools of thought." The psychologist should be prepared to explain to the jury what factors compel his or her adoption of a particular position in clinical psychology. Furthermore, practitioners should avoid attempts to discredit an opposing view. If they have failed to convince their colleagues, they will likely fail to convince a jury.

Q. Under what circumstances, if any, should the clinical psychologist reveal confidential information about a client?

A. In chapter 9 section C, the subject of confidential communications privilege is discussed at length. Of course, there are circumstances described in the chapter that compel the disclosure of confidential information. Perhaps the most frequently encountered area is that in which the patient by express waiver compels a clinical psychologist to reveal confidential information about a patient.

The State of California has frequently produced virgin law. Perhaps its most devastating production was announced in the case of *Tarasoff v. Regents of University of California*, Calif., 529 P.2d 533 (1975). If this view is adopted by other jurisdictions, the basic concept of confidentiality will be undermined. The substance of the California decision is that confidentiality must bow to considerations of public safety. The case involved a psychotherapist whose patient divulged his intentions to kill a certain person. The psychotherapist's superior, nonetheless, recommended the patient's release from confinement. No warning was given to the threatened person who was subsequently murdered by the patient. The trial judge, following well-established legal precepts, ruled that there was no affirmative duty imposed by law upon the psychotherapist to warn the decedent of the patient's threats. The trial judge's decision was reversed on appeal by a divided California Supreme Court holding that public policy compels the conclusion that an affirmative duty did exist between the psychotherapist and the decedent.

More likely than not this precedent will not sweep the nation with legal enthusiasm, since it creates far more problems than it solves. However, as long as it remains an unrejected opinion of a state's ultimate court, it will be relied upon as a basis for lawsuits.

The majority of the courts in this country are still applying the concept that successful psychotherapy depends upon confidentiality. The vitality of the practice of psychology depends upon the reputation in the community that the psychologist will not tell.

NEUROPSYCHOLOGY

F. R. J. Fields

Q.   What is the legal status of a neuropsychologic finding vis-à-vis a negative medical finding?

A.   The clinical neuropsychologist is concerned with the situation in which his or her test results point to subtle (or not so subtle) deficits in function of a child or adult in a head trauma case that are not always observed in the medical examinations and structurally oriented studies. It is noted that in the case of a child whose brain is developing and who has sustained head trauma, the neuropsychological deficits may have significant bearing on stinted future development of cognitive capacity.

The question posed could arise in the context of a negligence or malpractice suit brought against the clinical neuropsychologist at a distant time. Unfortunately, the answer is not quite as simple as would appear at first blush. The key factor to be considered is on whose behalf was the neuropsychological test conducted? The duty of the neuropsychologist then would appear to be to make a full disclosure of his or her findings and opinion to the person who engaged her or him. For example, if engaged by a parent or guardian, it would be the duty of the neuropsychologist to disclose the findings to them.

The question as put is also susceptible to the interpretation that it seeks a determination of the status of a clinical neuropsychologist in any given case where his or her testimony would be in opposition to the testimony of a medical doctor. This then leads to the question of competency versus credibility.

A psychologist is equally competent in his or her field as a medical doctor, assuming that the psychologist qualifies as an expert witness. A psychologist does qualify as an expert witness if he or she has been educated and has had experience, training, and skill in a particular field of psychology. In law, an expert witness is one who, because of possession of knowledge not within ordinary reach, is especially qualified to speak upon the subject to which his or her attention is called. The mere fact that it might be demonstrated that another witness is, perhaps, better qualified, does not render the psychologist's testimony incompetent and, therefore, inadmissible.

A jury is instructed that the weight to be given to the testimony of any expert witness is ultimately a jury function. They must look, not only to the witness' particular knowledge, skill, experience, training, and education, but to the witness' general credibility as well. A jury might very well accept the opinion of a lesser qualified expert if that expert witness had far greater opportunities for observation, study, and examination and who testified in a more credible, frank, candid, and honest manner. The relative qualifications of expert witnesses do not affect their competency as witnesses. However, the extent of their expertise is a matter which a jury, or other fact finder, must weigh in resolving the differences in the experts' opinions.

COUNSELING PSYCHOLOGY

W. F. Adams

W. F. Adams, the counseling psychologist, presented two areas for comment. The first area is the general subject of confidentiality. The subject of confidential communications privilege is discussed at length in chapter 9 section C, which should answer any questions raised by the counseling psychologist.

The second area of comment deals with the general subject of accountability. Again we have dealt in detail with the subject of legal accountability in chapter 9 section E.

Under the general category of accountability, the counseling psychologist is concerned with the applicability of licensure statutes to counseling psychologists. It would appear that the majority of the jurisdictions include the counseling psychologists as those who hold out to the public their title or description of their services to include but not be restricted to, counseling and the use of psychological methods with persons or groups with adjustment problems in the areas of work, family, school, and personal relationships. It would appear clear that a counseling psychologist must first obtain a license in order to engage in the specialty of counseling psychology.

A counseling psychologist also is concerned about accountability in the area of adherence to ethics. It would seem that a counseling psychologist comfortably qualifies for membership in the American Psychological Association. That association, in 1953, adopted ethical standards for psychologists, and the counseling psychologist should adhere to the principles described in the current standards.

Ethical standards adopted by professional societies do not have the status of law. Nonetheless, it is frequently argued that a deviation from ethical standards adopted by a recognized professional society, such as the American Psychological Association, is evidence of negligence. When a trial court is groping for an articulate standard of conduct applicable to a professional in a negligence (malpractice) suit, in the absence of any legal precedent, more likely than not the judge would refer to the ethical standards adopted by the recognized professional association as the yardstick for conduct expected of the professional.

COMMUNITY PSYCHOLOGY

P. L. Taylor

Q.   Is there any case law in Pennsylvania or other states clarifying what qualifies as psychological practice?

A.   In Pennsylvania, a licensure statute was adopted March 23, 1972. As of this writing, there have been no litigated cases concerning or clarifying the problem of what activity qualifies as "psychological practice." Section 2 of the Pennsylvania statute contains a comprehensive definition of what constitutes the practice of psychology. Section 3 describes the acts exempt from the licensure requirement. Both yin and yang are comprehensive and at times conflicting. By definition, the Pennsylvania statute requires that anyone who holds himself or herself out to the public as a community psychologist and under designation offers to render or actually renders advice as to the application of group relations to individuals, government agencies, or to the public in general for compensation must be licensed. The practice of community psychology addresses group, rather than individual, problems. Nevertheless, the licensure statute was written to protect groups as well as individuals. The compelled conclusion is that a practitioner of community psychology must be licensed.

Q.   What potential risks do community psychologists have for malpractice and/or negligence suits and, if so, what are some of the legal parameters of such suits?

A.   Initially, we note that there is no immunity from lawsuits against community psychologists merely because they are not treating patients under traditional medical concepts of doctor-patient relationships. A community psychologist is peculiarly vulnerable to the type of lawsuit known in our law as a *class action.* This type of lawsuit is instituted by one or more members of a class who have been injured as a result of either malpractice or negligent conduct on the part of a community psychologist. If the actions of a community psychologist result in injuries to members of the community generally, one or more members of that community may sue on behalf of all of its members if certain criteria are met.

Generally, a class action may be instituted if (1) the class of injured parties is so numerous that the joinder of all members individually is impractical; (2) there are questions of law or fact that are common to the community class; (3) the claims of the representative parties are typical of the claims of the class; (4) the representative parties will fairly and adequately assert the interest of the class; and (5) a class action will provide a fair and efficient method for adjudication of the controversy.

Thus, it is evident that a community psychologist is subject to the same standards of care and accountability for conduct as a practitioner who specializes in one-to-one relationships.

Both parameters and the character of the causes of action to which a community psychologist is susceptible are identical to those of other practicing psychologists. The only difference would be a group of plaintiffs rather than an individual plaintiff instituting the lawsuit.

Q. Is there professional insurance available to cover potential liability of community psychologists?

A. Insurance to indemnify professionals is available from most insurance carriers. Inasmuch as it is a special type of insurance, the scope of coverage and the premiums to be charged for the coverage would be a matter for negotiation between the community psychologist and insurer.

Q. Is evaluation research done on agencies receiving public funds in the public domain or can it be kept secret?

A. In the absence of a statute to the contrary, a psychologist employed by another to perform any professional service is subject to duties specified in the contract of employment, as well as such other duties which are implied by law.

It is fundamental law that an agent bears a fiduciary relationship to his or her principal and owes the principal the duty of good faith and loyalty. In addition, an agent owes a duty to obey the instructions of the principal, unless, of course, the instructions would oblige the agent to commit an illegal or criminal act. Thus, even though an agent is of the opinion that the principal is exercising poor judgment, or that the objectives could be better obtained by other means, the agent is not privileged to substitute his or her judgment for that of the principal.

If an agency of the government employs a community psychologist to undertake an evaluation, survey, or study of a matter involving the general welfare of the public, then the duties owed by the psychologist are to the agency employing him or her and not to the public. The ultimate decision as to whether to act or not, whether or not to inform the public, is a duty and responsibility delegated to the agency, not to an employee of the agency. The evaluation research performed by the community psychologist may be but one factor among many leading to the agency's decision. It would be disruptive of the orderly affairs of government if its employees undertook to make ultimate decisions they were neither authorized nor employed to make.

A typical "Right to Know" law was adopted in Pennsylvania by the act of the General Assembly on June 21, 1957, P.L. 390. The language of the statute appears to exempt from inspection and examination by the public research reports and evaluations contracted by an agency in the performance of its official duties. The statute specifically excludes access to documents or reports that would cause the agency to lose federal funding. The conclusion is inescapable that, when agencies contract for evaluations, there is no authority for the public to inspect the results of that research.

Public disclosure statutes generally impose duties upon agencies of government and not upon individuals employed by those agencies. Conceivably a statute could be written that would compel the public disclosure by the agency of a psychologist's project research. The legal duty to disclose would be imposed upon the agency and it alone would be legally accountable for violating its duties. Even though an agency violates its statutory duty of disclosure, there would be no license on the part of its employees to violate their duties imposed by law arising out of the relationship of employer-employee or principal and agent.

It has been pointed out that the scientific community adopts the principle that secret research is contrary to the scientific communication of knowledge. The conclusion to be drawn is that research is public. The simplicity of its statement belies the complexities. Duties imposed by law upon individuals who undertake to act on behalf of others, as well as duties voluntarily undertaken by contract, may very well render the psychology associations' platitude nothing more than that.

We can but conclude only that the typical "Right to Know" statute does not authorize public disclosure by psychologists employed by agencies of the results of psychological studies undertaken on behalf of and at the direction of the public agency. It is equally clear that there is nothing in law that would prevent a psychologist and an agency from contracting whatever terms they can agree upon concerning the publication of the results of research projects. Clearly, nothing in the Pennsylvania "Right to Know" statute would prohibit such a voluntary agreement between an agency and its employed research psychologist.

Pennsylvania's Licensure Statute

DECLARATION OF POLICY

The practice of psychology in the Commonwealth of Pennsylvania is hereby declared to affect the public safety and welfare, and to be subject to regulation and control in the public interest to protect the public from unprofessional, improper, unauthorized, and unqualified practice of psychology, and from unprofessional conduct by persons licensed to practice psychology. This act should be liberally construed to carry out these objects and purposes.
1972, March 23, P.L. 136, No. 52 Sec. 1.

DEFINITIONS

As used in this act:

(1) "Board" means the Pennsylvania Board of Psychologist Examiners in the Department of State.

(2) "Commissioner" means the Commissioner of Professional and Occupational Affairs in the Department of State.

(3) "Practice of psychology" means any one or more of the following: Holding one's self out to the public by any title or description of services incorporating the words "psychological," "psychologist," or "psychology," and under such description offers to render or renders to individuals, corporations, institutions, governmental agencies, or to the public for remuneration any service involving the following:

(i) The application of established principles of learning, motivation, perception, thinking, and emotional relationships to problems of personality evaluation, group relations, and behavior adjustment. The application of said principles includes, but is not restricted to, counseling and the use of psychological methods with persons or groups with adjustment problems in the areas of work, family, school, and personal relationships; measuring and testing of personality, intelligence, aptitudes, and emotions, and offering services as a psychological consultant.

(ii) Performing or offering to perform any one or more of the following acts or services; (a) "measuring and testing," consisting of the psychological assessment and evaluation of abilities, attitudes, aptitudes, achievement, adjustments, motives, personality dynamics, and/or other psychological attributes of individuals, or groups of individuals by means of standardized measurements or other methods, techniques, or procedures recognized by the science and profession of psychology, (b) "psychological methods," consisting of the application of principles of learning and motivation in an interpersonal situation with the objectives of modification of perception and adjustment, require highly developed skills in the disciplines, techniques, and methods of altering through learning processes, attitudes, feelings, values, self-concept, personal goals, and adaptive patterns, (c) "psychological consulting," consisting of interpreting or reporting upon scientific fact or theory in psychology, rendering expert psychological opinion, psychological evaluation, or engaging in applied psychological research.
1972, March 23, P.L. 136, No. 52 Sec. 2.

NECESSITY FOR LICENSE: EXEMPT ACTS

It shall be unlawful for any person to engage in the practice of psychology or to offer or attempt to do so unless he shall first have obtained a license pursuant to this act, except as hereinafter provided:

(1) Simple acts of persuasion or suggestion by one person to another, or to a group.

(2) Persons licensed to practice any of the healing arts in this Commonwealth shall be exempt from the provisions of this act. Nothing in this act shall be construed to limit the practice of persons licensed to practice any of the healing arts in any way and any persons offering services under the direct supervision of such persons licensed to practice the healing arts shall be exempt. Nothing herein shall be construed as authorizing any person licensed as a psychologist to engage in any manner in the practice of any of the healing arts as defined in the laws of this Commonwealth on the effective date of this act. The psychologist who engages in practice shall assist his client in obtaining professional help for all relevant aspects of his problem that fall outside the boundaries of the psychologist's own competence. Provision must be made for the diagnosis and treatment of relevant health care problems by an appropriate qualified practitioner of the healing arts.

(3) Nothing in this act shall be construed to prevent qualified members of other recognized professions from doing work of a psychological nature consistent with the training and the code of ethics of their respective professions.

(4) Nothing in this act shall be construed to limit the practice of psychology or use of an official title on the part of a person employed as a psychologist by a Federal, State, county, or municipal agency, or other political subdivisions, or those persons certified and employed as school psychologists in the public and private schools of the Commonwealth, in so far as such practice is a part of the normal function of his salaried position or is performed on behalf of or according to the usual expectations of his employer.

(5) Nothing in this act is to be construed as restricting the use of the term "social psychologist" by any person who meets the qualifications specified in section 6.1.

(6) Nothing in this act shall be construed to limit the practice of psychology or use of an official title on the part of a member of the faculty or staff of a duly accredited university, college, hospital, or State-approved nonpublic school in so far as such practice is a part of the normal function of his salaried position or is performed on behalf of or according to the usual expectations of his employer. Nothing in this act shall be construed to limit the practice of psychology or use of an offical title on the part of a student, intern, or resident in psychology, pursuing a course of study in a duly accredited university, college, or hospital or similar training facility for the qualified training of psychologists, provided that such practice and use of title constitute a part of his supervised course of study, and he is designated by such titles as "psychology intern," "psychology trainees," or other title clearly indicating such training status. Nothing in this act shall be construed to limit the activities of a faculty or staff member of a duly accredited university, college, or hospital, or research unit of a duly recognized business or industrial firm or corporation, in the performance of experimental and scientific research activities for the primary purpose of contributing to or enlarging upon scientific principles of psychology. Nothing in this act shall be construed to limit the use of the term, "psychology," "psychologist," or

"psychological," in connection with the aforementioned experimental or scientific research activities or for the purpose of publication of the research findings in professional and scientific journals, or for the purpose of providing scientific information to any user of such information.

(7) Nothing in this act shall be construed to prohibit the practice of psychology by a person who, in the opinion of the board meets the minimum qualifications for licensure under this act, provided said person is on temporary assignment in this Commonwealth.

(8) Nothing in this act shall be construed to prohibit employees of business and industrial organizations from applying the principles of psychology described in clause (3) of section 2ii to the employment placement, evaluation, selection, promotion, or job adjustment of their own officers, or employees or those of any associated organization. No business or industrial firm or corporation may sell or offer to the public or to individuals or to other firms or corporations for remuneration any psychological acts or services as are part of the practice of psychology unless such services are performed by individuals duly and appropriately licensed under this act.

(9) Nothing in this act shall be construed to limit the activities of a salaried employee in the performance of duties incidental to and necessary to the work of a psychologist, provided that the salaried employee acts at all times under the supervision of a licensed psychologist, and provided further that the employee does not assume to the independent practice of psychology.

1972, March 23, P.L. 136, No. 52 Sec. 3.

BOARD OF PSYCHOLOGIST EXAMINERS

There is hereby created the Pennsylvania Board of Psychologist Examiners as follows:

(1) Said board shall consist of seven members who are citizens of the United States, residents of the Commonwealth of Pennsylvania for a three-year period, six of whom are to be appointed by the Governor with the advice and consent of two-thirds of all the members of the Senate within ninety days from the effective date of this act and the commissioner shall serve, ex officio, as the seventh member of the board. At the first meeting the appointed members shall determine by lot two members to serve three-year terms, two members to serve two-year terms and two members to serve one-year terms.

(2) When the term of each member of the board ends, the Governor shall appoint his successor for a term of three years. Any vacancy occurring on the board shall be filled by the Governor by appointment for the unexpired term. Board members shall continue to serve until their successors are appointed.

(3) The board shall have at least two members who, at the time of appointment, are engaged primarily in rendering professional services in psychology and at least two members who, at the time of appointment, are engaged in research in psychology or the teaching of psychology, one of whom shall be from a university granting doctoral degrees in psychology, all of whom shall be eligible for licensing under this act. One member of the board shall be appointed by the Governor from nominations of members of the office of mental health and mental retardation submitted by the commissioners. One member of the board shall be appointed by the Governor from

nominations of mental health and mental retardation advocacy groups submitted by their boards of directors.

(4) No board member shall serve more than two consecutive terms.

(5) Each board member shall receive actual necessary traveling expenses incidental to board meetings, plus per diem expenses as approved by the commissioner upon recommendation of the board.

(6) The board shall within one hundred fifty days after the effective date of this act, and annually thereafter in the month prescribed by the board, hold a meeting, and elect a chairman and vice-chairman. The board shall meet at such other times as deemed necessary and advisable by the chairman, or by a majority of its members. Reasonable notice of all meetings shall be given in the manner prescribed by the board. A majority of the board shall constitute a quorum at any meeting or hearing. 1972, March 23, P.L. 136, No. 52 Sec. 4.

POWERS AND DUTIES OF BOARD

The board shall have the following powers:

(1) To pass upon the qualifications and fitness of applicants for licenses and reciprocal licenses; and to adopt and revise rules and regulations requiring applicants to pass examinations relating to their qualifications as a prerequisite to the issuance of license.

(2) To adopt, and, from time to time, revise such rules and regulations not inconsistent with the law as may be necessary to carry into effect the provisions of this act. Such rules and regulations shall include, but not be limited to, a code of ethics for psychologists in the State, based upon ethical standards for psychologists of the American Psychological Association.

(3) To examine for, deny, approve, issue, revoke, suspend, and renew the licenses of psychologist applicants pursuant to this act, and to conduct hearings in connection therewith.

(4) To conduct hearings upon complaints concerning violations of the provisions of and the rules and regulations adopted pursuant to this act and cause the prosecution and enjoinder of all such violations.

(5) To expend moneys necessary to the proper carrying out of their assigned duties.

(6) To waive examination and grant a license in cases deemed exceptional by the board.

Provided, however, that any one or more of the powers hereinbefore set forth may be assumed and exercised by the board at any time, upon its adoption of a resolution to so act, with notice thereof given in writing to the commissioner. 1972, March 23, P.L. 136, No. 52 Sec. 5.

QUALIFICATIONS FOR LICENSE

(a) An applicant shall be qualified for a license to practice psychology provided he submits proof satisfactory to the board that:

(1) He is of acceptable moral character; and

(2) He is either (i) a graduate of an accredited college or university holding a degree of Doctor of Philosophy or Doctor of Education in psychology plus two years

of postdoctorate experience acceptable to the board, or (ii) a graduate of an accredited college or university holding a doctoral degree in a field related to psychology, provided his experience and training are acceptable to the board as being equivalent to the above, or (iii) a graduate of an accredited college or university holding a master's degree in psychology or another of the behavioral sciences plus four years of experience provided his education and experience are acceptable to the board; and

(3) He has passed an examination duly adopted by the board; and

(4) His application has been accompanied by an application fee of fifty dollars ($50) or more as determined by the board, payable to the commissioner.

(b) Each applicant to the said board for examination or licensure shall have attached thereto the affidavit or affirmation of the applicant as to its verity. Any applicant who knowingly or willfully makes a false statement of fact in his application shall be subject to prosecution for perjury.

(c) In case of failure at any examination, the applicant shall have, after the expiration of six months and within two years, the privilege of a second examination by the board without the payment of an additional fee. The board may adopt rules and procedures governing the eligibility of applicants who have failed to pass two examinations in order to be admitted to subsequent examinations.

1972, March 23, P.L. 136, No. 52 Sec. 6.

LICENSE WITHOUT EXAMINATION

The qualifications provisions of section 6a shall not apply and a license shall be issued without examination to any applicant who has submitted an application for license accompanied by an application fee as specified by the board within two years from and after the effective date of this act and who is a resident of this State or who has practiced in the Commonwealth for a two-year period; and

(1) Who, on the effective date of this act, holds the Doctor of Philosophy or Doctor of Education degree in psychology or other equivalent doctoral degree from an accredited college or university acceptable to the board and has engaged in psychological practice acceptable to the board for two years, or

(2) Who, on the effective date of this act, holds a master's degree in psychology or another of the behavioral sciences from an accredited college or university plus four years of experience provided that his education and experience are acceptable to the board, or

(3) Who, on the effective date of this act, holds a permanent certificate as a public school psychologist in the Commonwealth of Pennsylvania.

1972, March 23, P.L. 136, No. 52 Sec. 7.

REVOCATION OF LICENSE

A license previously issued may be revoked, if the person licensed be:

(1) Convicted of a felony or enters a plea of guilty or nolo contendere thereto, or

(2) An habitual user of narcotics, or other habit-forming drugs, or

(3) An habitual drunkard, or

(4) Found guilty of the unethical practice of psychology as detailed by the code of ethical standards adopted by the board, or

(5) Found guilty of presenting false credentials or documents in support of his application for license.

1972, March 23, P.L. 136, No. 52 Sec. 8

SUSPENSION DURING PERIOD OF MENTAL INCOMPETENCY: OTHER GROUNDS FOR REMOVAL FROM PRACTICE

Any license under this act shall be automatically suspended upon the legal commitment to an institution of a licensee because of mental incompetency from any cause upon filing with the commissioner a certified copy of such commitment. Restoration of such license shall be made as hereinafter provided as in the case of revocation and suspension of licensure.

The Pennsylvania Board of Psychologist Examiners may for a definite or indefinite time, refuse, revoke, or suspend a license for the use of any substance or the presence of any condition which impairs intellect or judgment to such an extent as to incapacitate for the performance of professional duties. The board may so act upon satisfactory proof of grossly unethical practice or of any form of pretense which might induce persons to become a prey to professional exploitation or for violation of the rules and regulations of the board.

1972, March 23, P.L. 136, No. 52 Sec. 9.

HEARING: RESTORATION TO PRACTICE

Any person who is licensed by the board or who is an applicant for examination for licensure by the board, against whom are preferred any of the charges for causing the revocation or suspension of license or for causing refusal of the right to be examined for licensure, shall be furnished by the board with a copy of the complaint and shall have a hearing before the board or by attorney, and witnesses may be examined by said board respecting the guilt or innocence of said accused.

At any hearing the psychologist or applicant shall have the right to appear personally and by counsel, to cross-examine witnesses appearing against him, and to produce witnesses and evidence in his own defense. The board may subpoena witnesses and documentary evidence on its own behalf, and, if requested by the psychologist, shall subpoena witnesses and documents on his behalf. The board may administer oath, examine witnesses, and compel testimony. A record shall be made by the board, or under its direction, of such a hearing.

The revocation or suspension of the license of any person licensed by the board shall be removed when said narcotic drug or other habit-forming drug habit hereinbefore specified shall have been adjudged by the said board to be cured or overcome and said suspended licensee is deemed capable of practicing his profession. The revocation or suspension for any other cause of the license of any person licensed by the board may be removed at such time as it shall appear to the board to be just and proper to do so and upon any such removal of the revocation or suspension of license by the board, the name of any such person shall be restored and replaced upon the record in the office of the commissioner, by the board. Any action taken in regard to suspension or revocation of license, or removal of any suspension or revocation and the reinstatement of any license, must be by a four-fifths vote of the appointed members of the board.

1972, March 23, P.L. 136, No. 52 Sec. 10.

INJUNCTION AGAINST UNLAWFUL PRACTICE

After eighteen months from the effective date of this act it shall be unlawful for any person to practice or attempt to offer to practice psychology, as defined in this act, without having at the time of so doing a valid, unexpired, unrevoked, and unsuspended license issued under this act. The unlawful practice of psychology as defined in this act may be enjoined by the courts on petition of the board or by the commissioner. In any such proceeding it shall not be necessary to show that any person is individually injured by the actions complained of. If the respondent is found guilty of the unlawful practice of psychology, the court shall enjoin him from so practicing unless and until he has been duly licensed. Procedure in such cases shall be the same as in any other injunction suit. The remedy by injunction hereby given is in addition to criminal prosecution and punishment.

1972, March 23, P.L. 136, No. 52 Sec. 11.

LICENSE WITHOUT EXAMINATION

The board may recommend the granting of a license without examination to any person who, at the time of application, holds a valid license or certificate issued by a board of psychologist examiners of any state, provided in the opinion of the board, the requirements for such certification or licensure are substantially the equivalent of the requirements of this act, or at the time of application, holds a diploma awarded by the American Board of Examiners in Professional Psychology and upon payment of the fee specified by the board.

1972, March 23, P.L. 136, No. 52 Sec. 12.

PRIVILEGED COMMUNICATIONS

A person licensed as a psychologist under the provisions of this act cannot, without the written consent of his client, be examined in a civil or criminal action as to any information acquired in the course of his professional services in behalf of the client. The confidential relations and communication between a psychologist and his client are on the same basis as those provided by law between an attorney and client, and nothing in this act shall be construed to require any such privileged communication to be disclosed.

1972, March 23, P.L. 136, No. 52 Sec. 13.

SEVERABILITY

If any section of this act, or any part thereof, shall be adjudged by any court of competent jurisdiction, to be invalid, such judgment shall not affect, impair, or invalidate the remainder of any section or part thereof.

1972, March 23, P.L. 136, No. 52 Sec. 14.

RENEWAL: FEES: RECORDS

Provision shall be made for renewal of licenses on a biennial basis. The fee for renewal of license shall be ten dollars ($10) or more as specified by the board. A record of all psychologists licensed to practice in Pennsylvania shall be kept in the office of the commissioner. A duplicate record shall be kept by the board and published in such manner and interval as it deems necessary.

1972, March 23, P.L. 136, No. 52 Sec. 15.

Ethical Principles
of Psychologists

PREAMBLE

Psychologists respect the dignity and worth of the individual and strive for the preservation and protection of fundamental human rights. They are committed to increasing knowledge of human behavior and of people's understanding of themselves and others and to the utilization of such knowledge for the promotion of human welfare. While pursuing these objectives, they make every effort to protect the welfare of those who seek their services and of the research participants that may be the object of study. They use their skills only for purposes consistent with these values and do not knowingly permit their misuse by others. While demanding for themselves freedom of inquiry and communication, psychologists accept the responsibility this freedom requires: competence, objectivity in the application of skills, and concern for the best interests of clients, colleagues, students, research participants, and society. In the pursuit of these ideals, psychologists subscribe to principles in the following areas: 1. Responsibility, 2. Competence, 3. Moral and Legal Standards, 4. Public Statements, 5. Confidentiality, 6. Welfare of the Consumer, 7. Professional Relationships, 8. Assessment Techniques, 9. Research With Human Participants, and 10. Care and Use of Animals.

Acceptance of membership in the American Psychological Association commits the member to adherence to these principles.

Psychologists cooperate with duly constituted committees of the American Psychological Association, in particular, the Committee on Scientific and Professional Ethics and Conduct, by responding to inquiries promptly and completely. Members also respond promptly and completely to inquiries from duly constituted state association ethics committees and professional standards review committees.

Principle 1
RESPONSIBILITY

In providing services, psychologists maintain the highest standards of their profession. They accept responsibility for the consequences of their acts and make every effort to ensure that their services are used appropriately.

a. As scientists, psychologists accept responsibility for the selection of their research topics and the methods used in investigation, analysis, and reporting. They plan their research in ways to minimize the possibility that their findings will be misleading. They provide thorough discussion of the limitations of their data, especially where their work touches on social policy or might be construed to the detriment of persons in specific age, sex, ethnic, socioeconomic, or other social groups. In publishing reports of their work, they never suppress disconfirming data, and they acknowledge the existence of alternative hypotheses and explanations of their findings. Psychologists take credit only for work they have actually done.

b. Psychologists clarify in advance with all appropriate persons and agencies the expectations for sharing and utilizing research data. They avoid relationships that may limit their objectivity or create a conflict of interest. Interference with the milieu in which data are collected is kept to a minimum.

c. Psychologists have the responsibility to attempt to prevent distortion, misuse, or suppression of psychological findings by the institution or agency of which they are employees.

d. As members of governmental or other organizational bodies, psychologists remain accountable as individuals to the highest standards of their profession.

e. As teachers, psychologists recognize their primary obligation to help others acquire knowledge and skill. They maintain high standards of scholarship by presenting psychological information objectively, fully, and accurately.

f. As practitioners, psychologists know that they bear a heavy social responsibility because their recommendations and professional actions may alter the lives of others. They are alert to personal, social, organizational, financial, or political situations and pressures that might lead to misuse of their influence.

This version of the Ethical Principles of Psychologists (formerly entitled Ethical Standards of Psychologists) was adopted by the American Psychological Association's Council of Representatives on January 24, 1981. The revised Ethical Principles contain both substantive and grammatical changes in each of the nine ethical principles constituting the Ethical Standards of Psychologists previously adopted by the Council of Representatives in 1979, plus a new tenth principle entitled Care and Use of Animals. Inquiries concerning the Ethical Principles of Psychologists should be addressed to the Administrative Officer for Ethics, American Psychological Association, 1200 Seventeenth Street, N.W., Washington, D.C. 20036.

These revised Ethical Principles apply to psychologists, to students of psychology, and to others who do work of a psychological nature under the supervision of a psychologist. They are also intended for the guidance of nonmembers of the Association who are engaged in psychological research or practice.

Any complaints of unethical conduct filed after January 24, 1981, shall be governed by this 1981 revision. However, conduct (a) complained about after January 24, 1981, but which occurred prior to that date, and (b) not considered unethical under prior versions of the principles but considered unethical under the 1981 revision, shall not be deemed a violation of ethical principles. Any complaints pending as of January 24, 1981, shall be governed either by the 1979 or by the 1981 version of the Ethical Principles, at the sound discretion of the Committee on Scientific and Professional Ethics and Conduct.

Principle 2
COMPETENCE

The maintenance of high standards of competence is a responsibility shared by all psychologists in the interest of the public and the profession as a whole. Psychologists recognize the boundaries of their competence and the limitations of their techniques. They only provide services and only use techniques for which they are qualified by training and experience. In those areas in which recognized standards do not yet exist, psychologists take whatever precautions are necessary to protect the welfare of their clients. They maintain knowledge of current scientific and professional information related to the services they render.

a. Psychologists accurately represent their competence, education, training, and experience. They claim as evidence of educational qualifications only those degrees obtained from institutions acceptable under the Bylaws and Rules of Council of the American Psychological Association.

b. As teachers, psychologists perform their duties on the basis of careful preparation so that their instruction is accurate, current, and scholarly.

c. Psychologists recognize the need for continuing education and are open to new procedures and changes in expectations and values over time.

d. Psychologists recognize differences among people, such as those that may be associated with age, sex, socioeconomic, and ethnic backgrounds. When necessary, they obtain training, experience, or counsel to assure competent service or research relating to such persons.

e. Psychologists responsible for decisions involving individuals or policies based on test results have an understanding of psychological or educational measurement, validation problems, and test research.

f. Psychologists recognize that personal problems and conflicts may interfere with professional effectiveness. Accordingly, they refrain from undertaking any activity in which their personal problems are likely to lead to inadequate performance or harm to a client, colleague, student, or research participant. If engaged in such activity when they become aware of their personal problems, they seek competent professional assistance to determine whether they should suspend, terminate, or limit the scope of their professional and/or scientific activities.

Principle 3
MORAL AND LEGAL STANDARDS

Psychologists' moral and ethical standards of behavior are a personal matter to the same degree as they are for any other citizen, except as these may compromise the fulfillment of their professional responsibilities or reduce the public trust in psychology and psychologists. Regarding their own behavior, psychologists are sensi-

tive to prevailing community standards and to the possible impact that conformity to or deviation from these standards may have upon the quality of their performance as psychologists. Psychologists are also aware of the possible impact of their public behavior upon the ability of colleagues to perform their professional duties.

a. As teachers, psychologists are aware of the fact that their personal values may affect the selection and presentation of instructional materials. When dealing with topics that may give offense, they recognize and respect the diverse attitudes that students may have toward such materials.

b. As employees or employers, psychologists do not engage in or condone practices that are inhumane or that result in illegal or unjustifiable actions. Such practices include, but are not limited to, those based on considerations of race, handicap, age, gender, sexual preference, religion, or national origin in hiring, promotion, or training.

c. In their professional roles, psychologists avoid any action that will violate or diminish the legal and civil rights of clients or of others who may be affected by their actions.

d. As practitioners and researchers, psychologists act in accord with Association standards and guidelines related to practice and to the conduct of research with human beings and animals. In the ordinary course of events, psychologists adhere to relevant governmental laws and institutional regulations. When federal, state, provincial, organizational, or institutional laws, regulations, or practices are in conflict with Association standards and guidelines, psychologists make known their commitment to Association standards and guidelines and, wherever possible, work toward a resolution of the conflict. Both practitioners and researchers are concerned with the development of such legal and quasi-legal regulations as best serve the public interest, and they work toward changing existing regulations that are not beneficial to the public interest.

Principle 4
PUBLIC STATEMENTS

Public statements, announcements of services, advertising, and promotional activities of psychologists serve the purpose of helping the public make informed judgments and choices. Psychologists represent accurately and objectively their professional qualifications, affiliations, and functions, as well as those of the institutions or organizations with which they or the statements may be associated. In public statements providing psychological information or professional opinions or providing information about the availability of psychological products, publications, and services, psychologists base their statements on scientifically acceptable psycholog-

ical findings and techniques with full recognition of the limits and uncertainties of such evidence.

a. When announcing or advertising professional services, psychologists may list the following information to describe the provider and services provided: name, highest relevant academic degree earned from a regionally accredited institution, date, type, and level of certification or licensure, diplomate status, APA membership status, address, telephone number, office hours, a brief listing of the type of psychological services offered, an appropriate presentation of fee information, foreign languages spoken, and policy with regard to third-party payments. Additional relevant or important consumer information may be included if not prohibited by other sections of these Ethical Principles.

b. In announcing or advertising the availability of psychological products, publications, or services, psychologists do not present their affiliation with any organization in a manner that falsely implies sponsorship or certification by that organization. In particular and for example, psychologists do not state APA membership or fellow status in a way to suggest that such status implies specialized professional competence or qualifications. Public statements include, but are not limited to, communication by means of periodical, book, list, directory, television, radio, or motion picture. They do not contain (i) a false, fraudulent, misleading, deceptive, or unfair statement; (ii) a misinterpretation of fact or a statement likely to mislead or deceive because in context it makes only a partial disclosure of relevant facts; (iii) a testimonial from a patient regarding the quality of a psychologists' services or products; (iv) a statement intended or likely to create false or unjustified expectations of favorable results; (v) a statement implying unusual, unique, or one-of-a-kind abilities; (vi) a statement intended or likely to appeal to a client's fears, anxieties, or emotions concerning the possible results of failure to obtain the offered services; (vii) a statement concerning the comparative desirability of offered services; (viii) a statement of direct solicitation of individual clients.

c. Psychologists do not compensate or give anything of value to a representative of the press, radio, television, or other communication medium in anticipation of or in return for professional publicity in a news item. A paid advertisement must be identified as such, unless it is apparent from the context that it is a paid advertisement. If communicated to the public by use of radio or television, an advertisement is prerecorded and approved for broadcast by the psychologist, and a recording of the actual transmission is retained by the psychologist.

d. Announcements or advertisements of "personal growth groups," clinics, and agencies give a clear statement of purpose and a clear description of the experiences to be provided. The education, training, and experience of the staff members are appropriately specified.

e. Psychologists associated with the development or promotion of psychological devices, books, or other products offered for commercial sale make reasonable efforts to ensure that announcements and advertisements are presented in a professional, scientifically acceptable, and factually informative manner.

f. Psychologists do not participate for personal gain in commercial announcements or advertisements recommending to the public the purchase or use of proprietary or single-source products or services when that participation is based solely upon their identification as psychologists.

g. Psychologists present the science of psychology and offer their services, products, and publications fairly and accurately, avoiding misrepresentation through sensationalism, exaggeration, or superficiality. Psychologists are guided by the primary obligation to aid the public in developing informed judgments, opinions, and choices.

h. As teachers, psychologists ensure that statements in catalogs and course outlines are accurate and not misleading, particularly in terms of subject matter to be covered, bases for evaluating progress, and the nature of course experiences. Announcements, brochures, or advertisements describing workshops, seminars, or other educational programs accurately describe the audience for which the program is intended as well as eligibility requirements, educational objectives, and nature of the materials to be covered. These announcements also accurately represent the education, training, and experience of the psychologists presenting the programs and any fees involved.

i. Public announcements or advertisements soliciting research participants in which clinical services or other professional services are offered as an inducement make clear the nature of the services as well as the costs and other obligations to be accepted by participants in the research.

j. A psychologist accepts the obligation to correct others who represent the psychologist's professional qualifications, or associations with products or services, in a manner incompatible with these guidelines.

k. Individual diagnostic and therapeutic services are provided only in the context of a professional psychological relationship. When personal advice is given by means of public lectures or demonstrations, newspaper or magazine articles, radio or television programs, mail, or similar media, the psychologist utilizes the most current relevant data and exercises the highest level of professional judgment.

l. Products that are described or presented by means of public lectures or demonstrations, newspaper or magazine articles, radio or television programs, or similar media meet the same recognized standards as exist for products used in the context of a professional relationship.

Principle 5
CONFIDENTIALITY

Psychologists have a primary obligation to respect the confidentiality of information obtained from persons in the course of their work as psychologists. They reveal such information to others only with the consent of the person or the person's legal representative, except in those unusual circumstances in which not to do so would result in clear danger to the person or to others. Where appropriate, psychologists inform their clients of the legal limits of confidentiality.

a. Information obtained in clinical or consulting relationships, or evaluative data concerning children, students, employees, and others, is discussed only for professional purposes and only with persons clearly concerned with the case. Written and oral reports present only data germane to the purposes of the evaluation, and every effort is made to avoid undue invasion of privacy.

b. Psychologists who present personal information obtained during the course of professional work in writings, lectures, or other public forums either obtain adequate prior consent to do so or adequately disguise all identifying information.

c. Psychologists make provisions for maintaining confidentiality in the storage and disposal of records.

d. When working with minors or other persons who are unable to give voluntary, informed consent, psychologists take special care to protect these persons' best interests.

Principle 6
WELFARE OF THE CONSUMER

Psychologists respect the integrity and protect the welfare of the people and groups with whom they work. When conflicts of interest arise between clients and psychologists' employing institutions, psychologists clarify the nature and direction of their loyalties and responsibilities and keep all parties informed of their commitments. Psychologists fully inform consumers as to the purpose and nature of an evaluative, treatment, educational, or training procedure, and they freely acknowledge that clients, students, or participants in research have freedom of choice with regard to participation.

a. Psychologists are continually cognizant of their own needs and of their potentially influential position vis-à-vis persons such as clients, students, and subordinates. They avoid exploiting the trust and dependency of such persons. Psychologists make every effort to avoid dual relationships that could impair their professional judgment or increase the risk of exploitation. Examples of such dual relationships include, but are not limited to, research with and treatment of employees, students, supervisees, close friends, or relatives. Sexual intimacies with clients are unethical.

b. When a psychologist agrees to provide services to a client at the request of a third party, the psychologist assumes the responsibility of clarifying the nature of the relationships to all parties concerned.

c. Where the demands of an organization require psy-

chologists to violate these Ethical Principles, psychologists clarify the nature of the conflict between the demands and these principles. They inform all parties of psychologists' ethical responsibilities and take appropriate action.

d. Psychologists make advance financial arrangements that safeguard the best interests of and are clearly understood by their clients. They neither give nor receive any remuneration for referring clients for professional services. They contribute a portion of their services to work for which they receive little or no financial return.

e. Psychologists terminate a clinical or consulting relationship when it is reasonably clear that the consumer is not benefiting from it. They offer to help the consumer locate alternative sources of assistance.

Principle 7
PROFESSIONAL RELATIONSHIPS

Psychologists act with due regard for the needs, special competencies, and obligations of their colleagues in psychology and other professions. They respect the prerogatives and obligations of the institutions or organizations with which these other colleagues are associated.

a. Psychologists understand the areas of competence of related professions. They make full use of all the professional, technical, and administrative resources that serve the best interests of consumers. The absence of formal relationships with other professional workers does not relieve psychologists of the responsibility of securing for their clients the best possible professional service, nor does it relieve them of the obligation to exercise foresight, diligence, and tact in obtaining the complementary or alternative assistance needed by clients.

b. Psychologists know and take into account the traditions and practices of other professional groups with whom they work and cooperate fully with such groups. If a person is receiving similar services from another professional, psychologists do not offer their own services directly to such a person. If a psychologist is contacted by a person who is already receiving similar services from another professional, the psychologist carefully considers that professional relationship and proceeds with caution and sensitivity to the therapeutic issues as well as the client's welfare. The psychologist discusses these issues with the client so as to minimize the risk of confusion and conflict.

c. Psychologists who employ or supervise other professionals or professionals in training accept the obligation to facilitate the further professional development of these individuals. They provide appropriate working conditions, timely evaluations, constructive consultation, and experience opportunities.

d. Psychologists do not exploit their professional relationships with clients, supervisees, students, employees, or research participants sexually or otherwise. Psychologists do not condone or engage in sexual harassment. Sexual harassment is defined as deliberate or repeated comments, gestures, or physical contacts of a sexual nature that are unwanted by the recipient.

e. In conducting research in institutions or organizations, psychologists secure appropriate authorization to conduct such research. They are aware of their obligations to future research workers and ensure that host institutions receive adequate information about the research and proper acknowledgment of their contributions.

f. Publication credit is assigned to those who have contributed to a publication in proportion to their professional contributions. Major contributions of a professional character made by several persons to a common project are recognized by joint authorship, with the individual who made the principal contribution listed first. Minor contributions of a professional character and extensive clerical or similar nonprofessional assistance may be acknowledged in footnotes or in an introductory statement. Acknowledgment through specific citations is made for unpublished as well as published material that has directly influenced the research or writing. Psychologists who compile and edit material of others for publication publish the material in the name of the originating group, if appropriate, with their own name appearing as chairperson or editor. All contributors are to be acknowledged and named.

g. When psychologists know of an ethical violation by another psychologist, and it seems appropriate, they informally attempt to resolve the issue by bringing the behavior to the attention of the psychologist. If the misconduct is of a minor nature and/or appears to be due to lack of sensitivity, knowledge, or experience, such an informal solution is usually appropriate. Such informal corrective efforts are made with sensitivity to any rights to confidentiality involved. If the violation does not seem amenable to an informal solution, or is of a more serious nature, psychologists bring it to the attention of the appropriate local, state, and/or national committee on professional ethics and conduct.

Principle 8
ASSESSMENT TECHNIQUES

In the development, publication, and utilization of psychological assessment techniques, psychologists make every effort to promote the welfare and best interests of the client. They guard against the misuse of assessment results. They respect the client's right to know the results, the interpretations made, and the bases for their conclusions and recommendations. Psychologists make every effort to maintain the security of tests and other assessment techniques within limits of legal mandates. They strive to ensure the appropriate use of assessment techniques by others.

a. In using assessment techniques, psychologists respect the right of clients to have full explanations of the nature and purpose of the techniques in language the clients can understand, unless an explicit exception to this right has been agreed upon in advance. When the explanations are to be provided by others, psychologists establish procedures for ensuring the adequacy of these explanations.

b. Psychologists responsible for the development and standardization of psychological tests and other assessment techniques utilize established scientific procedures and observe the relevant APA standards.

c. In reporting assessment results, psychologists indicate any reservations that exist regarding validity or reliability because of the circumstances of the assessment or the inappropriateness of the norms for the person tested. Psychologists strive to ensure that the results of assessments and their interpretations are not misused by others.

d. Psychologists recognize that assessment results may become obsolete. They make every effort to avoid and prevent the misuse of obsolete measures.

e. Psychologists offering scoring and interpretation services are able to produce appropriate evidence for the validity of the programs and procedures used in arriving at interpretations. The public offering of an automated interpretation service is considered a professional-to-professional consultation. Psychologists make every effort to avoid misuse of assessment reports.

f. Psychologists do not encourage or promote the use of psychological assessment techniques by inappropriately trained or otherwise unqualified persons through teaching, sponsorship, or supervision.

Principle 9
RESEARCH WITH HUMAN PARTICIPANTS

The decision to undertake research rests upon a considered judgment by the individual psychologist about how best to contribute to psychological science and human welfare. Having made the decision to conduct research, the psychologist considers alternative directions in which research energies and resources might be invested. On the basis of this consideration, the psychologist carries out the investigation with respect and concern for the dignity and welfare of the people who participate and with cognizance of federal and state regulations and professional standards governing the conduct of research with human participants.

a. In planning a study, the investigator has the responsibility to make a careful evaluation of its ethical acceptability. To the extent that the weighing of scientific and human values suggests a compromise of any principle, the investigator incurs a correspondingly serious obligation to seek ethical advice and to observe stringent safeguards to protect the rights of human participants.

b. Considering whether a participant in a planned

study will be a "subject at risk" or a "subject at minimal risk," according to recognized standards, is of primary ethical concern to the investigator.

c. The investigator always retains the responsibility for ensuring ethical practice in research. The investigator is also responsible for the ethical treatment of research participants by collaborators, assistants, students, and employees, all of whom, however, incur similar obligations.

d. Except in minimal-risk research, the investigator establishes a clear and fair agreement with research participants, prior to their participation, that clarifies the obligations and responsibilities of each. The investigator has the obligation to honor all promises and commitments included in that agreement. The investigator informs the participants of all aspects of the research that might reasonably be expected to influence willingness to participate and explains all other aspects of the research about which the participants inquire. Failure to make full disclosure prior to obtaining informed consent requires additional safeguards to protect the welfare and dignity of the research participants. Research with children or with participants who have impairments that would limit understanding and/or communication requires special safeguarding procedures.

e. Methodological requirements of a study may make the use of concealment or deception necessary. Before conducting such a study, the investigator has a special responsibility to (i) determine whether the use of such techniques is justified by the study's prospective scientific, educational, or applied value; (ii) determine whether alternative procedures are available that do not use concealment or deception; and (iii) ensure that the participants are provided with sufficient explanation as soon as possible.

f. The investigator respects the individual's freedom to decline to participate in or to withdraw from the research at any time. The obligation to protect this freedom requires careful thought and consideration when the investigator is in a position of authority or influence over the participant. Such positions of authority include, but are not limited to, situations in which research participation is required as part of employment or in which the participant is a student, client, or employee of the investigator.

g. The investigator protects the participant from physical and mental discomfort, harm, and danger that may arise from research procedures. If risks of such consequences exist, the investigator informs the participant of that fact. Research procedures likely to cause serious or lasting harm to a participant are not used unless the failure to use these procedures might expose the participant to risk of greater harm, or unless the research has great potential benefit and fully informed and voluntary consent is obtained from each participant. The participant should be informed of procedures for contacting the investigator within a reasonable time period following participation should stress, potential harm, or related questions or concerns arise.

h. After the data are collected, the investigator provides the participant with information about the nature of the study and attempts to remove any misconceptions that may have arisen. Where scientific or humane values justify delaying or withholding this information, the investigator incurs a special responsibility to monitor the research and to ensure that there are no damaging consequences for the participant.

i. Where research procedures result in undesirable consequences for the individual participant, the investigator has the responsibility to detect and remove or correct these consequences, including long-term effects.

j. Information obtained about a research participant during the course of an investigation is confidential unless otherwise agreed upon in advance. When the possibility exists that others may obtain access to such information, this possibility, together with the plans for protecting confidentiality, is explained to the participant as part of the procedure for obtaining informed consent.

Principle 10
CARE AND USE OF ANIMALS

An investigator of animal behavior strives to advance understanding of basic behavioral principles and/or to contribute to the improvement of human health and welfare. In seeking these ends, the investigator ensures the welfare of animals and treats them humanely. Laws and regulations notwithstanding, an animal's immediate protection depends upon the scientist's own conscience.

a. The acquisition, care, use, and disposal of all animals are in compliance with current federal, state or provincial, and local laws and regulations.

b. A psychologist trained in research methods and experienced in the care of laboratory animals closely supervises all procedures involving animals and is responsible for ensuring appropriate consideration of their comfort, health, and humane treatment.

c. Psychologists ensure that all individuals using animals under their supervision have received explicit instruction in experimental methods and in the care, maintenance, and handling of the species being used. Responsibilities and activities of individuals participating in a research project are consistent with their respective competencies.

d. Psychologists make every effort to minimize discomfort, illness, and pain of animals. A procedure subjecting animals to pain, stress, or privation is used only when an alternative procedure is unavailable and the goal is justified by its prospective scientific, educational, or applied value. Surgical procedures are performed under appropriate anesthesia; techniques to avoid infection and minimize pain are followed during and after surgery.

e. When it is appropriate that the animal's life be terminated, it is done rapidly and painlessly.

Index

About the Editors
and Contributors

WILLIAM F. ADAMS, Ed.D., received his Ed.D. from Temple University, M.A. from Bowling Green State University, Ohio, and his B.A. from Gettysburg College. He served on active duty in the U.S. Navy, retiring on disability as a lieutenant commander. He is the Chief of the Vocational Rehabilitation and Counseling Division at the Veterans Administration Regional Office and Insurance Center, Philadelphia, Pa., and an evening school faculty member at LaSalle College, Community College of Philadelphia, and Philadelphia University.

FRANCIS R. J. FIELDS, Ph.D., is currently the Chief of the Psychology Service at the Veterans Administration Medical Center in Lebanon, Pa. He has served as a clinical neuropsychologist at VA Medical Centers in Coatesville, Pa., and East Orange, N. J. He was active organizationally in the establishment of the Philadelphia Clinical Neuropsychology Group which was established in 1979. Dr. Fields is on the editorial board of the professional journal Clinical Neuropsychology and currently is Vice-President of the Mental Health Association in Lebanon, Pa. Dr. Fields limits his private practice to the field of clinical neuropsychology, maintaining an office in Lebanon, Pa. He is neuropsychological consultant to Pennsylvania Psychological Services in Philadelphia, Pa.

The majority of Dr. Fields's research has focused upon brain-behavior relations.

Dr. Fields currently is in his second year of a four-year independent studies program in the field of law.

G. THOMAS GATES, Esquire, is a graduate of Brown University, obtaining his law degree from the Boston University School of Law. He is an adjunct associate professor of law at Dickinson Law School, Pa., Lebanon Valley College, Pa., and the Pennsylvania State University, Berks County Campus. He is a member of the American Association of University Professors, and is President Judge of the 52nd Judicial District of Pennsylvania.

ALLAN M. HORWITZ, Esquire, is a Pennsylvania general practitioner with law offices in Philadelphia and Chester County, Pa. He is a graduate of Temple University and received his J.D. from Temple University School of Law. Mr. Horwitz is a member of the Philadelphia and Pennsylvania Bar Associations, Philadelphia and Pennsylvania Trial Lawyers Associations, and the Association of Trial Lawyers of America.

RUDY J. HORWITZ, Psy.D., is a clinical psychologist in private practice in Pennsylvania. He received his B.A. and M.A. degrees from Temple University and Psy.D. degree from Heed University. He is currently Director of Pennsylvania Psychological Services, which operates a mobile psychological service unit in addition to several traditional offices in the greater Philadelphia area. He is President of Evalumatics, Ltd., which designs and manufactures automated psychological testing equipment. He has served as consultant to various organizations including the United Cerebral Palsy Association, Goodwill Industries, the Bureau of Vocational Rehabilitation, rehabilitation hospitals, vocational training schools, and police departments. He served two consecutive terms as president of the Council for Exceptional Children, Philadelphia chapter. He is a member of various professional associations including the American Psychological Association, American Personnel and Guidance Association, and the Pennsylvania Psychological Association. He has published articles of psychological interest in legal newspapers.

MICHAEL A. MAGAZINO, M.A., is a licensed psychologist who formerly directed a twenty-corporation, comprehensive employee assistance service-consortium. Currently he maintains a private practice in Lebanon, Pa. He is the founder and President of Theraxis, Inc., a psychological service for business, industry, and professional sports teams. He is also a partner in Psyforme (Psychology for Management), a service that provides management stress seminars and psychological testing to augment the personnel selection process. He is President of the Mental Health Association in Lebanon, Pa., and is a member of the Philadelphia Clinical Neuropsychology Group.

JOSEPH G. ROSENFELD, Ph.D., is a professor of school psychology at Temple University. He served as Chairman of the Department from 1974 to 1981. He is a certified school psychologist, having consulted in a number of schools and school districts, and has done clinical work in mental health clinics and hospitals. He has a Diplomate in Clinical Psychology from the American Board of Professional Psychology. He is a past president of the School Division and the Clinical Division of the Pennsylvania Psychological Association. He is a past president of the Philadelphia Society of Clinical Psychologists and the Pennsylvania Intercollege Council of School Psychology Professors. He has written a number of articles and has co-authored a book with Ralph Blanco entitled *Case Studies in Clinical and School Psychology*. Dr. Rosenfeld is also a hearing officer for the Pennsylvania Department of Education, dealing with right to education issues for special education children.

PHILIP L. TAYLOR, Ph. D., is a cum laude graduate of Harvard University. In 1971 and 1975 respectively he received Masters and Ph.D. degrees from New York University where he specialized in community psychology.

From 1974 to 1979 Dr. Taylor was a member of the faculty of the Pennsylvania State University, Capitol Campus, in Middletown, Pa. He is a member of the American Psychological Association, the Association for the Advancement of Behavior Therapy, the National Multiple Sclerosis Society, and the Pennsylvania Psychological Association. Dr. Taylor serves on the Advocacy Committee of the Family and Children's Service of Lancaster, Pa., where he has been active on its Children of Divorce subcommittee.

Dr. Taylor has conducted extensive research on various topics and has published professional articles and research reports as well as popular articles.

Dr. Taylor is currently consulting psychologist at Lancaster General Hospital (Lancaster, Pa.) and also maintains a private practice.

THOMAS N. TUMILTY, Ph.D., has been employed as a staff psychologist at the VA Medical Center, Lebanon, Pa., since 1973. Since 1976, he has maintained a private practice and has been listed in the National Register of Health Service Providers in Psychology. In public service and private practice he frequently has provided expert witness testimony at civil and criminal court proceedings.